AF334616

NORDIC SECURITY IN THE 1990s

OPTIONS IN THE CHANGING EUROPE

NORDIC SECURITY IN THE 1990s

OPTIONS IN THE CHANGING EUROPE

Edited by

Jan Øberg

Pinter Publishers

London

for

TFF

distributed exclusively in the USA and Canada by ST. MARTIN'S PRESS

First printed in Great Britain in 1992 by
Pinter Publishers Limited
25 Floral Street, London WC 2E 9 DS

Distributed exclusively in the USA and Canada
by St. Martin's Press, Inc.
175 Fifth Avenue, New York 10010, USA

British Library Cataloguing in Publication Data
A CIP catalogue for this book is available from
the British Library

ISBN 0 86187 080 8

The Transnational Foundation for Peace and Future Research *TFF*
Vegagatan 25
224 57 Lund
Sweden

Printed and bound in Great Britain by Billing & Sons Ltd, Worcester

CONTENTS

OPTIONS

About the Contributors

Clive Archer
Senior lecturer in international relations and deputy director of the Centre for Defence Studies at the University of Aberdeen, Scotland. He has published a number of books and articles on Nordic and Arctic security and cooperation and on international organizations.

Barry Buzan
Senior lecturer in International Studies at the University of Warwick and a senior research fellow at the Centre for Peace and Conflict Research at Copenhagen University; the author of numerous articles and books, among them *An Introduction to Strategic Studies: Military Technology and International Relations* (1987) and *People, States and Fear* (1991).

Johan Galtung
Founder of Peace Research Institute, Oslo (PRIO) and the *Journal of Peace Research*. Professor of peace studies in Hawaii, Germany and doctor *honoris causa* at several places around the world, consultant to numerous international organizations. The author of several hundred books and articles during the last forty years, member of the advisory board of the Transnational Foundationnfr Peace and Future Research (TFF).

Pertti Joenniemi
Senior research fellow at Tampere Peace Research Institute (TAPRI), author of books and articles on the Baltic Sea region, Norden in the new Europe and neutrality concepts and policies in the history of ideas.

Jyrki Käkönen
Ph.D., director, Tampere Peace Research Institute (TAPRI), lecturer at the Universities of Joensuu, Oulu and Turku in Finland, author of *Natural Resources of Conflicts in the Changing International System: Three Studies on Imperialism* (1988), director of an international project on 'Sustainable Development and Security in the Arctic'.

SVERRE LODGAARD
Director of Peace Research Institute, Oslo (PRIO) since 1987, chairman of the Norwegian Pugwash Committee and member of the Norwegian government disarmament commission, member of the TFF board and author or editor of numerous articles and books, among them *Naval Arms Control* (1990).

HÅKAN WIBERG
Associate professor in peace research 1971–80 and professor of sociology since 1980 at Lund University. Director, Centre for Peace and Conflict Research, Copenhagen University since 1988 and member of the board of TFF since 1986. Numerous books on public opinion, conflict theory, security issues, regional conflicts and on accidental war.

OLE WÆVER
Researcher at the Centre for Peace and Conflict Research at Copenhagen University since 1985. Part-time lecturer at Aarhus and Copenhagen University and at the European University Institute in Florence. Books and articles on Nordic security, European identities, the German question, peace movements, and foreign policy and international relations theories.

JAN ØBERG
Associate professor and director of the Lund University Peace Research Institute (LUPRI) from 1983 till its closing in 1989, professor at the International Christian University 1990–91, member of the Danish government commission on security and disarmament affairs since 1981; co-founder and director of the TFF, author of books on militarism, development, security, conflict resolution, alternative defence and peace.

1

Introduction: Norden in Europe 1990 – 1991

Jan Øberg, editor

THE EUROPEAN HISTORICAL PROCESSES

We held our meetings in 1989, 1990 and 1991. We witnessed the Berlin Wall crumble and the dissolution of the East European bloc and the Warsaw Pact. We followed the news about convulsions throughout the Soviet Union and woke up to news about the coup in August 1991. And, while writing this on December 9, another coup took place leading to the dissolution of the Soviet Union as we have known it for decades.

Earlier we saw the Gulf War, manifesting in its own brutal way, what some believe to be the post-Cold War world order. The German Democratic Republic disappeared, Germany reunited, Yugoslavia fell apart. Estonia, Latvia and Lithuania emerged, followed by Russia and the Ukraine. Thus, federations in the East disappeared and new states emerged.

In Western Europe elites worked, in a less dramatic fashion, to do the opposite and give substance to the idea of a new European superpower that has gained the attention of nation-states everywhere. In Maastricht, also on

---

December 9, they met to shape the foundations of a monetary as well as a political union by the end of this century.

Many central actors of European and world history are now "former" and new ones have appeared on the stage. Several are in transition, mostly knocking on the doors of Brussels such as Austria and Sweden, soon probably Finland, Switzerland, and Norway. Soon-to-be-states Slovenia and Croatia and other former Yugoslav republics will attempt to do the same.

We saw other states knocking on doors in Brussels – Poland, Czechoslovakia and Hungary – to become members of or associated with NATO. Simultaneously, we saw new nuclear weapons states being born.

In the wake of all this we Europeans became increasingly concerned about the manifest rise in Nazi sentiments, xenophobia, nationalism, anti-Semitism. The freedom of movement for capital, goods and services increased within the West, but not within the East, or between East and West. Some people also move more freely than ever, but not from underprivileged to overprivileged regions.

New walls – mental, cultural and economic – are being erected these days.

◆

Twenty or so years from now we may begin to understand the significance of all this. We are all witnessing events of world historical dimensions almost every day – but processes with few, if any, historical precedents.

What we *can* know – but seem to forget – is that this amazing turbulence takes place on top of all the fundamental problems facing humankind. None of us can escape them: the decaying world environment, global maldevelopment, intercultural conflicts and the overall crisis in the Western-based, liberal, capitalist market economy.

Elites worldwide proclaim the latter to be the victor in the post-Cold War era. At the same time, paradoxically, they struggle with the accumulating problems of that very economic system. With the breakdown of socialism and planned economies and the weakness of the mixed, social democracy, new millions pin their faith on integration into that single world market.

The risk for system overload, overextension, is evident. Years ago we used the expression of rising expectations about Third World peoples. Now it is relevant for hundreds of millions of people in the former Eastern bloc, the former Soviet Union as well as for many poorer segments of the ascending EC.

One must wonder what could happen when it dawns upon each and all that these expectations are either unrealistic or false promises? Furthermore, they are likely to be incompatible with the limited steering capacity of political systems, including democracies, and completely incompatible with internationally sustainable development and Nature's carrying capacity.

◆

It is easy to throw out all ideas of the past – mainstream as well as alternative – when the world changes so manifestly. We do need new thinking when the world of yesterday disappears. However, politicians, citizens, journalists as well as scholars and intellectuals are, more often than not, more inclined to look in the rearview mirror than to invent the exciting places we should try to reach and draw up maps for the roads that are most likely to lead to them. This volume does nothing to hide the fact that we all make deficient, biased assessments today about tomorrow. Rather, it shows that any single perspective or argument can be right today and somehow wrong tomorrow.

In a strange manner we increasingly have to ask ourselves what truth is – not The Truth, just today's truth – told without dishonesty or superficiality. One aspect of such a truth – and I think it will stand history's test – is that intellectual positions have tumbled, too. Many a theory about security, arms races and disarmament, causes of war, non-violence, democracy, tension and détente, human rights and overall change of western civilization will have to be revised. Few dare predict what, *for good or bad,* happens tomorrow.

At the same time, it is necessary to act. Those in Europe who sit and wait and hope to cope by means of the old thinking and paradigms will face alienation and isolation. The test of quality – in governance as well as in the intellectual enterprise – is intuition, vision, care, modesty, co-operation, a cultured good-will and mutuality. The challenge now is management of constant, unforeseeable – even to a large extent unpredictable – change, not of stability, and how to arrive at consensus in the increasingly interdependent world rather than using power or, when that does not suffice, violence.

Political power no longer means asserting oneself and requiring others to comply; rather, it will have to imply confidence-building, negotiation, good offices and willingness to experiment with safer modes of conduct for all. Intellectual power will consist in preserving the best of what was in thinking and reality, and devising structures and principles by means of which we are permitted not only to visualize the goals, but to help each other explore and travel along new roads, with new fellow travellers.

At the same time, it has become more difficult to foresee the consequences of our own, or others' actions. In decades to come, security will have to be sought and found in *change*, not in clinging to the post-1945 status quo. Europeans are condemned to live and act in a very unpredictable, but not necessarily more unstable or risky, environment than before.

The focus is that of Norden, i.e., the traditional five countries (Denmark, Finland, Sweden, Norway and Iceland) in the context of a larger area encompassing also the Arctic, Northern Central Europe, the Baltic states and whatever comes out of the transformations in the former Soviet Union.

How can we envisage and meet the new challenges of the 1990s and beyond? How can the Nordic countries respond in a constructive manner and help shape broader concepts and policies of security for themselves, and also for Europe and the global community still so painfully torn by inequalities, environmental decay and militarization?

We wanted to explore various themes. In which ways will Norden be affected by internal and external changes? What brings the Nordic countries closer together? What drives them apart? What governmental and people's actions are needed not only to respond to present and future trends but also to take upon ourselves the Nordic share of a larger, globally-oriented responsibility? How do we maximize the potential for acting as a subject rather than being an object within this area in the near and not-so-near future?

Significantly, almost all the writers in this volume start out from various fragments of what they define as a *Nordic identity*. Identities are mostly defined in terms of contrasts with others. Typically, human beings as well as nations focus on identity when it is threatened, when new and different people or circumstances arise, when they pass from one developmental phase to another or when they experience crisis. That the search for identity is closely related to a crisis sentiment is fairly obvious. So, too, in the case of the Nordic countries.

A Nordic identity can surely be found, a community and likemindedness which is an important asset. However, they all judge, from their respective angles that this post-1945 identity is outdated and, therefore, reactive. During the last few years Nordic governments have increasingly fallen back on wait-and-see policies or "we-have-only-one-option" policies.

The "new Europe" is slowly becoming a new point of reference and navigation, in real politics as well as in this volume. But there the commonality of perceptions ends. There seem to be as many conceptualizations today of that "new Europe", and views on how to relate to it, as there are authors.

The centralized, supranational Europe which aims at a future European Union creates, of course, its own countermoves or parallel streams towards a Europe of regions. The expanded Norden is one discussed here, a Baltic Sea region is another, and the Arctic dimension is a kind of third idea in this direction. Today we don't know whether any of these will have the required political, economic or cultural carrying capacity. Taking them up, looking at them from various angles and assessing their strengths and weaknesses in the light of the overall situation is a way of helping them to become a reality.

What you hold in your hand, therefore, is the results of a process, not its conclusion. We have attempted to look a little into "Nordic futures" under three headings. First, what if the Nordic identity – Nordicity – simply disappears? Second, how can the best of its elements be preserved and used – if at all – in the future? Thirdly, what if we redefine ourselves and adapt in a new way to a new world?

Speculative, indeed. In the future, research in these fields will have to be exploratory, self-critical, modest and rich in new thinking. There *are* no fixed frameworks or theoretical tools – or academic schools – which can help us understand these immensely complex developments. The safest we can do is to experiment – but with care in our every thought and action.

★

10

When the peoples in Eastern Europe and the former Soviet Union bear
the brunt of extremely painful transformations which carry existential and
civilizational implications, there is no way the West can be left untouched –
by its own increasing problems, as well as by the consequences of the
dissolution of the other.

To meet that challenge successfully a great deal of humility, competence,
ingenuity and self-appraisal is required. Will we in the West – in the super-
privileged Norden – manage?

THE BOOK PROCESS

The study group on Common Nordic Security Towards the Year 2010
(CONOSEC) held its meetings in 1989, 1990 and 1991 on the initiative of the
Transnational Foundation for Peace and Future Research, TFF, in Lund,
Sweden. We were nine members with a keen interest and experience in peace
and security studies pertaining to the Nordic region. Five lived and worked in
one or more of the Nordic countries plus there was one from Scotland, one
from London, a Norwegian from Hawaii, and a Dane living in Sweden and
working part-time in Japan.

To operate a project with a clearly exploratory aim under these
circumstances and under tight financial conditions is an experiment. It has its
advantages and disadvantages. Because of the depth, speed and breadth of
changes all around us, the traditional research project becomes irrelevant. A
book produced on the basis of traditional project management – developing
ideas, planning, finding people, fund-raising, analyzing, writing, editing,
publishing – would be outdated when arriving in the bookstore.

We have not aimed at putting this volume together as if it had been
written as an *end result*. It deliberately reflects a *process*. We did not want to
write only *about* changes in Norden and Europe, we let it be a *part of* those
changes as they have been discussed by the group and reflected in the minds

of each author. The manuscripts were written between summer 1990 and late summer 1991. Chapter 15 only was written in December 1991.

We want now to share this learning experience with our readers. An article is not bad because, after one year, it seems as if the author "did not recognize" this or that factor or foresee that his paradigm was tied to that particular time. Rather, studying what resembles the sketches of an artist is a treasure of learning – about what it means to be Europeans in the 1990s and what it means to be analytical observers who aim to go beyond commentarism and day-to-day journalistic coverage of events.

ACKNOWLEDGEMENTS

The TFF initiated this project and wants to thank all contributors to this volume, not only for these chapters but also for having stimulated us during days of discussions – important as it is to develop the competence of a young foundation like the TFF.

Financial support for the CONOSEC project and international conference was obtained from the Ministry of Foreign Affairs in Stockholm (100.000 SEK), from the Futura Foundation in Stockholm (20.000 SEK) and from the Peace Research Institute, Oslo (PRIO), the Tampere Peace Research Institute (TAPRI) in Finland and from the Centre for Peace and Conflict Research, Copenhagen University (each 10.000 SEK).

Finally, we thank Nicola Viinikka at Pinter Publishers for her patience and encouragement from the outset.

Lund, December 9–10, 1991

2

Norden in the Cold War Reality

Håkan Wiberg & Ole Wæver

WHAT KIND OF SYSTEM IS NORDEN?

Let us start by presenting some basic facts about the five Nordic countries, their size, location and economic and military relations to others. Some of these have been constant for a long time: the latest change in geography was in the 1940s, when the area of Finland was reduced – which also led to Norway getting a boundary with the Soviet Union (SU) that it had not had before. Others change very slowly and at about the same rate: the Nordic countries all have a population growth below 1% per year.

Trade patterns (data from 1988) also belong to this category, but there the accumulated changes over decades may become significant. The position of Germany (D) has increased in all these countries in the last few decades, while that of UK has decreased (its prime position in Norway is essentially due to the buying of oil; Norway imports more from Germany and from Sweden than from UK). The Nordic share of foreign trade is 20–25% for all countries, which makes the other Nordic countries a bigger market than any

---

single country outside Norden. It increased from the 1940s through the early 1970s, and has receded slightly since then.

The only marked change that has taken place since the mid-1980s is that the collapse of the Soviet economy has reduced its part of Finnish foreign trade from 20–25% to under 10%, so that it is no longer the biggest trade partner it has been for a generation.

	Denmark	Finland	Iceland	Norway	Sweden
Area (thousands of sq.km.)	43	330	102	324	445
Population (million)	5.2	5.1	0.3	4.3	8.5
GNP (bn. $ US)	110	120	5	95	200
Econ. bloc	EC	EFTA	EFTA	EFTA	EFTA
Main trade partners	D, S, UK	D, S, SU	UK, D, US	UK, S, D	D, UK, US
Alignment	NATO	None (FCMA)	NATO	NATO	None
Boundaries	D	N, S, SU	None	S, SF, SU	N, SF
Military expenditure (bn. $ US)	2.2	1.8	None	3.1	5.1

Another variable is military expenditures. All countries have had constant growth since the 1940s, calculated in constant dollars to adjust for inflation; and in all of them, this growth has been slower than that of GNP. Differential growth, however, has meant that Sweden is a bit less of the relative military giant in Norden than it was after World War II, when it accounted for more than half of the military expenditures in Norden.

Economic and military blocs, finally, have been constant for a long time. The military pattern in the table was in place in 1949 (see below), and the economic one in the early 1970s. Both are in flux today: Sweden has just applied for membership of the EC, and the others are expected to follow soon. No changes in either direction can be expected with respect to NATO; but the West European Union (WEU), of which no Nordic country is a member today, may be another matter, depending on how it will be related to the EC and on what its relationship to NATO will be.

These figures in the table tell us something about the components of the Nordic system, but they only give limited information about the system as such: its security problems, its economic structure and the pattern of mutual bonds of various kinds. Let us therefore focus on the security system, intertwining other aspects as they become relevant.

NORDEN AS A SECURITY SYSTEM

Norden has never been an isolated security complex of its own, but a part of wider ones surrounding it and finally of the single security complex that Europe merged into in the eighteenth century. During the last 500 years there have been about fifty wars inside Nordic countries, between these countries, or between them and their neighbours.

In some periods, foreign powers have intervened heavily in Norden; in other periods, Norden has been somewhat more self-contained, the states being each other's primary (but by no means only) security threats while being of secondary security interest only for its neighbours. There have also been some – short – periods when the doings of Nordic countries have had significant effects on their environment, the last one ending in the early eighteenth century.

From the late Middle Ages until the early nineteenth century, the Nordic state system essentially consisted of two actors: Denmark (with Norway and Iceland) and Sweden (with Finland). Both of them had wider possessions in the Baltic area; there were also some German provinces and Baltic islands under the Danish Crown, and Sweden at its maximum controlled the Baltic coast down to south of Riga, and several German coastal areas in addition. They had a number of wars with each other, some of them local, others regional and European, where Denmark and Sweden belonged to opposing coalitions.

Until the early seventeenth century, Denmark was the stronger power, which also comprised some of the southern and western provinces of what is today Sweden; these were then conquered by Sweden in a few wars, and in a few more wars Denmark failed to regain them.

The Napoleonic wars – and regional sideshows – were the last repetition of this. Denmark belonged to Napoleon's coalition, whereas Sweden was neutral for a long time. It lost Finland to Russia in a war in 1808–9, but nevertheless decided to join the British–Russian coalition in 1812, having been promised Norway as compensation for Finland by Russia. A short Swedish–Danish war in 1814 made Denmark confirm this outcome, and an equally short Swedish–Norwegian war later in the year forced the Norwegians, too, to confirm it, rescinding their recent declaration of independence.

This was a drastic rearrangement of Norden: both Norway and Finland had moved from a colonial relationship with a small power to a looser union with another and bigger power, from which they slipped away rather easily a century later, getting their independence in 1905 and 1917 respectively.

In hindsight, this was a blessing for Nordic unity. If the colonial relationships had prevailed, there would have been a risk of bitter struggles of liberation a couple of generations later (Iceland, however, got home rule in 1918 and complete independence in 1918 with little ado). It also largely transformed Norden into a system of nation-states where there were very strong coincidences between nations and states. There were two exceptions: there was a Swedish minority in Finland, reduced in the last two centuries from over 20% to about 6% by migration, differential fertility and inter-generational language changes; second, the King of Denmark was also the sovereign of the two principalities of Holstein (all German) and Schleswig (mixed), although these were not formally parts of Denmark.

The latter case proved problematic: a rebellion in 1848–50 was defeated by the Danes, but in the next one, in 1863, Prussia and Austria intervened, and Denmark lost both provinces. After World War I, it regained the northern part of Schleswig by a referendum in 1920, the Danish government being so far-sighted as not to want any territory where there was not a clear Danish majority, resisting offers for more from the victor powers as well as a domestic chauvinism calling for older boundaries to be re-established.

TOWARDS A – LIMITED – SECURITY COMMUNITY

The end of the Napoleonic wars also meant the beginning of the transformation of Norden into a security community in the sense Karl Deutsch speaks about. Several factors contributed to this. First, Norden had lost much of its strategic interest, so there were only occasional and rather half-hearted attempts from major powers to drag its states into coalition patterns. Second, the creation of nation-states meant that there was less to fight about than before.

Third, there emerged a strong tradition of neutralism, dominant until the formation of NATO. Fourth, there emerged an ideology of "Scandinavianism" (later "Nordism," including Finland), which started in the 1830s as a middle class ideology to reconcile Denmark and Sweden, but gradually became more encompassing in social basis as well as in scope.

While the ideological basis was laid in the nineteenth century, it is mainly in this century that the security community has solidified in several respects. Mutual trade and other forms of interaction have increased considerably. Common institutions have emerged on various levels, including assemblies of parliamentarians (the Nordic Council) and of governments (the Nordic Council of Ministers), a multitude of more specialized inter-governmental agencies and another multitude of non-governmental organizations. For professional associations, for example, there is often a Nordic one in between the national one and the European or international one, to which it is affiliated.

A number of tests have demonstrated the limits of this security community when there were calls for its being more than precisely that. Sweden/Norway remained neutral in 1863, and repeated attempts at creating a defence union have failed, the latest one in 1947–48. During World War II, Finland was a brother-in-arms with the same Germany that occupied Denmark and Norway, while Sweden remained neutral; it had stretched as far as to being "non-belligerent" (permitting it to send munitions) when the USSR attacked Finland.

After World War II, Denmark, Iceland and Norway joined the Western alliance, while Finland entered the FCMA (Friendship, Cooperation and Mutual Assistance) Treaty with the USSR, and Sweden remained non-aligned.

Another set of tests can be found in the economic area. Attempts at creating a common economic zone or customs union have always failed, and with the economic division of Europe we got just as complex a Nordic pattern in this area as in the politico-military one. Denmark joined the EC (but its home rule areas, the Faroe Islands never joined and Greenland left it), whereas Iceland, Norway and Sweden remained in EFTA, and Finland was associated with EFTA (later became a full member) and had a cooperation agreement with COMECON.

This, in a way, makes the Nordic security community unique. The other major cases also have defence pacts or economic pacts, or both, as institutional scaffolds. The Nordic one is "merely" based on a pattern of cooperation that is institutionally restricted to "low politics" with an ideology that is so vague that it might rather be referred to as a common sentiment.

This also tells something about the character of the Nordic security community. It differs from the Anglo-Saxon one by being too small and having too complex a pattern of dependence on external forces to be able to fend off these forces by creating some kind of institutional self-sufficiency. This pattern of dependence also differs from Benelux, where the problem could just be solved by joining the NATO and the EC since all the powers that they are dependent on are already there.

NEW PATTERNS AFTER THE SECOND WORLD WAR

World War II created a strong disturbance in the traditional patterns that seemed to have been confirmed by long and successful practice, including Norden staying out of World War I.

One fundamental component was isolated neutrality, common to all the states; in Finland, however, this was periodically combined with a policy of confrontation with the Soviet Union, looking for security reassurances from elsewhere (Poland, Germany, Norden). In the inter-war years, Denmark and Norway had a very low defence profile, whereas Finland and Sweden had a higher profile, corresponding to ambitions of existential defence.

Only Sweden proved successful by staying out of the war. It then continued and reinforced its traditional pattern. This isolated neutrality did not go quite as far as the Swiss, but it was only after some hesitation that it even joined the United Nations. For several years after 1945, it had the third strongest air force in Europe, and for even longer it continued to spend about 5% of its GNP on military defence.

The others had failed, and responded by doing largely the opposite of what they had done before. Denmark and Norway joined NATO and increased their armed forces. Finland lowered its defence profile (partly because of being obliged by the peace treaty), and based its policy of non-alignment on a policy of confidence vis-à-vis the USSR, rather than looking elsewhere for reassurance. (This, in fact, meant reverting to an older political tradition, from which the inter-war years had constituted an exception.)

This new Nordic pattern took a few years to sort itself out. During the years 1945 to 1947, there was a strong tendency in all countries to revert to the pre-war policies, and traditional Nordic neutralism was still strong in Denmark and Norway, too, while dislike of the Soviet Union was predictably strong in Finland. (It actually took Labour governments to usher the two into NATO – and a Conservative president to establish the good neighbour relations between Finland and the USSR.)

When the widening cleavage between the victor powers manifested itself in the spiralling Cold War, there came a time for choices; and none of the countries had a great power alliance as its first choice. In 1947, Denmark, Norway and Sweden began negotiations about the creation of a Scandinavian neutrality alliance (Finland was not invited). At least in Denmark and – even more – in Sweden, there was a strong desire for success, whereas Norway, including the Labour party, was split between this desire (being originally government policy) and those that wanted Norway to be part of an Atlantic alliance.

In 1948 the negotiations failed, however, for several reasons. It was seen as too costly for Denmark and Norway to rearm to Swedish standards; there was a split between those who wanted the pact to be precisely what it proclaimed to be and those who saw it as a first step towards cooperation with the West; the representatives of Norway did not feel sufficiently reassured as to its northern tip; and rumours were spread that the USA would not sell armaments to such a pact.

After that, Norway moved to trying to convince the Anglo-Saxons that Norwegian territory was of sufficient strategic importance to merit NATO membership. Denmark tried to get Sweden interested in a smaller version of the neutrality pact; when that failed, too, it preferred NATO membership to the old isolated neutrality that was seen as having failed and that was now the only other option.

The Swedes were very disappointed that the negotiations had failed, but did not regard a Danish–Swedish solution as second best; instead of NATO membership, they preferred the old isolated neutrality that was regarded as having succeeded and that was now the only other option. (There was a vociferous minority arguing for NATO membership, but it never even came to a parliamentary test and a national consensus was created within a few years.)

In the meantime, Finland had followed its own trajectory. The armistice in 1944 obliged it to participate in a third war, against the Germans, and an Allied Control Commission (*de facto* USSR) resided in Finland until the peace treaty in 1947. The armistice and the later peace in 1947 confirmed Finland's territorial losses from 1940. They mainly consisted of the Petsamo strip up to the Arctic Ocean and the Karelian isthmus close to Leningrad; in addition, Finland had to lease a military base (Porkkala, west of Helsinki) to the USSR for fifty years. (Its being handed back in 1956, after an agreement in 1955, was partly due to greatly improved Finnish–Soviet relations, partly to the Soviet 'détente offensive' in 1955–56 that also included the restoration of Austrian sovereignty, and some unilateral disarmament steps.) There were also clauses about war reparations and about limitations on Finnish armed forces, in terms of size, missiles, submarines and nuclear weapons.

The rise of the Cold War put Finland in an even more difficult position than the others. The conservative president Paasikivi managed to persuade the major political parties in Finland that the wisest policy was to try to establish good relations with the USSR, rather than relying on someone else to back Finland up, the experiences of which were – to put it mildly – not good. He then took up the negotiations that resulted in the FCMA Treaty in 1948, which has ever since been one of the cornerstones in Finnish security policy.

By 1949, then, the institutional pattern of security policies had been set that was then solidified for forty years. Within a few years after this, important parts were added by the NATO members (to which Iceland had now also been added) making unilateral declarations about peacetime conditions that amounted to 'NATO membership on minimal terms': neither of them would permit nuclear weapons on their territory, Denmark and Norway ruled out foreign bases, and Norway added even further restrictions on its own military presence in northern Norway as well as geographical limits for NATO exercises, flights of other NATO members, etc. These things together defined the preconditions for the preservation of Norden as a 'low tension' area, by means of the pattern of 'Nordic Balance'.

New European Constellations

A priori, an area can be characterized by low tension for two reasons: because it is strategically uninteresting for major powers, or because its strategic interest is counterbalanced by particular circumstances, whether internal or external to the area.

In the Nordic case, we seem to have different situations in different periods. In the nineteenth century, Norden was of little strategic interest. At the turn of the century, however, a new constellation emerged in Europe. In very abstract terms, it can be described as the Land Power/Sea Power situation. The two traditional rivalries in Western Europe had been those between France and Britain, and between France and Prussia/Germany. The former was largely a rivalry between a Land Power and a Sea Power, with Norden too far away to be of much interest; the latter was between two Land Powers, with Norden as markedly peripheral.

When Great Britain and Germany started to rival each other, and when in addition Germany developed ambitions to become a Sea Power as well as a Land Power, the Nordic situation became more precarious. Its western coast came to be of positive interest for a Land Power wanting access to the Atlantic, for which reason the Sea Power had an interest in preventing the Land Power from getting such control. Already at the turn of the century, young German naval officers had started thinking about the Norwegian coast; but it was only after World War I that they were senior enough to have any influence and get scenarios drawn up, and only after the ascent of Hitler that Germany had also had the resources to implement "Weserübung," as its code name was, against Denmark and Norway.

After World War II, the United States joined Great Britain in the role of Sea Power, whereas the role of Land Power was taken over by the Soviet Union. In the early years, its navy was very modest, primarily a coastal one designed to fend off possible Western attempts at invasion. Later on, Admiral Gorshkov managed to persuade the Soviet leadership to increase its naval ambitions to wield power across the oceans, in addition to which both surface vessels and killer submarines were thought necessary to protect the submarine leg in the Soviet nuclear armament.

Whatever the motives for the Soviet naval expansion from the 1960s, maritime geography dictated that much of it had to be based in the Murmansk area on the Kola peninsula. This in its turn could not avoid arousing NATO fears concerning its sea lanes across the Atlantic and the North Sea, and thus the strategic interest of Norden had once more grown highly problematic. The position of Norden was no longer enough to make it a low tension area; something more was needed, as long as it could last.

COLD WAR, NORDIC BALANCE AND LOW TENSION

When foreign ministries and establishment institutes write about Nordic security, they have tended to stress how the Cold War has conditioned and limited the options for it. Critical literature, on the other hand, often insists that the range of actual possibilities has been underestimated and that the Nordic elites have had more responsibility for developments than they pretend. Both perspectives overlook something important: how the Cold War furnished a basis for the *nicer* sides of Nordic security, in particular the Nordic understanding of it.

While holding different positions in the East/West arrangement, the Nordic countries remained concerned about the effects upon each other of their acts. They thus simultaneously participated – to some degree – in the East/West conflict and modified the competition in the subregion by taking each other's interests into account. Thus, a special system developed in one of the subregions of the European security complex generally dominated by East–West competition. The Nordic subregion did not establish a self-contained system of 'Nordic security'; but it was made a 'low tension area' by a system of mutual restraint that was in part designed, in part the upshot of trial and error.

A system of mutual restraint, of limited competition in a conflictual relationship – this is what the concept 'security regime' essentially refers to.

Such a regime clearly existed in Norden – but not in Europe – from the mid-1950s until at least the late 1970s. *There was a system of mutual self-restraint in a subsystem inside a greater system with full competition. Why was this possible and how was it brought about?*

One part of the answer is internal to Norden and has already been referred to: its character of a 'security community' where war is inconceivable as a means of resolving conflicts. Accounting for the external powers is far more complicated because of the following dilemma. If Norden was able to impose this system against the superpowers, this implies that it was an independent security complex, and that is not very credible even if it is sometimes heard in Nordic debates. And if it was not, it is hard to explain why the superpowers would behave differently in Norden than elsewhere.

While the Nordic states have made the local arrangements for such a 'low tension' system, it was neither derived from the initial interests of the global powers, nor would it have been possible to install it against them. What has happened is rather that the pattern of interlinking Nordic security considerations (by a combination of design and coincidence) *has created a subregional constellation in relation to which the superpowers have come to see self-restraint as lying in their own interests.*

The 'micro-mechanism' of this system is often referred to as 'the Nordic Balance'. This concept has achieved a dual function: on the one hand, it is used in academic analysis; on the other hand, it has served as a rhetorical device to legitimize a variety of policies in some of the Nordic countries. There could therefore obviously be no agreement on exactly what is meant by it or on what it can and cannot explain. We do not intend to get into that exegesis here, but we limit ourselves to one important insight that is conveyed by this concept: *it provides a clue to how the 'low tension' situation could be self-reproducing.*

In spite of the term 'balance,' the notion of 'Nordic Balance' cannot be reduced to a military balance in the traditional sense. It also – and essentially – refers to a system of political dissuasion, a balance of unexploited options; and in a slightly idealized version, the theory is about how Norden (and especially Norway) kept the superpowers out by elegantly using it.

Let us give a couple of examples. *If* the Soviet Union increased its pressure on Finland, the Nordic NATO members might ease their present bans on foreign bases and nuclear weapons in peacetime, thus making for a greater US/NATO military presence; the knowledge of this could dissuade the Soviet Union. On the other hand, such an increasing presence might lead to Soviet calls for closer defence co-operation with Finland – which could dissuade the USA from pressing for it.

In this – dynamic – version of the theory, an essential point is that the Nordic countries can keep tension down by keeping each other's superpower out. In addition, references to this 'Nordic Balance' can also help them to keep their own superpower out. A famous quotation in Danish foreign policy liturgy stems from the argument by Foreign Minister Per Hækkerup at the NATO Council meeting in May 1963, where he legitimized the Danish policy of no nuclear weapons by reference to "the inter-Nordic balance." Introduction of nuclear weapons "could upset this balance and cause reactions, not only detrimental to this vulnerable area but according to our view also to the NATO alliance as a whole," he argued.

As mentioned, the 'theory' was also used domestically to provide the NATO memberships of Norway and Denmark (and Iceland), as well as the non-membership and the high military expenditures of Sweden with a legitimization that went beyond national interests to be 'Nordic': "We are doing this for the sake of the Finns (Norwegians, Icelanders, etc.)."

In any case, the viable essence of 'Nordic Balance' seems to be that it has dissuaded the superpowers from increasing their military presence in Norden, because of the knowledge that such an increase would lead to a corresponding move from the other superpower. A precondition for this has been that the self-restraint of the Nordic countries has entailed that there *were* self-imposed restrictions that might be abandoned in favour of an increased 'threat' component in their postures – and that these instances of self-restraint were interlinked.

Both the local self-restraint and the interlinking of policies have, in their turn, depended on the local Nordic security community, which has permitted much more trust and mutual helpfulness than normally found among states with markedly different security arrangements.

All this taken together explains to some degree *why* it was possible to establish a Nordic 'low-tension' area. Because the Nordic states, the 'minimal members' of NATO and the non-aligned ones alike, *did* have some leeway and *would* take each other's interests into some account, the superpowers were dissuaded from 'forward moves' because they knew that the consequences would be harmful even to their own short-term self-interests.

Therein lay the true virtuosity of the Nordic arrangement.

This brings us to the second question: *how* was it worked out? It was decidedly *not* the design of some ingenious Nordic security expert, implemented by five Nordic countries in unison and in secrecy. The truth appears to be more prosaic: it gradually emerged, largely by trial and error, out of the policies of five countries that had chosen different 'roads to security,' but had the advantage of everybody knowing that the others *would* take their interests into account.

This implied being sensitive to the security needs of both superpowers, in particular the one that was an immediate neighbour in the East, and served to impose a local self-restraint that aided the self-reproduction of the 'low-tension' dynamism. Even if, as mentioned, this situation was only partly of Nordic making, it was highly advantageous for the Nordic countries which were thus able to develop their societies at a certain distance from the ideological clarion calls of the Cold War.

Finally, we have to take into account *the wider pattern* in which it was embedded. The Nordic system we here talk about was a *subregional security regime*, based on a *subregional security community*, inside a *regional security complex* (Europe), which was in its turn overlaid by the *superpower security complex*, neither of these complexes being a security community nor even a security regime.

That summarizes both the strengths and the weaknesses of the Nordic arrangement. Because it was *not* a security complex of its own, it continued to be dependent on the dynamics of the wider security complex of which it was an element. It could, and did, cushion some of the effects of that; but there were obvious limits to how far it would be able to avert any drastic changes in those dynamics.

NORDIC IDENTITY AND ITS SECURITY COMPONENT

The neat arrangement described above was in place for a long time, and it contributed something to Nordic identity. When the arrangement was challenged, first by an intensification of the Cold War and then by its disappearance, this also had effects on that identity. Let us therefore give a somewhat impressionistic picture of how the dimension of security arrangements has affected Nordic identity.

We first need to point out an apparent paradox. The post-war policies of the Nordic countries have been defined, underpinned and executed by cohorts of people that were predominantly Realists, and increasingly so (the interwar cohorts of people with a bit more Idealist colouring gradually leaving the arena). At the same time, their legitimization has used much of the Idealist language besides parts of the Realist language that was widely current among the NATO members, more limited in Sweden and Finland. (There is little relationship between the extent to which the Nordic elites thought in a Realist fashion and how much they spoke "Realese." In addition, the relative weight of the "Realese" and "Idealese" has depended much on the forum in which the argument was presented.)

In the largely Idealist language (that had to be) used in public legitimization, both the policies of the individual nations and the entire pattern of 'Nordic security' appeared as *virtuous*, as implying – at the very least – a more relaxed attitude and less of cold warrior mentality than among the European and Atlantic neighbours.

This was even more so in the two non-aligned countries: Finland with its low-key neutrality focused on confidence-building (for solid Realist reasons), and Sweden with its more high-profile neutrality with occasional Messianic overtones.

While all of the Nordic countries, individually and as a group, have been fairly engaged in international issues of security, disarmament and arms control, they have presented few proposals pertaining to *their own* areas; in the exceptional cases, such as a Nordic Nuclear-Free Zone or maritime CBMs, the initiative was normally Finnish. The *grand dessein* of the most active one,

Sweden, was seen by critical (and only partly unfair) observers as being about faraway countries in the Third World or about what to do with the nuclear weapons of the superpowers.

A public image of a special 'Nordic' way of handling security problems grew out of the interplay between Swedish/Nordic moral foreign policy and the structural arrangement described above (which was, as we saw, only partly of Nordic making).

This security-related dimension of the self-image harmonized well with the (self-understanding of the) social democratic welfare state, seen and known as the 'Scandinavian model' or 'Swedish model.' This also contained an element of creating distance from the Cold War, having found a 'third way' or 'the middle of the road.' Here, too, the very existence of the Cold War was among the preconditions for upholding this self-image because it was defined (partly) *by contrast*.

THE 'SECOND COLD WAR' AND THE FIRST EUROPEANIZATION OF NORDEN IN THE EARLY 1980S

The institutionalization in the Nordic countries of the 'low tension' regime – and thereby of the duality of living off the Cold War and keeping a distance from it – has helped the Nordic countries to modify circumstances in the past. *The collective ability to influence the direction of change is much smaller*. This was to become an important limitation during the 1980s and in particular the 1990s.

The first major challenge to this system in the 1980s came from the impact of naval competition between the superpowers, and more generally from the cold winds of the so-called 'Second Cold War'. The basic constellation was still there: Norden was still 'low tension' compared with Central Europe, but there were two disturbing factors: the tension was *increasing*, and it was *increasing more there than in Central Europe*.

The pressure that the Nordic region came under in the 1980s emerged from a superpower chain reaction that can be summarized as follows:

1) The Soviet Northern Fleet stationed in ports on the Kola peninsula was not directed against the Nordic states, but as it grew during the 1970s it actually threatened to shift the local power relations. NATO's Sea Lines of Communication across the Atlantic could possibly be threatened, and in particular Norway felt exposed by this. The Norwegian security elite started in the 1970s to ask for a counter move.

2) The American 'answer' was, however, much stronger than 'necessary' as a solution to the local problems. The new American 'Maritime Strategy' included a much more offensive approach than previously, an aggressive attempt to exploit the vulnerabilities of the Soviet Union, even if a war broke out somewhere else (so-called 'horizontal escalation'). The Soviet bases on the Kola were directly threatened, and this must have been seen as a serious security threat by the Soviet Union, whose maritime geography forces it to have a great part of its navy (including nuclear submarines) stationed there.

3) Given this, Soviet counter moves were then to be expected. An extended local defence zone would be a logical reaction, and an increase of the local forces on and around the Kola peninsula would be very unpleasant from a Nordic point of view, in particular for the immediate neighbours. Control of Swedish airfields might become more attractive, improving the possibilities of stopping the Maritime Strategy at the GIUK gap. Some analysts have also seen the submarine incidents in Sweden as part of a wider Soviet strategy for getting more influence in Norden.

4) What would the United States then do? If the Soviet Union had increased its presence in Norden, the United States would have to do the same. The mutual 'unused options' of the Nordic Balance would thus be implemented. Hence it would no longer be possible to build a 'Nordic Balance' arrangement, both superpowers would increase their presence in Norden, and *Norden would become divided – which is exactly what the special arrangement tried to avoid.*

In terms of possible future worst-case scenarios, the perspectives for Norden in the mid 1980s were even *worse* than those of Central Europe. Not only was Norden getting 'normalized' in the sense of 'full East–West competition;' some of the features described above might also, in this new situation, operate to exacerbate it.

For example, the submarine incidents in Sweden might have led to American moves in the form of grey zone activities, exploiting a situation after the murder of then prime minister Olof Palme and the revelation that different parts of the Swedish power elite used different parts of the intelligence system for their opposing aims. More generally, Norden might have become the arena for the 'coalition warfare approach' decribed as follows by Harvard professor Eliot A. Cohen:

The opposing coalition leaders strive to preserve the integrity of their bloc of states and expand it if possible. At the same time, they seek to dismember the opposing alliance, and to either woo, intimidate, or even coerce neutral powers into joining their bloc ... The strategic competition between the United States and the Soviet Union for advantage in Scandinavia takes place in peace time: that competition would intensify enormously in wartime or even in a crisis short of war.

Geopolitical trends are filtered through perception systems, among elites as well as in public opinion – and are often denied, exaggerated or reinterpreted. Official reports in all countries talked about the maritime situation as deteriorating, but saw this as a matter of degree, and as something that could be compensated for by use of the traditional instruments: increasing military preparations and getting stronger commitments from allies.

We get a first crude indicator of relative changes in perceptions by looking at defence expenditures in the 1980s. The closest neighbours to the Northern Waters and the Kola peninsula increased theirs: calculated in 1988 dollars, Norway rose from 2.4 to 3.1 bn. (and from 2.9 to 3.2% of GNP) and Finland from 1.5 to 2.1 bn. (and from 1.8 to 1.9%). Danish and Swedish defence expenditures, on the other hand, were almost exactly the same in 1989 as in 1980, and had thus reduced their percentages of GNP somewhat.

These differences between the two NATO members, Denmark and Norway, also underline the importance of geography. Norway was eager to strengthen commitments, and accordingly made some policy changes that might be seen as concessions to the USA, but were in fact Norwegian initiatives, e.g., pre-posititioning of NATO equipment. (The elements of diverging interests appeared when the location was to be decided: purely military logic pointed to northern Norway, whereas the prevailing logic of non-provocation led the equipment being stored in central Norway.)

The Danish government, in contrast, was repeatedly overruled by Parliament and forced to oppose a number of aspects of NATO nuclear weapons policy.

The new situation was as much of a challenge to the traditional critics of the establishment as to the establishment themselves. Some of the reactions among the critics were also 'traditional' ones. For example, the calls for a Nordic nuclear weapons free zone grew stronger in the early 1980s than before. (In fact, they got so strong that the governments had to give something: abstract declarations on its desirability in principle and on a number of conditions, and the appointment of an intergovernmental group of civil servants to study the question further.)

There were, however, also some new patterns of thinking. Many of the traditional critics had implied a combination of Nordism and globalism – which also meant keeping a distance from the superpowers and from a Europe shaped by military pacts and economic blocs. Some of the critics retained that pattern, whereas others began to think of a 'Europeanization of Norden' – at the same time as one found critical security thinking in Germany and elsewhere about a 'Nordification of Europe.'

The latter phrase – with subspecies such as the 'Finlandization of Eastern Europe,' the 'Swedification of Germany' and the 'Denmarkization of Western Europe' – points to some Central Europeans seeing the relative disengagement of Norden, with its shades of neutralism or semi-neutralism, as something to emulate in Central Europe. This did not call for a great amount of reorientation among these critics, since it essentially meant tagging a symbolic name, Norden, on a potential state of affairs that they had long been striving for.

For centre-to-left groups in Norden to call for 'Europeanization' called for more of a reorientation, whose essential logic was as follows. The Second Cold War was seen as essentially a superpower affair – and, from a Nordic perspective, with the American maritime strategy as the most threatening manifestation. Effective attempts to save or re-launch détente must therefore come from Europe, especially West Germany and its Social Democratic party, whose thinking on 'common security' was similar to that of Sweden under the Palme government and contained the essential preconditions for a security regime. It was therefore a good idea to reach out to a Europe that represented the more peaceful end in the intra-Western spectrum. At the same time, the notion of 'Europeanization' was so vague and general that it could be attractive in wider circles.

A good example is found in the Norwegian debate. Many of the EC opponents from the 1972 referendum were also opposed to the new American security policy. To oppose this, they needed to link up to Europe, and so they suddenly favoured an EC-orientation. For other and more mainstream groups in Norway, the "Europeanization of Norden" was thought of in more concretely military terms: it meant the Royal Navy and Bundesmarine replacing the US Navy in the high North, in order to avoid direct confrontation with the Soviet Union.

For the critics, however, the thinking behind 'Europeanization' was less in terms of the past (they certainly did not want Norden to take over the tradition European logic of competition) than in terms of perceived directions of change: they preferred a European situation where an emergent security regime was in the process of formation, to a Nordic one where a long-standing security regime was falling apart. The Europe they wanted to link up with was, as it were, one that was 'Nordified' in the good old sense – and that was also less sensitive than the small Norden to external influences.

THE END OF THE COLD WAR WAS THE BEGINNING OF NORDIC CONFUSION

Following the historical years of 1989–90, Norden faces a new set of challenges. East is no longer East; the East–West conflict is not what it used to be; Western Europe changes towards '1992'; and Germany has unified itself. *This is no longer the framework in which the Nordic countries had slowly evolved their ingenious little arrangement.* Until 1989, Norden was defined by having a lower level of tension than Europe. Norden has been dependent for its identity on Europe remaining divided, highly armed and marked by a certain level of tension.

Norden is in the process of losing that part of its identity. What is Norden if we have low tension in Europe? In a certain sense the old arrangement was ideal: Norden was embedded in a stable European constellation, with Norden's own situation somewhat better than the others.

What had previously not been noticed, now became clear: the Nordic arrangement was embedded in the European constellation, and in a dual sense. The Nordic security order was but a variation on the European one - Europe as a whole is the security complex. And the essence of 'Norden,' its identity, was based on the distinction in relation to 'Europe.'

This may account for an apparent paradox. For if we think of identity in absolute terms, as the central values and beliefs, then the European revolution in 1989–90 was very much what the peace-minded Norden had been asking for, and ought to have hailed enthusiastically. *In reality, however, the Nordic governments were among the slowest in Europe to appreciate that a dramatic change had taken place.*

If we think of identity in terms of relations and contrasts, however, the paradox disappears. The European transformation can then be seen as a painful loss to such central parts of Nordic identity as 'lower tension than in Central Europe' or 'more détente-oriented than Central Europe.' In the first case, it was no longer true: Europe had changed, but maritime geography had not. In the second case, it had become irrelevant: the change in Europe had gone far beyond degrees of detente, defining a major *transformation* where the traditional conflict pattern was broken up and quite new thinking called for.

By an ironical coincidence, the Parliamentary Defence Committees in all the four bigger Nordic countries were to present reports on long-term defence plans in late 1989 or 1990. These reports clearly illustrate the paradox, being more traditional than anywhere in Europe (except, possibly, Great Britain), at least in their practical conclusions. It is common to all of them to be largely

---

focused on the East–West conflict that has been so central to Nordic identity: seeing more 'détente' *inside* this conflict is about as far as their imagination carries them, and new themes of thought, such as 'Germany,' 'West–West controversies' and 'German–Russian interaction' are largely avoided, in spite of already being highly topical outside Norden.

The realities have changed too much, however, for such attitudes in Norden to have anything but bleak prospects. As some of the reports also acknowledge in their premises, the agenda of the early 1990s will have to deal with them, on several dimensions, and the Nordic system of perceptions will be forced to a number of reappraisals more painful than easily imagined by outside observers.

◆ ◆

3

Norden as a Mystery
The Search for New Roads into the Future

Pertti Joenniemi

THE WINDS OF CHANGE

The radical changes we have seen in recent years have shattered many of the time-worn accounts of political order on the European continent. With the dissolution of the old order, there is a growing sense of freedom and flexibility and an intensified search for new patterns of interaction – but also increasing uncertainty.

With the 'old world' in transition, there is an opportunity, if not a need, for new thinking. The previous order is caving in, and considerable repositioning is taking place among its different political agencies and policy configurations. All of them look less natural and permanent. Some of them are losers, and a few appear as winners. The Warsaw Treaty Organization and COMECON, which have disappeared altogether, are obvious cases in the category of losers while others, such as the CSCE or the European Community, seem to be less entrenched. They may even benefit from the changes, and emerge revitalized.

Norden is certainly one of the configurations on the scene of international relations that has been touched by the recent developments.

36

Traditionally regarded as quite stable, Norden is now turning into one of the more uncertain cases on the European agenda. It remains to be seen whether it will emerge as one of the central acronyms and configurations in the debate, such as 'Pentagonale,' 'Mittel-Europa' and the 'European Economic Space,' or rather discussed as something problematic, and considered to have a rather bleak future.

As a rule Norden is slotted in the latter category. As a spatialization that is becoming increasingly difficult to sustain, there are views according to which Norden, in its present form, is growing weaker and may eventually wither away completely unless a remedy is found. However, there are also those who are convinced that Norden still has a future: their argument is that it may be reconstituted and considered anew, although in a broader and different context.

The aim here is to address these questions on the future of Norden, although from a somewhat unusual perspective. The aim is not one of containment, of aspiring to control ambiguity or to restore normalcy, as often seems to be the case in research on the various European configurations that have been rendered problematic in recent years.

The aim, instead, is to penetrate a number of profound issues and fundamental questions that are often swept aside or taken for granted. This implies, among other things, that Norden is not understood simply as an object "out there," to be tackled in an objectifying and straightforward manner. It is not merely viewed as a politico-geographic delineation or a set of political relationships. On the contrary, Norden is regarded as being intimately bound up with the way in which it is understood and spoken of, including the treatment it is given in scholarly work. It is regarded as having a conversational and textual quality. If seen in this light, Norden seems to be currently in a process of being re-stated.

Norden, as a political configuration, is therefore problematized rather than treated as something self-evident and well-established in terms of analysis, as an entity that appears less natural and coherent that it did before.

Norden is increasingly in the focus of various modes of representations that clash over a preferred definition in the search for a broadly acceptable and durable ground. This clash, and the emerging understanding, is here seen as decisive for the future of Norden.

This approach means that we have to ask questions that touch upon the very essence of the 'Nordic:' how does it work in terms of constitutive practices, and how is it normally explained and understood? Such an insight is needed to probe into the question of whether Norden's current problems and paralyses are somehow related to the way these constitutive practices work.

The analysis therefore assumes a reorientation in the process of questioning by invoking a post-structuralist line of enquiry. It aims at pondering more closely than is usually the case into what a historian has called "the Nordic mystery."[1] More specifically: this chapter consists of unpacking those constitutive practices discovered and of inquiring into the way(s) the meaning of Norden is determined – and perhaps caught up and detained as a prisoner of the past – at this critical juncture.

In this our approach draws upon the rather fluid situation of Norden and its openness to alternative, less empirical, managerial and control-oriented approaches and interpretations than the ones usually offered. The aim is one of trying to order the debate on the future of Norden in a meaningful way, and thereby to offer perspectives needed for navigation in the current era of international relations.

THE MAIN IDEAS ABOUT THE ESSENCE OF NORDEN

Norden is certainly an established category of international relations, but even so it seems, upon closer examination, to be difficult to pin down in terms of analysis. It appears to have the quality of easily evading definition and turning into, despite efforts to arrest it, something rather vague and slippery.

1. The confusion starts with the term itself: in the English language there is no established and broadly recognized term that would cover the whole region and give it an autonomous and distinct identity. Should one speak of Norden – a delineation used in Swedish, Norwegian and Danish – or would it be more appropriate to resort to the familiar term of Scandinavia? Both solutions are problematic and their connotations remain diffuse and ambiguous. [2]

Another way of settling the question is simply to enumerate the actors involved and to list the countries belonging to Norden. The core comprises Denmark, Norway and Sweden, i.e., the Scandinavian countries. Finland is a non-Scandinavian latecomer, but by now it has achieved a recognized place in the Nordic family, even though it does not share the same main language with the rest of the members. Iceland has a less established position in the Nordic context and is sometimes forgotten, not to speak of Greenland, Faroe, the Åland Islands or the Same people up in the North, all of which have some autonomies of their own.

In other words, the politico-geographic delineations of Norden vary considerably, so much that it has not always been clear which countries and areas belong to "the Nordic area." There is, for example, no foundational text or basic treaty containing unequivocal definitions of the ones within and those outside. There are no grand schemes, either in the economic sphere or in defence policies, that would categorically nail down Norden as a political category or agent. There have been occasional efforts to establish such schemes of cooperation, but they have all notoriously failed; this was the case with the Nordic defence union during the late 1940s and the customs union at the beginning of the seventies, for instance.

The borderlines of Norden and the Nordic area have thus remained quite flexible. Norden would seem to be very much like a modern family: there are strong feelings of unity, homogeneity, concern and togetherness, but in practice everyone is at liberty to mix freely and to choose their own way. There are occasional joint meals around a table that is large enough to seat all the members. Some are entitled to more central positions and better seats than others, but in general the rules of conduct are quite liberal. In short: the trademark of Norden seems to be a certain openness, a lack of exclusive categorizations, as well as elusiveness.

2. Jan Øberg has expressed this in an exceptionally open fashion. Having looked into the various definitions, he concludes that there is no agreement as to what it means to be Nordic, feel Nordic, think Nordic or act Nordic.[3] Sometimes Nordism is taken to be an abstraction, as the ideology itself is regarded as more important than reality and concrete cooperation. Øberg recognizes the difficulty of grasping the essence of Norden and presents his own definition in terms of the peoples, rather than the states, in the region; the people who have affinities with each other and who feel a distinctness from the rest of continental Europe.

What precisely does he mean by this? Øberg's choice raises the question of whether Norden should be seen primarily as something statist, a formation composed of states located in northern Europe, or whether it deep down is something societal and communal, of which the cooperation among the states is merely a reflection. Øberg goes for the latter alternative. He provides Norden with a certain autonomy as a societal entity, rather than a security policy construct in the sphere of international relations.

3. Another way of putting it would be to say that the real story has been the one of Norden as a societal construct, or to put it differently, Norden may compete with any other text as a social text. As it has considerable self-sufficiency in the social sphere, Norden also gains a standing of its own as a security policy construct and a formation in the field of international relations. This is to say that Norden may not be depicted as a separate text in the field of international relations. It is seen, rather, as a subtext associated with and being dependent on the general text of East–West relations and European security at large. This may explain why researchers often, and Jan Øberg as one of them, search for the "real" Norden in the sphere of the societal, and allot it far less autonomy in the field of security policies and international relations.

4. There has often been wavering on this point, and many articulations settle it by skating over the problem entirely. The solution is one of addressing it only indirectly. The more statist and security policy oriented the argument becomes, the weaker are the claims that there is something

---

autonomous and distinct about Norden. It is thus taken, by a number of authors, to consist of a pattern, that is defined by using terms with considerable behavioural connotations, or approached as a network of relations. Those seeking to produce more concrete categorizations and trying to nail down Norden as something firm and measurable often define it in terms of a structure or load it with systemic properties.[4] In the same vein, they underline the status of the Nordic Council as the main institutional embodiment of Norden.

There can be no doubt that these approaches to Norden cover a good deal of its essence. Norden is indeed also an institution, a system or a structure and it is, largely, built around various practical, low-key aspirations. These have yielded many important results such as harmonized legislation, a special status for Nordic citizens on the labour market of other Nordic countries, a highly developed social security system, etc. Such results are quite important in providing Norden with a real content, and yet these ways of trying to capture the gist of Norden are far from perfect. It would be a gross simplification to assume that the essence of Norden can be grasped in structural or institutional terms or assumed to consist of a domain of practices.

Norden should not be reduced to something factual, manageable, homogeneous, ordinary and normal. In their endeavours at normalization, such reductionist approaches miss the aspects of Norden that seem to refer to something hegemonic, to a kind of master narrative. This is how a social text is transformed into a subtext of international relations. The factually oriented representations disguise more than they reveal; they downplay the constitutive practices that portray Norden as a case above the ordinary. They objectify, and thus discipline, more than they should, particularly when we assume that the aim is to provide insights into the essence of Norden.

5. The indicators and aspects that are downplayed in the constitution of Norden as a configuration of international relations tend to be value-oriented and immaterial. They consist of instigating Norden in terms of a number of rather positive features, such as peacefulness, stability, affinity, concern for the interests of each other and closeness in terms of values, culture and political systems. These features or properties are such that they tend to

evade objectification. They are not systemic, structural or institutional, but have to be expressed through categorizations such as identity, culture or heritage, i.e. in terms of something soft and elusive rather than factual and concrete.

This frame of Norden in terms of value-orientation and some societal features allows it to be delineated as something special in the sphere of security policy as well; it is ascribed features that are understood to distinguish the northern sub-region from the rest of Europe. Instead of normalizing and pursuing Norden as an entity among others, the endeavour translates into one of capturing it in terms of its exceptional features.

It is therefore often pointed out that Norden constitutes a zone of relative stability and peace, a barrier in the confrontation between East and West. The parties to this conflict are thought to have tempered their security policy ambitions considerably, and there has been less rivalry and more neighbourly cooperation in the northern part of Europe than elsewhere on the continent. Norden has thus been described as an exceptionally stable and peaceful region. It has been seen to consist of a subregion conditioned by a broader European setting – as better-off and privileged in relative terms.

6. This means that Norden is not a self-reliant region. The reference point is the post-war European security order, or to be more precise, the major actors in the security constellation of which Norden has been a part, are represented by the superpowers and the East–West conflict in general. As to political space, the scene of the drama has been Europe and the European security pattern.[5] Within that setting Norden has had a profile of its own, being less ridden by ideological controversy and less influenced by the Cold War.

The formula for the politics pursued in Norden has often been described as one of participating in the Cold War on minimalist terms.[6] Norden has been viewed as an area outside the normal sphere of power politics, that of the Europe of the two alliances competing without self-limitations. Europe has almost fully abided by the power-political dictates of the superpowers, while Norden has adopted a different line. Norden is less militarized, it has a lower level of tension and a less distinct bloc structure than the rest of Europe. The major powers are thought to have contributed to this by

---

deliberately de-emphasizing their offensive aspirations – as indicated by the downgrading of the nuclear threat and various restrictions on conventional armaments, including the decision not to station foreign troops in the region and to keep the military presence of the major blocs in and around Norden at a comparatively low level.

Such delineations of Norden as something special, but as part of a larger setting, may almost be described as the standard approach. There has been less interest in finding explanations as to how and why Norden has developed into such a partial exception. The few explanations that do exist are mostly in the form of historical accounts, and they – too – tend to lead to problems, as it often turns out that the history of the region has not been an altogether peaceful one. In fact, the more recent history of cooperation has been preceded by a long period of conflicts.

Some scattered efforts to develop a joint identity and to strike agreements to counteract the efforts of external major powers to divide Norden into spheres of interest took place during the two centuries following the end of the Napoleonic wars, but the early twentieth century was a clear turning-point in intra-Nordic history in the sense that the tendency towards peaceful resolution of conflicts then strengthened considerably. This goes for the Norwegian secession from Sweden in 1905, and the settling by peaceful arbitration the status of the Åland Islands (1921) and East Greenland (1933).

This more recent history has invited some revealing interpretations concerning the basic nature of Norden. It has been correctly observed that the quality of being less divided and conflictual than most other regions in the world does not follow simply from the application of pragmatism and de-ideological approaches, nor from joint institutional arrangements. Håkan Wiberg, for example, argues that this specificity of Norden "must be sought more in common ideology and practical politics than in formal arrangements on a grand scale." [7] Again there is a pondering into the social and communal background of Norden to figure it out as a construction of international relations.

This ideological and almost utopian nature of Norden has its roots in the mid nineteenth century. At that time 'Scandinavianism' was an internationalist-idealist movement with a wide following among Danish,

Swedish and Norwegian university students and teachers, and it was manifested in a series of joint student meetings and publications.[8] This ideology, carried by social forces arising from civil society, then started to spill over into the political system and was of major influence around and after the mid nineteenth century. Later it receded as a manifest ideology; great feelings and explicit idealism were left behind and everyday policies, referred to by Wiberg, took over. The neutralist or semi-neutralist tendencies also began to recede, and the ideology became primarily one of pragmatism and functionalism.

However, the early period left profound traces behind and may help to explain the lack of serious intra-regional rivalry and conflicts in the region. There has been an unusual lack of expansionism, selfishness and pursuing of 'national interests' in Nordic policies. The pacific secession of Norway from Sweden in 1905 is a case in point, representing as it does a rather exceptional event according to the standards of international relations.[9]

This line of politico-historical argument seems to catch something quite essential. It illuminates the nature of Norden as a political idea and a social text with merits of its own. The message conveyed is that Norden has been less coloured than many other regions by nationalism and calls for differentiation and exclusive spatialization. There have been unifying values and goals – nationalism in this sense – but not traditional nationalism and feelings of an exclusive national heritage.[10] Beate Børresen, the Norwegian historian, speaks of the Nordic countries as having been "de-nationalized" in the process of history.[11]

Unlike most European countries, there has been a 'middle way' present in Nordic policies. Policies have consisted of compromises and solutions based on consent, rather than enforced or dictated settlements. One possible explanation is that the Nordic countries have not been detained by soaring class relations or ethnic rivalry that, in turn, would have called upon a very strict sense of nationalism and a strong central state as a unifying element in order to counterbalance the divisive effects of intra-societal conflicts. The relationship between the state and society has been a relatively harmonious one and the word 'solidarity' has had a real meaning in Norden.

All this has had consequences for external security and an impact on Norden as a security policy configuration. The usual bifurcation of political identities into exclusive categories of "us" and "them" as something demanding inviolable sovereignty has not been present in the region. With the lack of strong nationalist movements and a strong state, one that has to gain legitimacy in the eyes of society, Nordic national borders have been less sacrosanct than in many other places. This implies that Norden has been less detained by the usual power political understanding of the word than most other regions.

In the absence of any pressing need for distinct national borders or firmly established national identities, efforts at secession have not led to the standard employment of violence and resort to war. With no stringent identities and borders, Norden has managed to escape this dilemma. There has been an exceptional degree of tolerance, flexibility and reformism, allowing deviations – within reasonable limits – from the status quo. This is why it became possible for Norway in 1905 to achieve sovereignty merely by political emancipation.

This ability to cope with conflictual issues without resorting to violence has transformed Norden into a region symbolizing hope and representing a moral authority. Certainly the Second World War was a blow to such a hope and authority, in the sense that the war provided ground for arguments about Norden being too illusory and idealistic about power politics and the nasty realities of international relations. However, some of the hope and authority remained there even after the war, and the impact of the Nordic model found its way into the policies of other European countries. This happened to some extent through major politicians who stayed in the Nordic countries during the war. Willy Brandt, Herbert Wehner and Bruno Kreisky are among the most prominent ones.

The trademark of Norden is thus plurality, a tolerance for deviation, and a lack of strict and categorical delineations. This may have been reflected in analysis: Norden has been less distinctly articulated than most other categories and agents of international relations. This elusiveness seems to be a conscious choice: it is one of Norden's basic properties, perhaps even a condition for its success. The ambiguity may be perceived as deliberate, rather than resulting from a neglect of analysis or failure to perceive its essence correctly.

NORDEN AND THE OTHERS

Another distinctive characteristic of Norden is that it seems to have been constituted in an exceptionally positive vein, rather than in terms of counteracting fear, even in relation to the external and foreign. The chief concern of the foundational texts has not been with (in)security, and the articulation of danger has been far less central to the construction of Nordic identity than is usually the case. Nordic communality is not constructed and imposed in terms of an existence and identity threatened from the outside. Rather it seems to operate by negotiation, mutual consent and co-operation. Therefore there has been no real need to construct some external otherness or perceptions of threat to ensure the articulation of the Nordic.

Norden has frequently been depicted in terms of something unprovocative and intimate, such as "family" and "home." The lack of any serious threats has been articulated through descriptions such as "the quiet corner of Europe." These articulations provide Norden with connotations of an escape, a refuge, or turn it into an expression of hope in an otherwise nasty and dangerous world, one burdened with endemic conflicts. These ways of constituting Norden set it aside, but do not explicitly contrast it with a threatening environment or make security a prerequisite for its subjectivity.

This is not to say that there are no contrasts involved in the constitution of Norden. The definition of Nordic identity has not been possible without some "otherness." The aim of the Nordic has been historically one of counteracting outside major powers and preventing them from getting a foothold in the region. Intra-regional co-operation has been aimed particularly against the major Eastern power – originally Russia and pan-Slavism and later the Soviet Union and Communism. These have served –

---

externally – as the prime constituting element of the Nordic. The Russian revolution at the turn of the century seems to have been an important event in strengthening the barriers towards the East. Russia was depicted as non-Nordic, that is Oriental and "the Other" in relation to the values and points of departure that constituted the core of Nordic as a policy configuration.

Given this difference Norden could be defined *in contrast to* the Soviet Union: as a democratic, progressive, rationalist and reformist entity, a carrier of such values as individualism, as an advocate of welfare combined with egalitarianism. It has been said the Nordic countries share a joint puritan and Protestant, although secularized, culture and that they rank among the most advanced and modern countries in the world. There are researchers labelling them as the true incarnation of the programme of the Enlightenment. The vocabularies used contain articulations such as 'The Progress Machine' or 'Prototype of Modern Society.'[12] There are also references to a societal "people's home" ideology in contrast to the imperial, authoritarian and statist Russia. And last but not least: there has been a temporal distinction between the backward and the advanced, with Norden representing the avant-garde.

The same factors – lack of democracy, authoritarian rule and backwardness – placed the semi-feudal, imperial Prussia, which later evolved into Germany, into the category of the non-Nordic. In the 1930s this barrier towards Germany was further strengthened by the rise of Fascism. These views of the external environment did not change with the world war; nor was there any need to tear down previous barriers or to distance oneself from the German and the Russian in the post-war years. Nordism was not an explicitly anti-German or anti-Soviet ideology, but nevertheless it was thought to have features that set it clearly apart from the Soviet model and the German set of values.

For these reasons it was relatively easy for Norden to adjust and find its own place in the post-war setting, which was very much dominated by Anglo-Saxon values. Culturally the Anglo-Saxon became the criterion for similarity, while difference was indicated in relation to the Eastern, the Russian and the Soviet.

There was continuity in certain other respects as well. The world war had undermined the pre-war efforts at joint Nordic neutrality. After that war there was no going back to such policies, but there was enough plurality in international relations to allow for the constitution and articulation of Norden as something specific, although at the same time it was important to avoid giving the impression that Nordism was mutiny in the ranks, a claim for neutrality, or that Norden would refuse to acknowledge the general bipolarity of the East–West system.

Generally, the post-war period has seen a downgrading of the various ideological or utopian – some might say illusory – elements associated with Nordism. With the prevailing pragmatism and non-celebration mood, these have continued to recede. The erection of barriers against the external has become less conspicuous, and the essence of the Nordic has increasingly been phrased in techno-rationalist and instrumentalist terms. Nordic togetherness and affinity have become something quite natural and ordinary, and the once prominent internationalist or idealist-pacifist elements have receded into the background. Certain features of model societies representing some universal values and moral purity have prevailed, however, and provide the Nordic countries with a profile and image of their own.

In terms of security, Norden is there as a *de facto* political agency, downgrading rather than elevating its exceptional features. It existence is recognized without giving too much thought to its background and without contrasting it with the outside. The discourse within Norden has thus increasingly taken on features of normalization, the aim being to de-emphasize Norden's deviant and specific character. This is to say that Norden, as a social text, has been transformed into a subtext of international relations, and of the East–West setting in particular.

Interestingly enough, Nordic analysts and those viewing it from the outside seem to articulate Norden in somewhat different ways. The analysis presented by Nordic scholars easily turns into legitimation and taking things for granted; they tend to deal with Norden as an unproblematic given. The focus is either on the intra-Nordic in societal terms or on the foreign and security policies of the Nordic countries, but the different aspects are rarely mixed in the same analysis.

For those providing an outside view, things are less clear from the outset. One often sees mixes of the societal and the statist, for example.

Norden's quality as a social text has an impact on the way Norden is categorized in the field of international relations. Outsiders seem to be more curious about Norden. They are more serious about trying to uncover its essence, and are interested in Norden precisely because of its exceptional features and because of the challenge it presents. Outside analysts are of course also well aware of Nordic successes: the prosperity of the Nordic countries, the successful elimination of national barriers and their relatively favourable position in terms of security. Some have described Norden as Paradise, that is to say something quite far beyond the ordinary.[13]

NORDEN AS A CATEGORY IN INTERNATIONAL RELATIONS

To the extent that this way of depicting Norden mainly refers to the various societal features of the Nordic countries, it is not a particularly problematic term. However, if it is also intended to cover Norden more broadly as a category of international relations, then these references to something heavenly are clearly more dubious. Such idealizing conceptualizations raise questions that cannot be addressed without at least some conceptual and theoretical discussion.

The notion of 'Paradise,' indeed, sounds somewhat idealistic. Such connotations do not easily mix with the ordinary understanding of international relations that denies the possibility of positive alternatives in the first place. No state, no region or arrangement is assumed to escape the dictates of these conditions as long as they belong to the domain of the external. The metaphors used in describing qualities pertaining to relations between states usually refer to hell rather than heaven.

The use of such utopian terminology is obviously out of place. It is, by definition, an impossible condition in the sphere of international relations. It is precisely to avoid such issues and problems of definition that Norden has had a low profile as an agency in regard to the surroundings. The Nordic countries have refrained from dealing systematically and collectively with foreign affairs and security policies. They have abstained from any formal security policy arrangements, not to speak of joint institutions or any central authority that would manage security affairs. There is a Nordic Council, but no Nordic Community or Nordic Alliance. According to modernist accounts of political space, this leaves the Nordic countries in the category of fragmentation, that is, the ordinary negative state of affairs in terms of security.

It appears then that the Nordic countries are well aware that they must not challenge the conventional understandings of international relations too openly. They stay in their role as subtext, and tend to demonstrate concern only if adverse development affects their own area. One reflection of this aspiration for a low profile is that foreign policies, and particularly defence issues, are still banned from the Nordic Council. [14]

In practice, Nordic foreign and security policies consist of regular joint meetings of the foreign ministers, plus a fairly complex network of contacts and consultations between the respective officials. There is also a consultative caucus within the United Nations and other similar forums seeking to establish ground for the possible adoption of a joint profile. These efforts have quite often been successful and led to joint action and a common pattern of voting. There is less cooperation in the field of security policy, but even that is not totally absent. Recently the Ministers of Foreign Affairs from the five Nordic countries launched a joint study on the subject matter of a Nordic nuclear weapons free zone.[15]

In sum, joint Nordic foreign and security policies are there, but only in terms of a profile, an image and a perception of togetherness rather than in a rigidly coordinated institutionalized form. The Nordic countries have a sense of mutual affinity, they listen to and take into account the interests and concerns of each other if this is necessary and possible. They are all enlightened and progressive countries, strong on normative and moral power but relatively weak in coercive power, and they mix easily with each other as a group of like-minded countries. However, it would be wrong to describe them as a coherent bloc, not to speak of anything as formal or regular as an alliance.

50

SUCCESS BEYOND THE ORDINARY SCHEME

The question might be articulated as one of how and why the Nordic countries have such a good security policy record. Norden has managed very well without the power and organizational framework that is usually required for such achievements. And more precisely: the task is to find conceptualizations that can help us to understand the success of the Nordic countries, first, in their mutual relations and, second, *vis-à-vis* their external security policy environment. They have been able to avert war and preserve a low level of tension. They pose no military threat to one another and they have maintained rather good relations, relatively speaking, with all external powers without having to formalize their foreign affairs and security policy cooperation. It is almost a contradiction in terms: a positive security relationship within a setting where only negative relationships are assumed to exist.

The issue is thus the absence of the ordinary security dilemma among the Nordic countries. They are not opponents or rivals conditioned by the requirements of an anarchic state of affairs in the foreign policy sphere. By showing mutual concern and self-limitation, the Nordic countries have succeeded in forming a pattern that all parties want to preserve. The parties to this pattern abstain from pursuing short-term interests if these might undermine or destabilize the relationship. This kind of concern for others, reciprocity and reconciliation of conflicting interests has not been possible in the rest of Europe during the Cold War.

The issue that needs to be conceptualized is therefore the lack of the ordinary negative pattern and binary divisions, rather than endeavouring to explain something which is firmly established, concrete and easy to point out. Nordic security policies contain alternatives that should not be there and that amount to an unusual profile, pattern, or image. Norden, as a set of political relations, is quite puzzling: it lacks the enmity that is assumed to be ever-present according to an ordinary, that is to say a realist account of relations between states.

THE EMPLOYMENT OF OPPOSITES

This non-compliance with the rules of the game, and the identity thus achieved, seems to be the mystery lurking in the background. Norden is not to be defined against the background of some particular conflict or configuration of interests, but more generally in relation to the 'nature' of international relations. This is what makes it difficult to tackle Norden conceptually.

Instead of the usual, straightforward way of portraying a configuration, a double move has been needed to come to grips with Norden: first, it has been explained through conceptualizations that make it part of something general; and second, properties have been attached to Norden that turn it into an exception with regard to the rules that constitute the whole.

Upon closer inspection we can see an element of tension between these two constitutive moves: one is generalizing and standardizing, the other is specifying and builds on difference. The former denies the possibility of alternatives, while the latter modifies the power-political game and allows exceptions.

An example of this tension, and an operation of reconciliation, is the portrayal that says that Nordic policies contain elements of both linking and de-linking.[16] The basic, normalizing move is to present Norden as an integral part of a whole, and linked, in terms of security, to an Atlantic and European setting. The second move of de-linking is to provide it with some indigenous and autonomous features that turn Norden into a case beyond the ordinary. The concepts of linkage and de-linkage have sometimes been used in a rather dynamic fashion. The Nordic countries have been described as being able to regulate and control this relation of engagement and disengagement to a degree that is unusual for small countries. They are portrayed as being linked to a larger setting, and yet de-linked in certain ways, thus escaping some of the negative features of such a constellation and, more generally, the dictates of power politics.

There is similar wavering on the point of whether the Nordic countries should be primarily seen as strong on subjectivity with a determination, awareness and resourcefulness of their own, or as objects reflecting the

---

endeavours of the major powers to avoid confrontational policies in the northern part of Europe. There have been presentations which elevate the Nordic countries to masters of their own fate and depict them as fully in command of their external security environment. In some presentations, however, Norden has been reduced to a "flank" in the power-political game and the general confrontation between East and West. In those descriptions Norden is considered to possess very little subjectivity.

The most common approach, however, has been a compromise in which Norden is portrayed as containing elements of both objectivity and subjectivity. The Nordic countries have thus been set apart into a category of their own, although at the same time it has been stressed that they are small countries with moderate resources, and therefore very much at the mercy of general developments. They are considered to have had considerable influence on their external security environment, in spite of their being basically dependent on the rules of the general power-political game.

A further dichotomy and combination of opposites is found in the way that Norden has been related to trust and threat – two basic conceptualizations used in describing any security-related constellation of international relations. Here again, the Nordic countries are seen as deviating in their security policies from the standard application of principles such as deterrence. It is argued that there is an unusual degree of trust in intra-Nordic relations, and that such a positive relationship also has beneficial consequences for Nordic relations with external powers.

The general feeling is that somehow the Nordic countries have been able to escape the basic rules of international relations: they are frequently portrayed as countries trying both to avoid provocation and to maintain some distance, by policies of dissuasion, from the East–West confrontation. The element of trust is seen as being rather strong within Norden, but the Nordic countries are also presented more as partners, rather than opponents, of outside powers in their effort to reduce tension and to sustain a stable and predictable pattern of relations in Northern Europe.

This duality of trust and threat, cooperation and division is clearly manifested in the simultaneous use of such concepts as "deterrence" and "reassurance" in the vocabularies aiming to delineate key elements in the

Nordic repertoire of security policies.[17] Policies based on the application of threat have been qualified by something that moderates it. In a sense, Nordic security is seen to be based on the simultaneous use of two pedals: the accelerator and the brake.

The main problem seems to be that political agencies in the sphere of international relations are usually defined in terms of inclusion or exclusion. This is to ensure the dominance of one single text. However, the constitutive moves may not be ones of inclusion or exclusion. There is little understanding of configurations that operate in terms of 'both–and', as texts having their roots simultaneously in two different spheres. They are anchored, in the latter case, in the sphere of international relations, but have properties that pertain in the domain of the domestic and the societal.

Norden does not easily meet this criterion of 'either–or'. It falls in between and therefore remains difficult to come to grips with even in terms of the vocabularies and conceptualizations used. The constitutive moves applied do not correspond to the rules of analytical agencies or to constructs operating in the field of international relations.

THE ELIMINATION OF OPPOSITES

Karl W. Deutsch adhered to this rule, although twisting it around, in his classical study on political communities. Deutsch is one of the analysts for whom Norden has been an important source of inspiration and insight in waging an alternative, de-militarizing security discourse.

The way in which Deutsch depicted Norden allowed him to circumvent the usual dilemmas. For him the matter of security did not follow from the nature of international relations as such, but it was something to be explored empirically by analyzing and comparing different cases under different circumstances. He therefore easily transcended the usually untouchable borderline between the external and the internal, the domestic and the

---

foreign. Using a functionalist approach, Deutsch made a clear-cut choice in arguing that the Nordic region had become a pluralist "security community," a community not in terms of common security with some specific arrangements to provide for it, but in the sense of an island of peace amidst a broader setting based on the perpetual presence of the danger of war.[18]

In attempting to explain why war has become unthinkable among the countries of the region, he ascribed to them properties that are usually understood as located within states. Thus he set Norden clearly apart from the rest of the European constellation, attributing to it a communality that transcends the usual boundaries of the state. Such a constitutive move implied the breaking of the standard formula in international relations research of community inside and threat outside.

In other words, Deutsch was not seeking to strike a balance between two basically different conceptualizations and thereby to square the tension between the general play of power politics and the features characteristic of the Nordic region. He placed it clearly within the domain of the domestic. Deutsch depicted Norden as something quite separate, making it synonymous with difference and elevating it into a sphere with specific norms and with the consensual features of normal politics.

For Deutsch the Nordic countries were no longer a case in between, a peculiar meeting-point of different conceptualizations. He saw them as configurations outside the usual ambit of international relations. In his view Norden was not explicable in terms of the properties usually ascribed to states and the relations prevailing between states. Deutsch emphasized the significance of communality, i.e., properties that are normally considered to have their location within states but absent in relations between them. When such properties exist, inter-state relations would be labelled by continuity and merely be an extension of the internal. They would not form a domain of their own. Communality is precisely what is assumed to be, according to the usual accounts, missing in inter-state relations.

Karl W. Deutsch thus made a very forceful move in his constitution of what he thought to be the essence of the Nordic: he blurred the borderline between the internal and the external, the very line that distinguishes international relations from politics in general, the domestic from the foreign and the societal from the statist. He made this important move by ignoring the strict separation of theories of political community and those of inter-state relations as well as the thesis that political assumptions must not be transferred from within states to the analysis of relations between them. In doing so he also undermined, without explicitly saying so, the assumption present in traditional realist discourse on the timeless ontological quality of danger and anarchy attributed to international relations, and substituted it with perceptions of the presence of political community.

Many other analysts concerned with the essence of the Nordic have followed the path opened by Deutsch. It has often been stated that the hallmark of Norden is that war has become an impossibility amongst the countries of the region, and this without any hegemonic or strong institutions to quash the disorder assumed to be inherent outside the sphere of the domestic. Deutsch's functionalist approach to explaining this state of affairs has faded, and Nordic peacefulness and lack of enemy images among the countries of the region *vis-à-vis* each other have assumed something of a dogmatic status. Its presence is so strong and so obvious that no particular explanations are considered necessary. Norden has frequently been labelled as a security community outside the domain of war, without any deeper reflection.

The functionalist approach was based on an upgrading of the societal and a downgrading of the statist. Although this argument – as one form of the so-called Idealist view – has since been losing ground in the debate, there are still those who insist that the special character of Norden is explicable in similar terms. Their assumption is that the fragmentation and conflicts endemic in the "high politics" of inter-state relations can be overcome through cooperation on a mundane functional level and in the sphere of "low politics." The hope is that such cooperation – or a movement from fragmentation to integration – might relocate the place of war and the place of peace. Thus, Norden is explained in terms of success in the sphere of practical politics, that is its focus on "low" rather than "high" politics.[19]

If we take a closer look at these delineations, we see that they profoundly challenge the ordinary understanding of inter-state relations, for the essence of these relations, in contrast to intra-state relations, is precisely that the threat of war is assumed to be ever-present. The argument is that peace and order can only prevail within states, that is, where the community is located and where politics is made in the real sense of the word. There can be no community between states as the threat of war is always present, and therefore a community of states, or conceptualizations such a "security community," is taken to be misnomer, an impossible state of affairs. Communality is located on the inside, while the outside is invariably characterized by lack of communality.[20]

Peace between states cannot, the argument continues, rest on something as positive as communality, as peace rests by nature on negative and enforced conditions. Peace can only exist in the form of absence of war. It is taken to be a negative relationship achieved by repressive rather than emancipatory policies. States are assumed to be selfish to the border of obsession, so why should the Nordic countries be different? Why should they be able to accommodate and to adjust, to demonstrate flexibility and have enough power over themselves to show concern for the security interests of their small neighbouring countries? Many of the characteristics attributed to Norden as a region of democracy, justice, virtue, openness and legitimate authority are such that it almost becomes a projection of an account of life within states into the realm outside states. The demarcation of the outside is blurred, in view of the dominant accounts, as the external is no longer depicted as the sphere of Realpolitik, *raison d'état*, and the necessity of violence.

The crux of the problem is that the standard accounts have drawn a clear-cut borderline between intra- and inter-state relations governing the location of war and anarchy, and somehow Norden seems to have been misplaced in view of these arguments. In other words, the Nordic cannot be explained merely by reference to the ordinary properties, singularly or jointly, of the participating states. An adequate explanation also requires intrusion into the societal and communal, analysis of such features as progress and democracy. According to customary accounts, the delineation of such properties is largely irrelevant for the understanding of inter-state relations.

These points could be elaborated to demonstrate that in many of the articulations of Norden, the strategy is one of radically eliminating opposites. This is done by transcending the borderline between the internal and the external, and by viewing Norden in terms of qualities that belong to the sphere of the internal and that of order in public life. The move is based on a refusal to follow the traditional realist argumentation of international relations. The challenging of these accounts, albeit implicitly, has been one of the major ways of understanding and depicting the essence of Norden.

The choice of such a strategy implies, from the perspective of traditional theory, that Norden becomes an anomaly, something peripheral and outside the mainstream of international relations. It assumes features that are negative in terms of "high politics" and the perspective of Realpolitik. Such a strategy may be useful for descriptive purposes, but at the same time it implies that Norden is silenced as an alternative security discourse and a way of rethinking the nature and possibility of political community as compared to the understanding of these questions within the dominant discourses of security and international relations.

NORDIC BALANCE: A STRATEGY OF STANDARDIZATION

Since the beginning of the 1960s, it has become commonplace to use the concept of balance within the Nordic security policy context. This way of representing Norden has the benefit of making it comprehensible within the conventional categories of international relations theory, as part of the main text.

It ascribes a major role to the superpowers and the blocs in conditioning the circumstances upon which subregional security rests. It is, in this sense, a move of standardization and one of hiding the exceptional nature of Norden. The Nordic countries are seen as states among other states, as no different from the others. The impact of the Nordic countries is seen as a minor factor;

they get the credit for skilfully exploiting the conditions determined by others. The task of the concept is to confer upon Norden a much more central position within the main text. This is done by qualifying similarity and by purporting Norden to be a part of a continuum, although with some peculiarities of its own.

There are different understandings of the essence of Nordic Balance; for the most part it has been portrayed as a description of the Nordic pattern, providing an understanding of how the mechanics of security work, but it has also been presented as a model, system or doctrine – and ultimately, as a theory. Nordic Balance serves chiefly as a conceptual tool for analysis, but occasionally it has also been given normative and programmatic functions, particularly in political or journalistic parlance. It has also been used to obtain legitimacy for the policies pursued in the various Nordic countries.

In the context of research, the primary purpose of Nordic Balance has been to provide an explanation for the prevailing conditions of peace and stability in the Nordic area. The greatest merit of this approach is that it builds upon the ordinary assumptions of international relations. Within this approach the issues of security can be tackled without having to trespass across the borderline between the internal and the external or the societal and the statist. Balance is a statist concept firmly rooted in the domain of the foreign. It operates without any intrusion into the internal or communal. Furthermore, it draws on assumptions of security as an enforced condition and depicts it as an interplay between states.

Conceptualizations of Nordic Balance allow Norden to be conceived as a specific region and portrayed as a configuration with favourable security policy consequences. It boils down into a subtext, a micro-mechanism, a pattern or a system of statist policies. The region has security-related functions without being itself a state or an alliance with state-like security functions. The concept of Nordic Balance rests on assumptions of a bipolar East–West system, with the Nordic region as one of its components, and a perception of an interplay between regional policies and those of a larger system of blocs and major powers.

Basically the employment of such a configuration leads to conceiving Norden as a subsystem of a larger balance-of-power system, although the

Nordic countries are considered to have been able to influence the way in which these two levels interact with each other. The striking of a balance has been depicted as having produced quite useful security policy bargains for the small, Nordic players of that configuration. These countries are perceived as exceptionally sophisticated and skilful players: after all, they have fended off aggressive major powers and kept them at arm's length.

As a rule Norden is not considered to form a traditional military balance. Rather, the argument is that it constitutes a system of political deterrence, a balance of unexploited options with the intention of keeping the superpowers out of Norden and preventing them from applying maximalist policies of confrontation in the region. They are assumed to have skilfully used pressure, threats and some form of deterrence, e.g., coercive politics. The overall result is a subregional constellation influencing the calculations of the superpowers so that self-restraint becomes their own interest as well.

The system is one of influencing, and in a sense of exploiting the superpowers by keeping them at a distance, and thereby keeping the tension down. Each Nordic country is seen as regulating its own security policy in response to any provocation or change in the security policy conditions in the Nordic area.

This 'theory' focuses particularly on Norway and Finland, which both have their own superpower to keep out. If the United States and the Soviet Union pursued normal policies of confrontation and containment in the Nordic region, that would cause a chain reaction involving all the other actors and result in greater engagement and cause aggravated tensions in Northern Europe. Norden would become divided, and the normal rules of confrontation would become effective. This is what Nordic Balance, as a dynamic principle, aims at avoiding. It succeeds in doing this, so it is argued, by a moderation of security policy ambitions. This restraint is considered to be in the interests of each and everyone. With a certain measure of reciprocity, the argument continues, the Nordic countries have been exceptionally successful in their endeavours, especially because they are such small countries and have no formal cooperative security arrangements.

As Erik Noreen and Håkan Wiberg have clearly demonstrated, there are obvious shortcomings in such theory or thinking. Indeed, it is questionable whether one can speak of a theory at all.[21] All versions of Nordic Balance have been criticized for their lack of accuracy or for making statements that are empirically unfounded.

The important point, however, is that the 'theory' formalizes and represents one understanding, or one prominent branch of thinking in trying to come to grips with the Nordic mystery – and it does so mainly by explaining it away and hiding the tension between the various elements employed.

For instance, the theory makes no attempt to explain the reciprocity that is recognized as crucial to Nordic Balance. Where does this automation modifying ordinary power politics come from, and what is it that allows the Nordic countries to coordinate their security policies in such a peculiar and uncommon way? Why do the Nordic countries concern themselves with each other's interests if intra-Nordic relations do not essentially differ from inter-state relations? What allows the Nordic countries to be the prime subjects in running the micro-mechanism of Nordic Balance? Why are the superpowers' pooicy objectives pursued by the small powers of the region rather than the other way round?

These are some of the inadequacies of Nordic Balance as a resolution aiming at standardization and downplaying Norden as something specific and hiding its potential for becoming an autonomous text.

This conceptualization of Nordic balance was originally elaborated by Nils Ørvik, Arne Olav Brundtland and Johan J. Holst, i.e., analysts belonging to the Realist school of thinking.[22] Their aim has been to fit Norden into the normal world of power politics and to produce explanations that are not based on idealization or on elements that are in conflict with modern accounts of international relations theory.

The criticism has come mainly from peace researchers, and perhaps most explicitly from Erik Noreen. Noreen found that it has usually been unclear what the balance is assumed to consist in: a balance of resources, a political balance, or a homeostatic balance. Instead of balance, one could speak of efforts to regulate and control various operational factors pertaining to security policy. Noreen concluded that the concept of balance in the Nordic context is more confusing than elucidating. He thought it would be more

---

fruitful in certain situations to talk of an interplay of security policies with the purpose of keeping great power tensions and conflicts out of the Nordic area, but not balancing anything within Fenno-Scandinavia. As the concept involves contradictory elements, it should be excluded from regional security policies, Noreen argued.[23]

The concept of Nordic Balance is now surrounded by increasing controversy. At one point it served as a vehicle for communication, and almost consensus-formation, among the Nordic countries, but this is no longer the case. The criticism it has encountered from the strong Nordic peace research community may have contributed to this change. There may be other factors involved as well, but in any event the portrayal of Nordic Balance has grown quite thin at least in the scholarly debate. If explicitly used, it is immediately qualified and turned, for example, into a pattern of "subtle cooperation" instead of adhering to the analogy of a balance.[24]

More generally: the decline of the configuration of Nordic Balance has left room for other ways of depicting Norden. The development has been twofold: either there has been less trust in the specificity of Norden, with the Nordic Balance invaded by notions of a central balance, or analysts have abandoned notions of standardization or playing on a continuum. Instead, they have been going over to the vocabulary of "assurance" and "reassurance," that is, an approach based on opposites and differences.

This would seem to imply that it has become more difficult to ascribe to Norden some exceptional features and yet to perceive it in terms of the standard approaches of international relations theory. The tensions that are built into such an approach seem to have accumulated and the solution has been increasingly to deny the specificity, or to resort to explanations that clearly depart from the repertoire of dominant international relations theory.

NORDEN AS A DISCOURSE – "NORDEN"

Summarizing the above discussion, it would seem that there are problems with all the main strategies used in portraying Norden, whether their aim is to do away with the

---

opposites or to strike a balance between contrary elements. They are each problematic in their own way. Neither of the basic approaches produce very convincing results, and both fixate and impose limits on the way that Norden may be perceived as an international relations construct.

Either the dilemmas become too obvious, as in the case of operations based on the concept of balance, or they turn Norden into something of an anomaly and a peculiarity that endangers, if generalized, the modernist accounts of political space. These approaches fail to deal adequately with the plurality of international relations, with Norden as one indication of such a plurality.

Norden therefore seems to be one of those cases that have fallen victim to the binary divisions sustaining the rhetoric on international relations, war and peace, idealism and realism. It is provided a legitimate but marginalized and decidedly subordinate place within a given order. Since all the efforts to provide a credible explanation revolve around this rhetoric, they are bound to fail in articulating the full potential of Norden and providing it with the more varied treatment it would need.

As the basic dilemma seems to be that Norden is not in tune with the conventional debates of war, peace and security, alternative perspectives are called for. These should avoid offering the state as the only resolution to the issues of sovereignty, freedom and autonomy and accordingly allow modifications of the power-political game as well as greater flexibility in depicting various configurations of international relations.

It *does* seem possible, however, to perceive Norden in terms of a security policy relationship that has not been dichotomized and militarized in the ordinary way. "Norden" is something that unites, functions as a bridge between the Nordic countries, and provides a delineation and an identity with regard to the foreign and the external. It could also be taken to consist of a relationship based on trust and communality. It is an ideology, a political culture, a joint political spatialization.

Thus, "Norden" has been created in terms of a discourse. It is exceptional precisely because it is a security policy relationship that has not been allowed to be militarized or bureaucratized to the same extent as is normally the case with various security policy conceptualizations.

Norden may thus be described as a positive security policy relationship; it is something uniting and unifying, but created without resorting to the usual security policy institutions and without erecting barriers against the external in exclusive and militarizing terms.

This notion of Norden as a discourse could be a promising avenue in placing Norden into perspective. Norden could be seen as a multitude of voices or articulations, which coincide and share the idea of Norden as something positive and worthwhile affiliating to as an identity, value-formation, or policy. In this sense Norden could consist of many "Nordens." It is not a singular master narrative, but a variety of interpretations aspiring to articulate Norden each in its own way. The various participants in the discourse are allowed to have, within certain limits, their own understanding of the core of the discourse.

This in turn would make it pointless to try to define "Norden" as something concrete, firm or one-dimensional, for it is precisely the opposite: a joint field of understanding that prevails only if the participants in the discourse are allowed to adhere to their respective understandings of the Nordic and are not confronted too harshly with the question of what is "real," and what it is not.

In other words, Norden is a multitude of voices, although not too distinct from each other. It is a meeting-point of a number of understandings, some representing the Idealist and others the so-called Realist school. It is a textual field with room for both these schools of thinking. There have been both peace researchers who have perceived Norden as something potentially beyond ordinary power politics, and Realists who have played on notions of balance, stability, credibility and such like.[25] There has been room for both, and they have both had a significant role as voices in the constitution of Norden as a configuration of international relations. The basis for the agreement and meeting of minds is that Norden is seen as something positive, useful and worthwhile preserving in relation to other options and discourses.

The understanding that there is a qualitative difference between the domains of the internal and external, or a borderline between Norden and the outside, is important. Such a borderline is required in the constitution of

---

Norden, but it exists only in the sphere of understandings. The inside does not comply with the dictates of realism, while the outside consists of the ordinary world of the power-political game.

The Nordic countries comply with the rules of the outside without explicitly challenging them, and as one reflection of this they do not articulate the inner sphere in terms that would too drastically break with the ordinary, realist understanding of international relations.

The discursive constitution of Norden is primarily an intra-Nordic affair, and each Nordic country seems to come in with a somewhat different understanding of what security in the region is basically about.[26]

However, in a sense the superpowers and the blocs are also an integral part of the discourse. They have been the guardians of the main text, of which Norden has been the subtext. Norden cannot be something that is established and sustained explicitly against the will of these powers. There is no way of forcing them to accept the existence of Norden and the existence of a region with a special setting of policies that the superpowers have to abide by. They have to be persuaded to do so, and therefore allowed to enter and discipline the basic text.

SECURITY ISSUES AS DISCOURSES – SOME EXAMPLES

In this sense the special character of Norden results from a bargain struck within a frame common to the Nordic countries and the crucial external powers. The consent of the superpowers and the blocs is achieved by playing down the challenge inherent in the Nordic as an alternative text in regard to the ordinary rules of the power-political game. The Nordic countries have to convince the superpowers that it is also in their interest to have Norden as a subjugated entity and refrain from fully integrating it into the main text.

The dialogue has been most explicit in such questions as Swedish and Finnish neutrality, Danish and Norwegian "footnote" policies at the beginning of the 1980s, and the case of port calls by nuclear-capable ships in Nordic harbours.[27] In the mid-1980s the superpowers gave signals of incorporating Norden increasingly into their confrontational policies, and the Nordic countries replied by giving signals of increased defiance. For example, the decision to establish a joint Nordic foreign affairs officials study group was clearly a discursive move, and one aimed at the strengthening of the Nordic.

The message was clear: the Nordic countries would consider measures of disengagement, in the form of a nuclear weapon free zone, unless the superpowers started to apply their usual strategic logic also in and around Norden. They were asked to continue with their policy of respecting the specificity of Norden. The pledge was for the United States and the Soviet Union to return to their customary policies of moderation and regard for the subtext. The aim of the Nordic countries was to communicate profound concern and to signal uneasiness, not one of proceeding towards the implementation of a zone.[28]

The conversation showed clear signs of defending Norden as a subtext; it indicated unity, demonstrated concern for the interests of other Nordic countries and gave signals of the zone proposal developing into a joint and legitimate topic to be discussed among the countries of the region, although in a way that would not seriously challenge or undermine the main text, that of the East–West setting and superpower policies. It was made clear to outsiders that the zone proposal was something to talk about, but not something to be implemented.[29] Thus, the idea of a zone became, during the 1980s, an important site for the articulation of the Nordic under changing politico-military circumstances.

The message sent in that context was an exceptionally strong one. It ranked quite high on the scale of discursive diplomatic moves, as the Nordic countries decided for once to join hands and make a common appearance in the sphere of security policy. To prevent their security policy setting from unravelling, the Nordic countries took a number of countermeasures in the form of various statements and calls for naval arms control, restrictions on the introduction of cruise missiles, including as an operational measure the establishment of the foreign affairs officials study group.

The moves of the Nordic countries complied with the ordinary discourse on Norden in the sense that the these countries were the ones calling for moderation as well as pledging allegiance to the prevailing rules of the game. The superpowers were the receivers, but now Norden and its surroundings were spatially the target area of the discourse, not Europe or changes in European constellations. The crux of the issue was that the superpowers seemed to be on their way to transferring their confrontational logic, and especially the tough logic prevailing in the strategic sphere, to apply also in Norden and its vicinity. This threatened to undermine the nature of Norden as a subtext, depriving it of any distinct nature of its own and incorporating it fully into the main text.

The perception of Norden as a discursive field that also involves the superpowers helps us to understand why both the themes of the 'Nordification of Europe' or the 'Europeanization of Norden' have never struck a very favourable chord in either the Nordic or the European debates. Such moves would produce unwarranted mixtures and distort borderlines that are essential to the constitution of Norden.

The pursuit of these themes would endanger essential demarcations of borderlines in two different ways. On the one hand the 'Nordification of Europe' suggests that the subtext would spread all over Europe, and become far more representative and powerful as it would comprise a much broader region and contain a number of major European powers.

On the other hand, the flooding of Norden with the more recent European logic of policies would transform Norden into something more than merely a subtext of power-politics. 'Europeanization' would elevate Norden into a different, competing text. Qualitatively the step would be quite moderate as 'Europeanization' nowadays consists largely of the same elements as the Nordic. It would, however, magnify the challenge inherent in the Nordic, and distort its position as a subtext in relation to the East–West setting in general.

The "Greying" and the "Europeanization" of Norden

This distinction between two different texts, one consisting of the superpower confrontation and another European in essence, is quite helpful in providing a background to why the challenges of the 1980s, which to some extent still prevail in the northern waters, and the current pressures originating with European integration, are quite different in character. They have endangered, each in their own way, the constitutive moves that place Norden simultaneously on the inside and the outside.

The intensification of strategic competition that occurred in the late 1980s around the Kola region and in the northern waters with the American 'new naval strategy,' threatened to draw Norden into the normal sphere of power politics, one characterized by clear-cut divisions into "us" and "them." This borderline between the opposites, if fully implemented in all of Northern Europe, would have cut the Nordic countries off from each other and erected barriers across Norden. Under such confrontational conditions Norden would have been merely one region among others. It would have been no different from the ordinary sphere of rivalry between the two superpowers. The competition would have been played out in the Nordic arena in exactly the same way as elsewhere. By changing their view and by intensifying their rivalry, the superpowers threatened to undermine the understanding of Norden as a region with modified rules of the game, and erode its position as a subtext.

Norden, as a configuration simultaneously on the inside and the outside, was thus under pressure. It became the target of an attack ascribing to it merely a position on the inside without any tolerance for specific Nordic security policies. The Nordic response was to try to impose normalcy, that is, to aspire for a return to business as usual. The spreading of the general power-political rules endangered the specific ones, and Norden replied by underlining its specificity within the general rules of the game.

The pressures generated by the strategic developments were considerable, but they did not present, in conversational terms, any basic threat to Norden. There was no danger of the main text collapsing and

---

transforming into something qualitatively different; on the contrary, it was becoming so strong that it endangered Norden's position as a distinct subtext. It remained for Nordic countries, within this frame, to send signals emphasizing their specificity and to resist absorption into the ordinary competition between the two superpowers. The Nordic countries used their veto power against being dragged into the strategic equation, and performed a variety of discursive countermoves to restore the status quo.

In the vocabularies used this change of scenery has been depicted as one of the Nordic 'buffer' translating into 'a grey zone,' an arrangement consisting of a very different security logic. The buffer logic is understood to be an exercise in moderation, with restraints in the presence of one superpower to limit the presence of the other. The grey zone logic is understood to work differently, as it implies the countering of the presence of one side by the presence of the other. The latter does not pay heed to the interests and policies of the smaller powers in the region, and goes therefore against the type of arrangement that has prevailed in Northern Europe.[30]

It turned out that the Nordic countries were able, without any great difficulty, to deal with the threat of being swallowed up into the main text of superpower rivalry. In the traditional terminology, the buffer logic continued to prevail. To some extent that challenge added to the appreciation of Norden and made clear that the Nordic countries had joint interests to take care of. The threat common to all of the Nordic countries became the focal point for an increasingly strong articulation of Nordic distinctiveness.

Over time the significance of the strategic challenge has declined, but another one has gathered momentum in the form of the alternative text of 'Europeanization.' It has become a competing master narrative which places Norden, if Norden were to become part of it, clearly on the outside from the point of view of the traditional East–West setting. The Nordic countries are now faced with more dramatic and difficult issues to deal with than previous ones. This is to say that the challenges of the 1980s consisted of an intensified discourse within an unchanged frame, while the current ones have the character of a shift in the discourse that deprives Norden of its traditional constitutive references.

The problems are complicated by the partial overlap of these two challenges; or, to be more precise, they have appeared in sequence in such a way that there are still traces of the former while the latter is becoming increasingly dominant in the debate. This simultaneous confrontation with two different, and in some respect contrary, challenges has left Norden in a state of disarray.[31]

In conventional parlance only the intensification of strategic confrontation has been understood as a security policy threat. It seriously endangered Nordic security and 'stability' in the region. Rivalry between the superpowers presented challenges that could easily be discussed within the framework of traditional security analysis. The security dimension of 'Europeanization' is much more difficult to establish and analyse. It evades analysis based on concepts such as balance, stability or credibility. The security policy consequences of European developments are positive rather than negative, and therefore 'Europeanization' is usually not taken to be on a level with strategic confrontation.

It becomes clear, however, if viewed discursively, that 'Europeanization' is at least an equally serious challenge to Norden. Continental developments endanger the very framework of which Norden has been a part. The European setting has slowly evolved into a text of its own, adopting quite a number of features that have also been characteristic of Norden. Moreover, it is not only the European Community that has contributed to this; during the Gorbachev years the Soviet Union has also pursued policies conducive to the demise of the Cold War constellation. Europe, as a narrative, has achieved a status that Norden has refrained from aspiring to in settling for the position of a subtext; Europe has used the opening available and developed into an alternative text that undermines much of the traditional power-political game. Integration in Western Europe has reached a state which implies that the prospect of war among major European powers has become very distant. Europe is more than a subtext; it has discursive potential that openly challenges the rules of the traditional East–West setting.

These developments present Norden with complicated challenges. There is, on the one hand, less reason than earlier to remain on the inside, and to remain in the position of a subtext to the power-political game. On the other hand the identity and the specificity embodied in a position on the outside as part of 'Europeanization' would be modest as well.

The dilemma seems to consist in a lack of any ideal and obvious solutions; both choices fail to to provide Norden with a firm and indisputable ground. The 'old world' is fading away, and there is no obvious place for a distinct Norden in the new one. There is no way of ignoring the challenges either, as the constitutive horizons of all the European political configurations are changing. From a security perspective, Norden used to be, in relative terms, better off than the rest of Europe. Now this distinction is far from self-evident. Europe, as a measure of difference, is no longer there to the same extent as a point of departure. It has become difficult to argue that Central Europe is the core of the East–West confrontation, or to ascribe to Northern Europe the position of a side-show and a region of low tension compared to the rest of Europe.

In present-day Europe the features of Norden as something privileged, ideal, progressive and worth aspiring to have also turned pale in another sense. There is clearly less admiration for the Nordic model than there used to be. The previous East European countries, for example, seem to be aspiring to membership of the European Community. In their search for different ways and models of reforming their post-communist societies, they are less interested in Norden. That is to say that Norden is no longer as distinct as it used to be in terms of well-being, democracy, progress or modernity. It has become difficult to establish the "otherness" of Germany, and even the borderline with the Soviet Union is growing rather thin in terms of social systems. In sum: Norden has become less distinct as a social text. This, in turn, undermines the position of Norden as a subtext in the sphere of international relations, and more specifically in the East–West setting.

There are thus good reasons to argue that the separateness and the exclusive nature of Norden is seriously in doubt. It can no longer be constituted against the otherness of the rest of Europe. Norden has to be defined as part of Europe, and constituted in inclusive terms. This is so because there are hardly any reference points left for the demarcation of difference between Europe and Norden.

It seems that the crucial voices in the debate in which Norden is constituted are also changing. Both the Soviet Union/Russia and the United

States have declined in importance, while new voices, such as the European Community, Germany and the Baltic states are beginning to emerge. These voices give a new twist to the debate.

The European Community, and Germany in particular, is not aspiring to establish the same kind of firm borderlines as the two superpowers have traditionally done. These new forces tend to see Europe more in terms of continuity, perhaps containing different spheres of influence, rather than a continent provided with distinct divisions into "us" and "them," with pockets for countries such as the Nordic ones that do not fit into the basic duality composed of blocs and opponents.

The Baltic countries are, for their part, a problematic case for the Nordic countries. They breach the previous duality and aspire to penetrate into the inside, establishing at least some linkage with the Nordic Council. They thereby problematize the demarcation of Norden's south-eastern border. The Baltic countries transcend the previous division and claim affinity with the Nordic countries across the Baltic Sea. They join may of the sites that have previously been important for the articulation of the Nordic, such as the debate on the nuclear weapon free zone in the northern part of Europe.

THE DEBATE ON NORDEN

All this seems to have divided the debate on Norden into two clearly separate spheres. There is, on the one hand, the traditional security policy debate based on the perception that the Nordic countries still have to cope with their respective national security dilemmas. It is thought that the security problem inherent in international relations may have changed in appearance, but it has yet to be encountered. On the other hand an extensive debate has evolved in which the whole question of security, in its traditional form, is no longer present, or has faded into a side-issue of marginal importance. The existence of a variety of problems is recognized, but none of the relevant ones are thought to pertain to military developments.

The underlying assumption in this debate is thus that there has been a significant shift: the quality of international relations is no longer what it used to be, at least in Europe. On the part of the Nordic Countries, the problems perceived to be really important are those related to finding a position in the new, post-Cold War Europe. They are discussed as issues of marginalization, vulnerability and the threat of being deprived of influence on the crucial decisions that determine the future of Norden and the Nordic countries in the European constellation.

The former, neo-realist debate hinges on the assumption that international relations remain conflictual in essence, and that this state of affairs also presents the Nordic countries with national security dilemmas. It is argued that this is the case in spite of the demise of the Cold War, the settlement of major European conflicts, political changes in Eastern Europe and the Soviet Union, and further integrative developments in continental Europe. These changes are quite drastic, but they have not altered the quality of international relations.

The most obvious way of trying to prove this point has been to refer to the continuation of the US–Soviet strategic competition in northernmost Europe and around the Arctic. There the naval developments and the strategic bipolarity of nuclear weapons seem to have survived and continue to have an impact on the politico-geographic scenery. It has also been argued that the unpredictability of Soviet developments, combined with conflicts between central authorities and some of the republics, makes the world quite uncertain and presents other countries with eventual security issues.

There seems to be four basic scenarios of potential conflicts that need to be taken into account in national security planning:

1. The continuation of US–Soviet rivalry;
2. Conflictual relations developing between the European Community and the Soviet Union/Russia;
3. Rivalry between the European Community and the United States;

4. The emergence of traditional major power conflicts in Europe if the European Community project fails and turns into a fragmented Europe.

Let us take a closer look at these scenarios.

1. If US–Soviet/Russian rivalry continues the Nordic countries would remain divided. Intense superpower rivalry around the Arctic entangles northern Norden into the conflict and implies that Norway, Iceland and Greenland remain Atlanticist in their orientation. Denmark, Finland and Sweden are less touched by this strategic bipolarity of the Arctic. One possible scenario, although a less probable one, could be that Norway, Finland and Sweden would try to shield themselves against the consequences of such bipolarity, and join each other in policies aiming at moderating the conflict. Their cooperation would have features of a Nordic-Arctic Alliance, if taken far and institutionalized.

2. The emergence of rivalry between the European Community and the Soviet Union/Russia would produce a quite different constellation among the Nordic countries. Denmark and Sweden would associate themselves with the Community, Finland would slide into an eastern direction, or Finland and Norway would remain neutral as best as they could.

3. The emergence of a conflict between the European Community and the United States as the main dividing axis in European politics would again split Norden in different fractions. Norway, Iceland and Greenland, with their strong Atlanticist traditions and structural links, would land in the American camp or become neutral, while Denmark, Sweden and presumably also Finland would associate themselves with the Community, and become part of the defence arrangements within that setting.[32]

4. The scenario of a fragmented Europe torn by major power rivalry would carry the promise of joint Nordic policies. The Swedish Chief of Defence, General Bengt Gustafsson has presented this as one potential scenario in an interview on future Swedish defence policy options.[33] As the Nordic countries would no longer be divided by the East–West conflict, they could enter into an alliance with each other in order to avoid being drawn

into the camp of any of the rivaling major powers. This would lay the basis for a Nordic Defence Union.

In general the *neo-realist* argumentation tends to be rather conservative and has been presented mainly to defend existing arrangements. If there have been pressures for change, these have been reflections of the dialogue within the European Community. Denmark, as a member of the Community, has been forced to take a stand on a potential European defence union.[34] Similarly, the other Nordic countries have to take into account that if they eventually end up as members of the European Community, this may involve membership of a European defence arrangement as well. Such an arrangement would bring the Nordic countries, or most of them, under the same security policy roof, but hardly allow them to establish a profile of their own within that setting.

The *neo-functionalist* debate is a more acute one in the sense that the Nordic countries are under pressure to settle for a line concerning their ties to the new Europe, and the European Community in particular. When an EES agreement between EFTA and the EC materialize, Finland, Iceland, Norway and Sweden will presumably be part of it. Iceland has had some reservations towards the negotiations, but Sweden has applied for membership in the EC. An EES agreement will draw those Nordic countries party to it ever closer to each other. They would form something of an EES–Norden, with joint interests to take care of within the framework of the arrangement.

The position of the European Community as a new master narrative challenges the Nordic countries with the choice of either joining or staying out. Those resisting the Community and searching for alternatives to membership have sometimes played with the idea of using Norden as some kind of counterweight to integrative developments on the continent. This would imply that Norden, that is all the Nordic countries except Denmark, would be given the features of a closely knit Nordic Community. Among the Finnish politicians Christoffer Taxell, and more recently Paavo Väyrynen and Ulf Sundqvist, have presented scenarios along these lines.

A much more favoured idea has been the one of all the Nordic countries joining the Community, and evolving into a club of their own within the Community. This is argued to be the only realistic way of arriving at a reunion of the Nordic countries. The idea has been pursued mainly by Danish politicians, including the Minister of Foreign Affairs, Uffe Elleman-Jensen. It would require a profound change in the attitudes of the countries concerned. Instead of moderation and abstentionist small-state policies pursued at the fringes of the East–West system, the aim would be one of aspiring for a considerable role and influence within the Community.

Sweden is well equipped for such a role, taking into account its traditional ambitions in international relations at large. Denmark has recently shown signs of being on its way in the making of the shift needed, and Finland could capitalize on some of its traditional experiences in pursuing policies beside a major power. Norway and Iceland would be the two countries having the most obvious difficulties with the requirements of such a new position.

The Community has obviously become the centre of gravity for the Nordic countries, and the issue of membership has become an increasingly serious concern for each of those still on the outside. The more probable candidates for joining are Sweden and Finland, while Norway is a somewhat more uncertain case. Iceland, as well as Greenland, will presumably remain outside. This implies that the membership scenario is one that divides, although it could turn out to be a uniting one for the core of the Nordic countries.

If the Community turns out to be a relatively loose and pluralist arrangement, this might allow for regional formations in various parts of Europe. The Nordic countries could capitalize on this option by extending their relations and cooperation in a Baltic or Arctic direction, or both. The dimension of the Baltic Sea might be perceived as an interesting one to exploit by Denmark, Finland and Sweden. Arctic cooperation would be more in the interests of Finland, Greenland, Iceland, Norway and Sweden.

Thus, to summarize, a more systematic presentation of the alternatives circulating in the neo-realist and neo-functionalist debates can be categorized as is done in the Table below.

It thus seems that the current debate is still rich in different Nordens; actually the number of conceptualizations in circulation might have increased rather than decreased. However, they are no longer debated within the same, unifying frame. Norden has been losing its function as a meeting-point of various conceptualizations and as a spatialization above the ordinary. Instead of being something autonomous and a distinct political configuration, Norden is debated in reactive terms. This deprives Norden of the ideal and hegemonic aspects it has previously had.

Norden	Neo-functionalist view	Neo-realist view
Reconstituted in a more limited form	EES–Norden	Nordic–Arctic defence arrangement
Strengthened	EC–Norden Baltic Sea Norden Arctic Norden	Nordic Defence Union
Modified	Nordic Community	–

Both the neo-realist and the neo-functionalist debates represent strategies of standardization. They do not contain, and this goes particularly for the neo-functionalist one, delineations which would allow the Nordic to develop into a sphere of its own; that is something distinct, yet part of a broader setting. The debates distort the constituents of difference, and thereby deprive Norden of its very essence.

However, both allow for Norden to turn into a group, institution or interest configuration within a larger setting, either totally inside or outside a general set of rules. The EES–Norden alternative could be a solution in between, but the prospects for such an option have grown weaker over time, and may disappear altogether. It seems, therefore, that there is hardly any space left for a configuration within these debates that aims at leading simultaneously a life outside and a life inside.

BY WAY OF CONCLUSION

Norden, as a discourse, is now at a crossroads. The issue is not whether it will survive in institutional terms, in terms of interests, or as a structure. Norden will quite probably remain in its old form, or it may assume new forms in view of some specific conflicts or patterns of cooperation. It may even generate some new interest and curiosity, as is evidenced by the research projects recently started both within peace research and at the Nordic institutes for foreign affairs studies. What has happened is that with the European 'revolution' of recent years, and the consequent plurality in international relations, the foundations of Norden have changed.

Norden is not going to fade away as a result of problems in the domain of practice. Norden is not controversial in any significant way, and we may now see the Nordic countries developing a much closer cooperation among themselves – if they so wish – than was possible during the Cold War.

The heart of the matter lies elsewhere. Norden has lost its nature as a borderline case and its character as an entity out of the ordinary. It has value, it is appreciated, it has a long and honourable history, but its creative potential has been exhausted. It appears that Norden has been caught up with by its own success, by the world around it. For a long time there was no reason to aspire for change, and now the confusion is too profound for any major reforms to be carried out. It is no longer as fashionable as it used to be. Norden is now increasingly at the mercy of new hegemonies and their discourse, and these do not provide it with the same foundation as the old ones.

In a sense, Norden has turned into a gold watch in the Rolex era. It is based on constituents embodied in the very nature of international relations that are no longer fully in tune with the development of today, at least in the part of the world relevant to the Nordic countries. Norden has connotations referring to the past rather than the future, and it provides a weak shelter against changing conditions in Europe.

This means that Norden may have outlived its usefulness as a common frame outside the ordinary discourse on security, as a meeting-point or joint ground for different understandings. However, the change of ground of the discourse is producing, or laying the basis for, new and contemporary formations much like the Nordic one, and by this process much of what is "Nordic" may live on – although under a different name and in the form of an alternative text rather than merely a subtext.

NOTES & REFERENCES

1. Ebbe Kløvedal Reich speaks about Norden as a mystery (den nordiske "gåde") in his book, *En engels vinger*, København 1990, p. 321.

2. "Norden" is actually a quite old concept that was used as early as the eighteenth century. It originally referred to the countries north of Germany. The term "Scandinavia" came into use later, denoting ethnic communality in a period when Finland had become part of Russia, see Beate Børresen, "Enhetstanken i Norden," *Norden i Europa*. En skriftserie från projektet "Norden i Europa," NUPI 1991.

3. This view is provided by Jan Øberg in "Towards Understanding Common Nordic Security Alternatives," *Current Research on Peace and Violence*, No. 1–2, 1986, p. 74.

4. For an application of the systemic approach, see Wallensteen, P., & Vesa, U. & Väyrynen, R., *The Nordic System: Structure and Change, 1920–1970*. Tampere Peace Research Institute, TAPRI Research Reports, No. 6, 1973, and Department of Peace and Conflict Research, Uppsala University, Report No. 4, 1973.

5. This dimension of Norden is emphasized by Ole Wæver, 'Region, Sub-region and Proto-region: Security Dynamics in Northern Europe in the 1990s.' Paper for the annual BISA-conference, Newcastle, December 1990. The paper has been published as a working paper 21/1990, Centre for Peace and Conflict Research, Copenhagen.

6. I have used these terms and ways of coming to grips with Norden in an earlier article, "Norden and the Development of Strategic Doctrines: From a Buffer Zone to a Gray Area?" in *Current Research on Peace and Violence*, No. 1–2, 1986, pp. 54–74.

7. For this view, see Håkan Wiberg, "The Nordic Countries: A Special Kind of System?", *Current Research on Peace and Violence*, No. 1–2, 1986, pp. 2–12.

8. On this early history, see Otto D. Dethlefsen, "Die Nordische Einheitsbewegung" in *Deutsch-Nordische Schriftenreihe aus dem öffentlichen Recht*, Rostock 1941.

9. For this evaluation, see Håkan Wiberg, *op. cit.*

10. Arne Ruth refers in this context to Margaret Coles, who wrote in 1938 that: "The Swedes are far less possessed by a national history than most other nations in Europe," see Arne Ruth, "The Second New Nation: The Mythology of Modern Sweden," *Daedalus*, Spring 1984.

11. Cf. Beate Børresen, "Enhetstanken i Norden," *Norden i Europa*. En skriftserie från projektet "Norden i Europa," NUPI 1991, p. 5.

12. These connotations are mostly associated with Sweden, but apply to the other Nordic countries as well. See Arne Ruth, "Det andra nya riket: det moderna Sveriges mytologi," *UNDR.*

13. This is the expression used by Susan Sontag in describing her experiences of the Scandinavian countries, interview with Nils Gunnar Nilsson in *Sydsvenska Dagbladet,* January 26, 1986.

14. In recent years this ban has come under increasing pressure, but formally it still holds. For example the Baltic states have appeared on the agenda increasingly openly, and policies of European integration have also been discussed. The ban was initiated by Finland, which continues to adhere to it. The Finnish foreign policy leadership resisted the idea of rewriting the statutes of the Nordic Council also to include treatment of external issues, see "Norden starkare" in *Dagens Nyheter,* March 1, 1991.

15. This group consisted of foreign affairs officials from all five Nordic countries. The project was initiated in March 1987 and it submitted its report to the Nordic Foreign Ministers in March 1991.

16. Osmo Apunen has approached Norden by employing a vocabulary composed of the systemic and sub-systemic. The strength of the sub-systemic is taken to be the specific feature of the Nordic region. Apunen describes the relationship between the systemic and the sub-systemic as one characterized by continuity but as one being dichotomic in nature. See Osmo Apunen, "The Nordic Area – Systemic and Sub-systemic Functions" in *Peace and the Sciences,* International Institute for Peace, Vienna, No. 3, 1976, pp. 106–113.

17. For the use of these concepts in descriptions of Nordic security, see for example Clive Archer, "Deterrence and Reassurance in Northern Europe" in *Centre Piece,* No. 6, Winter 1984. Centre for Defence Studies, University of Aberdeen.

18. For this, see Karl W. Deutsch, *Political Community and the North Atlantic Area.* Princeton; Princeton University Press 1957.

19. These terms have also been applied by Håkan Wiberg, *op. cit.*, p. 4.

20. For this argument, see R. B. J. Walker, "Security, Sovereignty, and the Challenge of World Politics" in *Alternatives*, No. 1, Winter 1990, pp. 3–29.

21. For this, see the chapter by Håkan Wiberg on the concept of the Nordic balance, in Nils Petter Gleditsch et al., (ed.), *Svaner på vildveje? Nordisk sikkerhed mellem supermagtsflåder og europæisk opbrud*. Vindrose, Copenhagen 1990.

22. Arne Olav Brundtland has been developing a theory of Nordic balance in a number of articles and research notes since the sixties. See, for example, "Nordisk balanse før og nå" in *Internasjonal Politikk*, no. 5, 1966, pp. 491–541. The most recent contribution is an effort on "Nordic Security at the End of the Cold War," which appeared in *Cooperation and Conflict*, 1991.

23. For this, see Erik Noreen, "The Nordic Balance: A Security Policy Concept in Theory and Practice" in *Cooperation and Conflict*, No. 1, 1983, pp. 43–56.

24. For such a qualified use, see for example John H. M. Hagard, "Nordic Security" in *Occasional Paper series*, Institute for East–West Security Studies. New York 1987.

25. For an effort to depict Norden as a security policy alternative, see Jan Øberg, "Towards Understanding Common Nordic Security Alternatives," *Current Research on Peace and Violence*, No. 1–2, 1986, pp. 74–94.

26. This point has been elaborated by Ole Wæver, "Supermagterne i Norden," in B. Møller (ed.), *Norden som Atomvåbenfri Zone*. Egtved 1985.

27. For an analysis of Nordic port call policies, see the report of the Nordic Study Group, "The Port Call Issue: Nordic Considerations" in *Bulletin of Peace Proposals*, No. 3, September 1990, pp. 337–352, or an updated version, Pertti Joenniemi, "The Port Call Issue: Finnish Policies in a Nordic Perspective" in *Occasional Papers*, Tampere Peace Research Institute, No. 43, 1991. These two

studies demonstrate that port calls constitute an exceptionally interesting discursive field with a complex system of overt as well as covert signals. The Nordic countries seem to comply with the dictates of power politics much more in their covert than overt policies.

28. Håkan Wiberg has described the zone proposal in cultural and conversational terms, see "The Nordic Nuclear Weapons-Free Zone as a Process," in Torben Størner et al. (eds.), *Peace and the Future.* Proceedings of the Second International Peace University, Aarhus, October 1985, pp. 191–212.

29. This symbolic and discursive nature of the zone proposal has been well taken by Jakob Andersen and Ole Wæver, "Den nordiske forzoning," *Krig og fred*, Nr. 3. 1986, pp. 4–9.

30. For the use of these terms in a Nordic context, see Ola Tunander, "Gray Zone and Buffer Zone: The Nordic Borderland and the Soviet Union" in *Nordic Journal of Soviet & East European Studies*, Nr. 4, 1987, pp. 3–34.

31. For a more detailed elaboration of this thesis, see Pertti Joenniemi, "Europe Changes; The Nordic System Remains?" in *Bulletin of Peace Proposals*, No. 2, 1990, pp. 205–217.

32. For a creative discussion on the alternatives available to the Nordic countries, see Sverre Jervell, "Norden i en ny europeisk arkitektur," *Parlamentarikernas roll i regionernas Europa.* Rapport från Nordiska Rådets seminarium i Snekkersten, November 13, 1990, pp. 32–44.

33. This theme has been elaborated by Ola Tunander, " The Two Nordens: The North and the South, or the East and the West?" in *Bulletin of Peace Proposals*, No. 1, 1991, pp. 55–65.

34. Denmark for long supported NATO in order to avoid a European defence union. The establishment of such a union could further divide Denmark from the other Nordic countries; it might exclude Greenland from Europe and thus

divide Denmark into European and Atlantic parts, and it would weaken the possibilities of the USA and NATO balancing the strength of a strong Germany close to Denmark. However, recently the Danish position has become more favourable *vis-à-vis* a European defence arrangement. The Gulf War may be one of the catalyzing explanations for this change of attitude. The Danish position has been elaborated in *Den europeiske sikkerhetsordning set i lyset af CSCE-processen og den tyske samling*, Det Sikkerheds- og Nedrustningspolitiske Udvalg, September 1990.

4

Framing Nordic Security
European Scenarios for the 1990s and Beyond

Barry Buzan & Ole Wæver

INTRODUCTION

Nordic security is not a self-contained system. Nor was it derived directly from the superpower relationship. The most important framework for analysing Nordic security is the dynamics of the region in which Norden is located: Europe (Wæver, 1990b). Europe is in security terms a 'natural' unit. If the globe is divided into regions on the basis of intensity of security relations, one will find a number of regions which are more than analytical tools in as much as they reflect a real patterning of global politics.

The term 'security complex' has been coined to capture this phenomenon. Thus, one can argue about the correct interpretation of the dividing lines, but one cannot just use the term 'security complex' on any group of states (Norden, the Warsaw Pact, the Non-Proliferation Treaty members). There is a European security complex but not a Nordic one, a South East Asian, a South Asian, a North East Asian and a Middle East complex, but not an Asian one.

To the extent that this approach is accepted, it follows that one can gain much in understanding a subregion like Norden, by approaching it around the region, Europe. Talking about future security, one will need to 'know' the future of the security complex, and fortunately it happens to be that the concept of 'security complex' is a useful tool for generating *scenarios*. Thus the present chapter will first introduce the key concept, then outline the scenarios for European security, and finally sketch briefly how the security agenda of Norden will be defined by the different scenarios.

SECURITY COMPLEXES

The central concept, *regional security complexes*, is about distinctive patterns of security relations within regions. The basic definition of a security complex is a set of states whose major security perceptions and concerns are so interlinked that their national security problems cannot reasonably be analysed apart from one another. The idea derives from the interplay between, on the one hand, the anarchic structure and its balance of power consequences, and on the other the pressures of local geographical proximity.

Simple physical adjacency tends to generate more security interaction among neighbours than among states located in different areas. Adjacency is potent for security because many threats carry more easily over short distances than over long ones. Security complexes embody durable patterns of amity and enmity occurring within geographical patterns of security interdependence (Buzan and Rizvi, 1986, ch. 1; Buzan, 1991, ch. 5).

The impact of geographical proximity on security interaction is strongest and most obvious in the military, political, societal and environmental sectors. Military power and environmental damage are much more easily projected over short distances than over long ones. Thus Pakistan is more concerned about the capabilities of the Indian Air Force than is Japan, and Canada is more concerned about American emissions of sulphur dioxide than is Britain.

Political and societal threats and tensions also operate more easily over short distances. Ethnic and religious groups often straddle adjacent state boundaries in politically significant ways.

Being adjacent to an antagonistic ideology is usually discomforting. The conditioning of security perceptions by historical memory also operates more strongly with adjacency, as illustrated by relationships between Greeks and Turks, Vietnamese and Chinese, and Arabs and Persians.

The general rule that adjacency increases security interaction is much less consistent in the economic sector. For many Third World countries, even ones with substantial economies such as India, economic interaction with neighbours is relatively insignificant. What counts is a far flung network of trade and finance, in which distance plays little role. There is evidence that proximity plays a role among advanced capitalist states, as indicated by the moves towards common markets in Western Europe and North America, but the function of geography in economic security is much more uneven than for the other sectors.

All the states in the system are to some extent enmeshed in a global web of security interdependence. But because insecurity is often associated with proximity, this interdependence is far from uniform. Anarchy plus geographical diversity yields a pattern of regionally-based clusters, within which security interdependence is markedly more intense between the states inside such complexes, than it is between states inside the complex and those outside it.

South Asia provides a clear example, where the wars and rivalries of the subcontinent constitute a distinctive pattern that is little affected by events in the Gulf or in South-East Asia (Buzan and Rizvi, 1986). The analysis in this book hinges on the idea that Europe can be seen as a security complex: a group of states whose securities are sufficiently interdependent to make them a type of subsystem within the overall pattern of international security.

Many variables affect the basic premise that security interdependence tends to be regionally focused. One such intervening variable is power. At one end of the power spectrum, superpowers such as the United States have such wide-ranging interests, and such massive capabilities, that they can conduct their rivalries over the whole planet. Superpowers, by definition, largely transcend the logic of geography in their security relationships. At the other end are states whose limited capabilities confine their interests and activities to their near neighbours, as in South-East Asia or Southern Africa. Possession of great power thus tends to override the regional imperative, small power to reinforce it.

The great powers form a kind of global security complex amongst themselves, taking the whole planet as their region, and it is for this reason that neo-realist theory focuses on them. Lesser states will usually find themselves locked into a regional security complex with their neighbours. The particular character of a local security complex will often be affected by historical factors such as long-standing enmities (Greeks and Turks, Arabs and Persians, Khmers and Vietnamese), or the common cultural embrace of a civilizational area (Arabs, Europeans, South Asians, North-East Asians, Latin Americans).

Local security complexes are defined by indigenous patterns of security relations, but this does not mean that they are immune from the system-dominating influence of the great powers. The idea of the distribution of power (the number of great powers in the system) links to that of security complexes through the mechanism of penetration. Penetration occurs when outside powers make security alignments with states within a regional security complex. An indigenous regional rivalry such as that between India and Pakistan provides opportunites for the great powers to penetrate the region.

Balance of power logic works naturally to encourage the local rivals to call in outside help, and by this mechanism the local patterns of rivalry become linked to the global ones. South Asia again gives a clear example, with Pakistan linked to the United States and China, and India linked to the Soviet Union. Such linkage between the local and global security patterns is a natural feature of life in an anarchic system. One of the purposes of the security complex concept is to combat the tendency to overstress the role of the great powers, and to ensure that the indigenous local factors are given their proper weight in analyses of regional security.

Although regional security normally involves a mixture of local and global patterns, there are occasions when great power interests dominate a region so heavily that the local pattern of security relations virtually ceases to operate. This condition is called *overlay*. It usually results in the long-term stationing of great power armed forces in the local region, and in the alignment of the local states according to the patterns of great power rivalry. Overlay can occur across a whole spectrum of degrees of local support for the intrusion of an outside power.

In theory, it could occur with total local support (i.e. against a hated common enemy), or against total local opposition (i.e. in the face of colonizing imperialism by a great power), though such extremes are rare in practice. More likely is overlay either with the consent of the dominant local governing elites, as in Western Europe after the Second World War, or with the support of local minority factions, such as the communist parties in Eastern Europe. The period of European colonization in Asia, Africa, and the Americas gives a mixed picture of the overlay process, with some cases of substantial elite support for the penetrating power (India), and some cases of sustained opposition (Afghanistan).

For overlay to occur without substantial local support requires a massive superiority of power in favour of the overlayer, like that enjoyed by the Europeans in their conquest of technologically and organizationally less developed societies in the Americas, Africa and Australasia.

The concept of overlay plays a major role in the analysis of European security in the book on which the present chapter is based: Buzan et al., 1990. Scenarios are set up against the background of understanding the history of the European security complex, and an assessment of how the breakup of the Cold War order affects it. The traditional European security complex collapsed after the Second World War, and was overlaid by the two superpowers. That overlay has lasted for more than forty years, and is now rapidly breaking up. The European complex has not operated independently since the period of the world wars, and the question is what local patterns lie dormant under the imposed rigidities of the superpower rivalry?

Overlay is an intensely political process, and it is highly unlikely that four decades of it has had no effect on Europe. Colonial overlay, for example, reconstructed the political organization of five continents on the model of the European territorial state. On this basis, there is little reason to expect a

---

resumption of business as usual in Europe on the pre-1945 pattern. What kind of metamorphosis has occurred within the cocoon of overlay, and how will those changes evolve as overlay recedes?

SCENARIOS

The scenarios are deduced logically, and it is our claim that they actually constitute *possibilities*. The first is no longer very likely, and we therefore end up with the second and third as real possibilities for Europe, while half-and-half outcomes are seen as less stable, and therefore in the long run as less possible. This is in contrast to the way 'scenarios' are often set up these days. Most often scenarios take off from 'tendencies' or are conceptualized around organizations (an EC scenario, a CSCE scenario, a German scenario, a German–Russian scenario, and what have you). Then the author states that they are actually ideal types, and the most likely is a mixture.

What does that mean? It amounts to a method where the 'scenarios' are in the end that which is *not* possible. They are extreme appearances of each tendency, and therefore not possible. But what does it then tell us? In the present framework the idea is that the scenarios contain inner mechanisms that stabilize each as a likely outcome, and the intervals between the scenarios are the less likely outcomes.

A security complex can exist in four different conditions:

1. The 'normal' complex: a regional pattern of rivalry, balances, alliances, etc. (Example: South East Asia.)

2. Overlay, as defined above. (Example: South Asia under British rule.)

3. Centralization of political decision making in a region to the point where it is primarily to be seen as an actor at the highest level: a participant in

the global security constellation among the greatest powers, whereas the regional dynamics can no longer be seen as a system where the primary fears and concerns of a group of states are defined by each other. (Example: North America.)

4. Below a certain level of security interdependence, local states are so weak that their power does not project much, if at all, beyond their own boundaries. These states have domestically directed security perspectives, and there is not enough security interaction between them to generate a local complex (Buzan 1991: 197ff). (Example: some parts of Africa.)

Europe has been in the condition of (2) for some forty years, and the theory of security complexes claims that the possible states of a security complex define the main options for a possible future European security order.

In our book, we presented the scenarios in terms of three variables: power, fear and interdependence. This might have misled some readers to believe the scenarios were *generated* by the use of these variables. However, these three would make possible many more scenarios, and furthermore the three existing scenarios can be differentiated without the help of the variable interdependence. The scenarios are *defined* or *generated* from the theory of *security complexes* but they are in *The European Security Order Recast* (chapter 8) *introduced* by way of explaining the conditions for each scenario in terms of power, fear and interdependence.

Looking at the four possible states, we can first note that number 4 is impossible in the case of Europe. The technological level in Europe is such, that this kind of tribalism and non-interconnectedness is irrelevant. Thus, we are left with three possible roads, and if we spell out in a little more detail how they look in the case of Europe, we get these three basic scenarios for European security.

---

1. The Return of Overlay: Cold War III?

This scenario is about the re-imposition of overlay onto Europe. Its main requirement is a major reversal in the current trends towards a general lowering of fear between East and West. Such a reversal would require either a massive change of policy in the Soviet Union, such as an attempt to use military power to reassert control over Eastern Europe, or an aggressive attempt by the West to exploit current Soviet weakness. Either type of action would be filled with dangers under present conditions. It would also require a reversal of the trends towards a stronger Europe and a weaker Soviet Union, such that the United States was forced to continue to support Europe as part of its own forward defence against the Soviet Union. This scenario would foreclose any major changes in the low level of interdependence between the Soviet Union and the West.

2. The Triumph of Integration: Western Europe as a Pole

This scenario is about the replacement of the European security complex by an actor sufficiently integrated to constitute a pole of power in the international system. Its key is a Europe grown much stronger in relation to both superpowers, but particularly the Soviet Union. The key to Europe's strength is the degree of its political cohesion. There is room here for a variety of mixtures between stronger Europes and weaker Soviet Unions. It requires a general reduction in the level of fear all round. Only in the very extreme and unlikely case of a much stronger Europe (one integrated up to the level of a single state, and therefore a great power) and a much weaker Soviet Union (disintegrated down to its Russian core), is the distribution of power a sufficient condition for this scenario. There would be a great increase in interdependence between Western and Eastern Europe, some, but much less between Europe and the Soviet Union, and perhaps some decline in the high level between Europe and the United States.

3. The Triumph of Anarchy: Fragmentation

This scenario is about the re-emergence of the European security complex. The necessary conditions for it are a reversal of the trend towards a stronger Europe, plus a decline in fear between both the United States and the Soviet

Union, and Europe and the Soviet Union, sufficiently large to enable both superpowers substantially to disengage their national security concerns from Europe. Where fear would rise is inside Europe, pushing a return to some form of balance of power behaviour amongst the European powers. A weak Soviet Union would facilitate the scenario. Its most likely triggers would be either reaction against an overmighty Germany, or a breakdown of the organization adaptation mechanisms in NATO, the EC and the CSCE in the face of changes to big and too fast to handle collectively.

NORDEN IN THREE EUROPES

Cold War III – Buffer

Should East–West tension return it would not mean a recreation of the Soviet empire in Eastern Europe. What used to be 'Eastern Europe' has already reached the status of 'buffer zone,' and the closest to a Cold War would probably be something like a 'stop here' development (See Figure 1).

The Cold War scenario is the least interesting to deal with here. It is the one we know best, and it is the least likely one. The Cold War would never be itself again. The worst case is probably the buffer scenario with an Eastern Europe having to pay some attention to Soviet interests while economically and politically penetrated from the western side. This would not be too far from a 'Nordification of Europe' scenario. This could be slightly unpleasant to Sweden and Finland who would share a category with the countries of Eastern Europe, and could come to feel the increased tension along the border of Soviet/Russia. And yet this would probably be the scenario easiest for the Nordic countries to accommodate to – it is closest to the known.

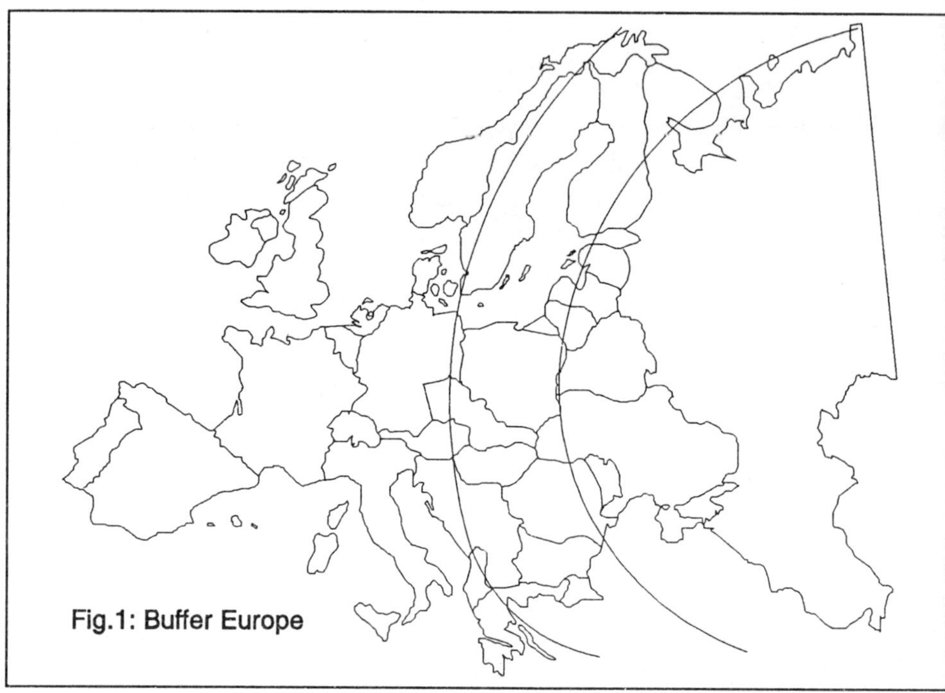

Fig.1: Buffer Europe

Pole – Integration – Grand Bargain

The basic image to use when thinking about the pole scenario, especially as the EC relates to the rest of Europe, is *concentric circles* encompassing ever-larger areas: the EC – EFTA – Eastern Europe – the Soviet Union/Russia. This differentiation makes it possible for Europe (*de facto* materialized in the EC) to *act*, because all do not have to agree. And when the hard core has made its decisions, they *de facto* obtain validity for a larger circle, i.e., a European unit emerges which is able to *act*, and most of the impulses for *all of Europe* emanate from Bruxelles, although only a part of Europe is a member of EC. Should all European states sit around one (CSCE) table, they could not reach the same amount of 'agreement' as is now produced by the slightly unbalanced procedure of concentric circles (Figure 2).

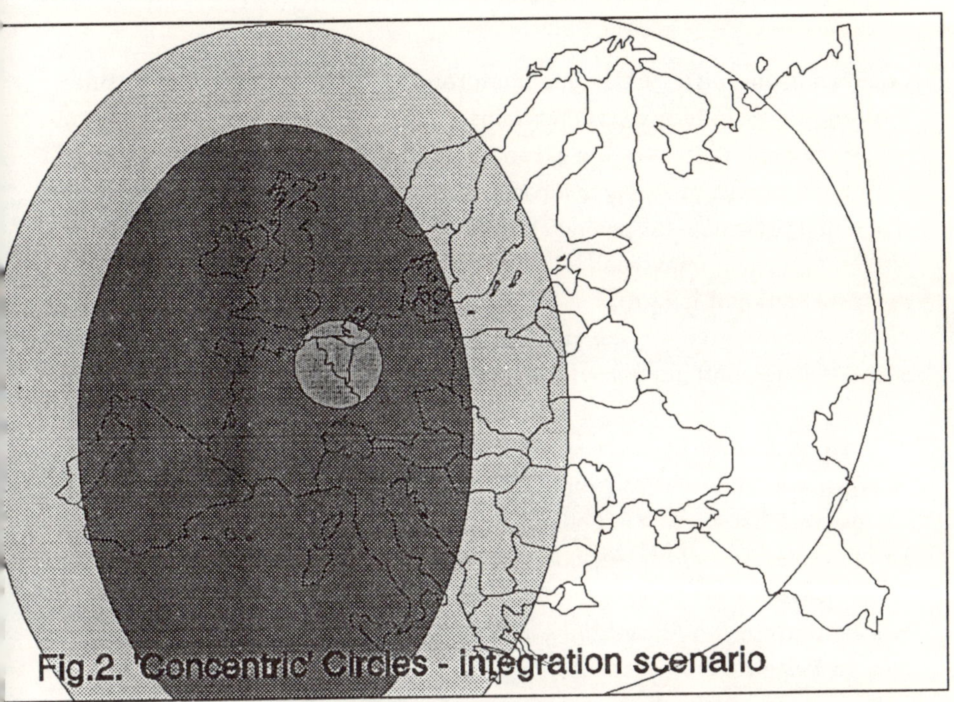

In the short run this pattern is a problem to Norden. Not to Denmark, but to the others. It means a hierarchical Europe. And there is a considerable danger that eventually EFTA merges with 'ex-Eastern Europe.' All these countries flow together as 'in-between-Europe.' Sweden, Finland and Austria are allocated the role of therapists for broken post-planning economies.

Under such conditions, EC policy might well go in the direction of treating the two outer circles increasingly as one zone. For political reasons, Eastern Europe will have a higher profile than EFTA, and thus tend to determine the terms for EC policy towards the whole outer European zone. The prospect is of a two-level Europe: the EC is first class, and then there will be a second class of 'in-between Europe'.

Within the EC core, the idea of concentric circles gained increasing support in the late 1980s as it seemed to be a meeting point for French and German thinking about Europe. The Germans tended to emphasize openness towards the East, and the French insisted on a clear line of demarcation on borders, on an identity, on defence, in other words on an EC with state-like

---

qualities. Concentric circles is a compromise in the sense that it includes Eastern Europe in Europe, but it retains a major difference between the EC as a core actor and those who are led and helped by it. (Wæver, 1990a).

Enlargement probably *will* come, but only to the extent and at the speed that a first priority to deepening allows for. Thus some elements of concentric circles logic seem unavoidable if the dynamism of the European project is to be sustained, and if Europe is to become a pole. An element of concentric circles is necessary for the relationship between the EC and the former socialist states, and for some time probably also in relation to the neutrals in EFTA.

Finland never liked the word 'Finlandization.' Not when it was applied to Western Europe and connotated deliberate submission to the Soviet Union; nor did they like the talk of Finlandizing Eastern Europe. This was on the one hand because it could be seen as a subversive policy in relation to the Soviet Union. On the other hand was it because closing the gap between Finland and Eastern Europe would not only be a Finlandization of Eastern Europe, but also an 'Eastern Europeanization' of Finland.

Norway is the only country that can be sure it will always be welcome in the EC, since she has already been invited once, and she is a NATO member. But Norway is also the country where the internal situation makes EC membership most problematic. This follows from the nature of *norskhed* (Norwegianness). Norway is founded on the belief that it is possible to keep the whole territory populated, that there is a fisher on each island and a farmer on each fjell (Enzensberger, 1987:235–314). This would hardly be possible in the EC. Thus it is possible that at a very deep level the EC and Norway are not compatible.

On this point it will always be easier for Sweden to join. However, it is less guaranteed that Sweden is always welcome – which is almost completely overlooked in the Swedish debate. It is impressive how fast the Swedish debate has swung to taking the EC membership application for granted. The 'risk' of grass roots revolt of the Norwegian type seems not to be relevant in Sweden. But it is equally impressive how this Swedish decision is taken to be synonymous with a Swedish membership (where the theme is already how much Europe will benefit from the progressive Swedish input) and there is likely to be a Swedish shock reaction when it is discovered that although the EC is unlikely to hand out 'no's (even in Eastern Europe) due to its legitimacy as 'Europe,' it will be rather busy testifying "waits." Even to Sweden.

Thus, the scenario of pole/integration created immediate difficulties for Norden. The scenario, however, needs to be elaborated a little. It does not consist only of concentric circles, but they have been emphasized because they are the immediate source of concern in parts of Norden. The EC project is not possible without an overall stability of the European security order (and vice versa). This means that the position of Russia also has to be acceptable, there has to be some mechanism for handling conflicts in the Balkans, and Germany has to take a general route compatible with French self esteem.

Europe of Regions: The Pole Scenario, Later On
Paradoxically, it is the pole scenario which in the longer run leaves most space for Nordism. In the Europe of regions, there will be more possibilities for overlapping patterns of cooperation (Figure 3).

European unification spells differentiation. The dynamic behind this is not only the often noticed "weakening of the nation-state," but also (and possibly mainly) the fact that the security dynamics tend to move out to the edges of Europe. Until now patterns of cooperation and coalitions in Europe have been conditioned and limited by concerns of security policy. The current tendencies point to a future where security concern will be located as a question of 'Europe in the world.' There will still be numerous conflicts and concerns in Europe (as inside any state), but Europe will be sufficiently *centred* (due to EC integration and the weakening of the Soviet Union) that these conflicts inside Europe cannot become *security* problems.

This makes room for the regions. Deep splits are not running through Europe any more. Furthermore, there will be less need for one-dimensional identities. When intra-European conflicts are not polarized or handled on the basis of exclusion, there is *no need to define oneself up against any European neighbour.*

In a Europe where security problems are moved out on the outside, there will be more room for shifting and overlapping patterns of co-operation. It

---

will be possible to identify oneself as belonging to Slovakia, Czechoslovakia, Central Europe, Europe and the "Pentagonale" group.

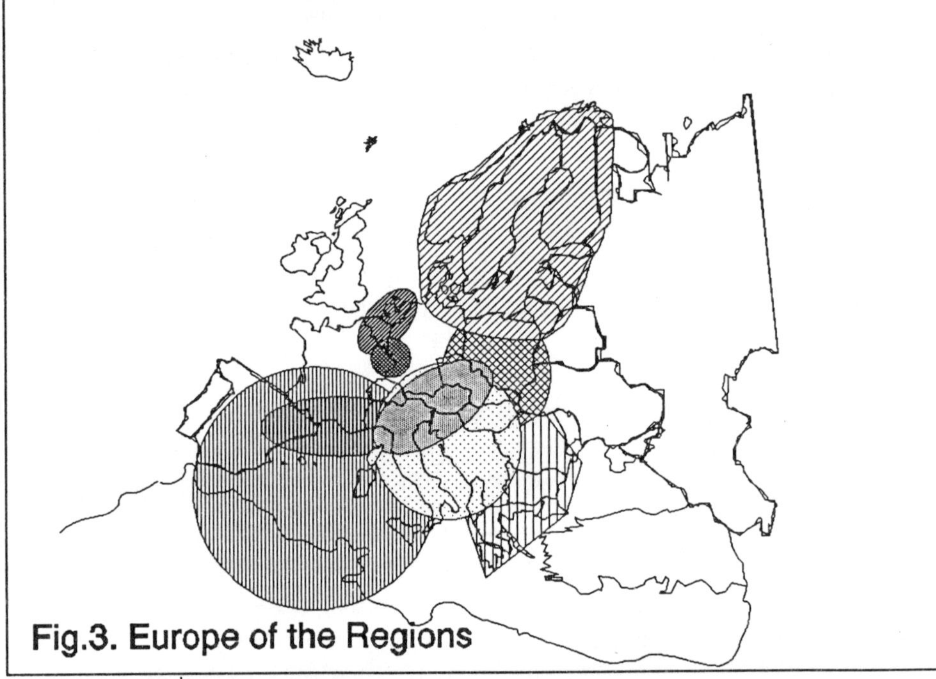

In the Cold War, political security borders were cutting through Europe. If Europe again disintegrates into independent nation-states balancing each other and establishing spheres of interest, there will again be lines cutting through Europe. And smaller states will be forced into adjusting their patterns of cooperation according to the security arrangements. Not in the more integrated scenario. Here overlapping identities will get the higher chance.

Fragmentation

This scenario comes around if the 'grand bargain' fails, if the German-European process does not unfold as a balance of French, German and Russian Europes leaving a meaningful place for each of the greater powers. The grand bargain can fail at many points: the depth of the EC process makes it touch sensitive areas triggering national reactions. And this depth is matched by the breadth of the Russian project, the CSCE project for handling security in all of Europe. Finally, the internal developments in each of the key actors are problematic; the French EC policy is extremely vulnerable at present; so is the Soviet European policy as everything in the country; and the whole arrangement rests on the premise that the Germans continue to orient themselves away from classical nation-state aims of political power and influence and instead continue to enjoy the economic freedom of manoeuvre made possible by their low profile in politics.

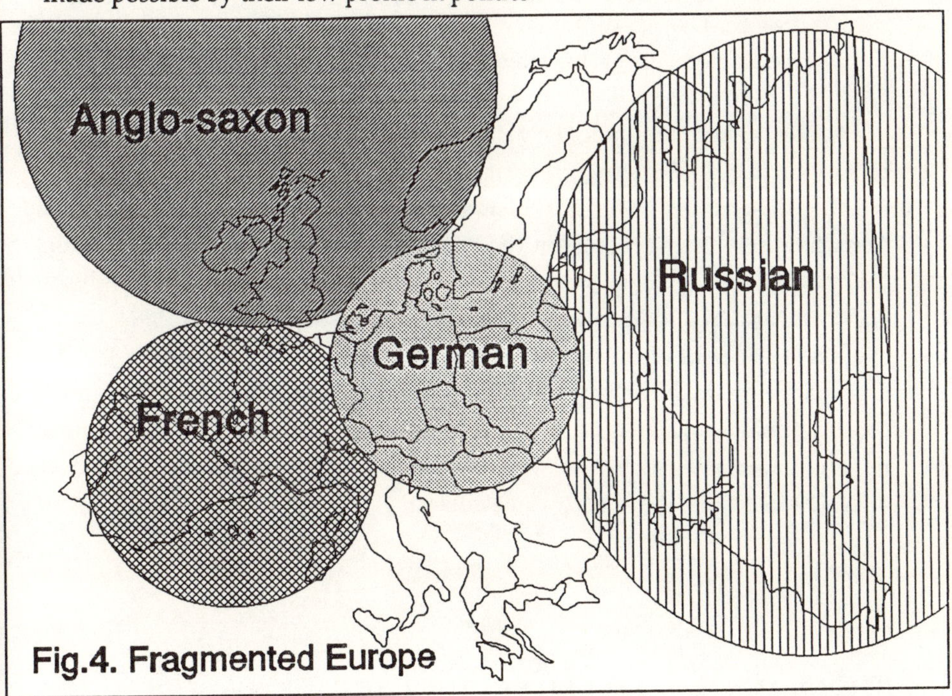

Fig.4. Fragmented Europe

If the very ambitious package deal breaks down in one place or the other, it is likely that the whole thing will unravel, and structures of cooperation will be weakened in the EC as well as the CSCE, whereupon Europe's smaller states will group themselves around regional great powers who will enter the classical games of alliances, balances and spheres of interests.

This will, first, be a problem to Denmark – a German problem. Probably it will be less of a problem to the other Nordic countries (contrary to the pole scenario). This is the 'old' constellation, and for Denmark the problem will again be that no local balance of the great powers is established, and Denmark ends up in one-sided dependence on Germany. One does not have to make nasty assumptions about the character or policy of Germany – such a *position* will always be unpleasant.

The other Nordic countries will find it easier to balance different powers against each other.

Therefore, Danish diplomacy was in 1990 and 1991 very strong in its support for all elements of the 'grand bargain'. This led to a combination of:

a) a new more pro-integrationist policy towards the EC;
b) support for all-European security structures. At the Copenhagen CSCE meeting in summer 1990, Uffe Ellemann Jensen was more Genscherist than Genscher, and the Germans on their side wanted the strengthening of the CSCE because they believed this to be in the Russian interest. The end result was Denmark on a confrontation course in relation to the United States;
c) explicit criticism of the other Nordic countries for not working sufficiently towards *rapprochement* with the EC. It is very uncommon that the Nordic countries make such direct statements on each other's policies. The latter must be interpreted as a call for assistance in the handling of Germany – a modern 1864. (At that time, they didn't come either.)

THE MEANING OF SECURITY IN THE 1990S

With the general mood of change, unpredictability and instability, there is a danger that all kinds of threats are listed – and then mixed up. For instance, the so-called 'German problem' is discussed in relation to economic growth, classical balance of power arguments, influence in the EC, etc. Very seldom is the question addressed whether all these versions of the 'German problem' can actually materialize in the same world; i.e., we rarely distinguish and say if *this* occurs we will have certain kinds of problems, but some others are not relevant anymore. This could be an important function of the scenarios.

For instance in Denmark, 'the German problem' has reappeared as an unclear combination of classical Danish concerns, and the obvious reality of German economic expansion. If discussed without differentiation, there is a considerable risk that problems of a new type will be seen as vindications of classical modes of thinking, and treated accordingly. These prophecies then become self-fulfilling.

Hopefully this is more clear after the scenarios. In the one possible scenario – fragmentation – the *form* of security problems will be (rather) 'classical'. Denmark's security problem Number One will be the one that pertained from 1864 until 1945: how to manage the relationship with Germany, how to move to a certain distance without being able to escape basic dependence, and knowing if in one form or the other there was a direct, bilateral contest, there would be no chance for Denmark of carrying it through – whether the means be economic or whatever.

In the other possible scenario – pole/integration – the security problems will be of a completely different character. Therefore, it should be possible, with the use of the scenarios, to discuss on the one hand the merits of one or the other scenario and the possible actions that might influence the directions taken by developments, and on the other hand to discuss more clearly the security problems in one scenario or another. National policies of security and integration can then be designed so they contribute to the preferred development, and with a realistic assessment of what risks should be given what weight.

Security problems take a completely different form in the integrated scenario (pole scenario). This is evident in the case of Sweden and Norway where the EC question triggered governmental crisis from the second half of 1990. But the general argument can also be shown with the case of Denmark. *Most of Denmark's security problems are related to the ever-deeper processes of integration in various forums and at various levels.* Most obvious is the problem of the EC on an economic and social level; but in addition the aspiration of the

EC to become a major political actor means that Denmark will be part of certain political games it previously stayed outside of.

Thus, does Denmark want to take part in multinational forces in a NATO or Western European context? Should these be stationed in Denmark – since it has now lost its argument for a special status, one might ask: why not in Denmark? What if the CSCE comes to involve peace-keeping forces in Europe? Conflict-resolution in relation to minority rights in South Eastern Europe is also a type of issue Denmark would be involved with.

The nature of security problems will be less Denmark *versus* another state than the effects on Denmark stemming from the internationalization of various issues; i.e., it will be less a problem of some other political actor challenging Danish sovereignty (political security) than that of *processes* undermining (or being perceived as undermining) essential elements of Danish culture and identity (societal security).

In a Europe of integration the security problem of integration will probably be rivalled by only one security problem, that of non-integration. The name of the game in the already-emerging Europe is centrality/distance: how far away from the core group will our country/region/company land, and what will be the effects of this? What is the price of being too far away from the centre? What is the price of moving closer to it? Clear indications of the power of this agenda with its ensuing fear of a marginalized Norden, can be found in the formation of the business lobby group, the 'North European Club', and its role in rushing through a decision about a Danish–Swedish bridge (across the Sound, Øresund) with a speed and in a form not very akin to (at least) Danish democratic tradition.

The price of participation is discussed in Denmark and even more in Norway and Finland. But the price of non-participation seems to dominate the Swedish debate and to some extent the Finnish. Positioning on the economic map of Europe is today felt to be so important that the elites often judge it necessary to compromise on long-held principles in relation to classical security. This has been seen in the Swedish flexibility in interpreting 'neutrality' and it can be read as a subtext in the Danish debate on possible membership of the Western European Union where membership is probably not very important for Danish defence as such (and the argument of 'taking part where decisions are made' seems a little like hypocrisy in the light of traditional Danish behaviour in alliances); it seems more likely that the felt need relates to Danish pride in being admitted to the core group in the EC in terms of inflation rate and candidacy for a possible forerunner core group in the Economic and Monetary Union (Wæver 1991b).

Balance of power, alliances, security, sovereignty – the old security agenda remains of importance due to the continuing possibility of fragmentation or Cold War III, but it is increasingly rivalled by another agenda following the logic of centre–periphery, participation and downplaying formal sovereignty.

Nordic security in the 1990s will remain exposed to this dual challenge. Beyond the 1990s it is more likely that one scenario will have won out to such a degree that one agenda will dominate. Since it is most widely assumed that the winning Europe will be that of integration, the discussion of the longer perspective is mainly couched in terms of economy and culture. Where should Norden be placed in relation to Europe? In the centre? On the periphery? Or is it possible to articulate a new way of being European *and* different, being European in a Nordic way and thereby transcending the choice between centre and periphery?

The *old Nordism revived* will mean a fighting, anti-European periphery. Centre-orientation as well as a subdued periphery will lead to the *dissolution of Norden*. Only a *rearticulation of Norden* can lead to an original input into the European process, a distinct voice which adds a new kind of Europeanness. Whether this is only an ideal or an emerging reality, and more generally how these three Nordens are unfolding at present, is investigated elsewhere in this volume.

★ ★ ★ ★

104

REFERENCES

Buzan, Barry and Gowher Rizvi *et al.*, *South Asian Insecurity and the Great Powers*, Macmillan, London 1986.

Buzan, Barry, *People, States and Fear: An Agenda for International Security Studies in the Post-Cold War Era*, 2nd ed. (original 1983), Harvester Wheatsheaf, London and New York 1991.

Buzan, Barry, Morten Kelstrup, Pierre Lemaitre, Elzbieta Tromer and Ole Wæver, *The European Security Order Recast: Scenarios for the Post-Cold War Era*, Pinter Publishers, London 1990.

Enzensberger, Hans Magnus, *Ach Europa! Wahrnehmungen aus sieben Ländern. Mit einem Epilog aus dem Jahre 2006*, Suhrkamp, Frankfurt 1987.

Wæver, Ole, 1990a, "Three Competing Europes: German, French, Russian," *International Affairs*, Vol. 66/3, July 1990, pp. 477–493.

Wæver, Ole, 1990b, "Region, Sub-region and Proto-region: Security Dynamics of Northern Europe in the 1980s and 1990s," paper presented at the annual BISA-conference, December 1990 in Newcastle, *Working Paper*, no. 1990/21.

Wæver, Ole 1991a "Danmarks Sikkerhedspolitiske Situation År 2000", *Militært Tidsskrift*, Vol.120/4, April 1991, pp. 96–129.

Wæver, Ole, 1991b "Nordic Nostalgia: Northern Europe after the Cold War," *International Affairs*, October 1991.

Wæver, Ole, Ulla Holm and Henrik Larsen (forthcoming), *The Struggle for 'Europe': French and German Concepts of State, Nation and European Union.*

5

From Confederation to Federation
Consequences for European Security

Johan Galtung

EUROPE AND THE OUTER DIALECTIC: A MACRO-HISTORICAL IMAGE

Europeans have a tendency to focus on dissimilarities and they are numerous, such as the three major types of Christianity (Orthodox, Catholic, Protestant) and the three major families of languages (Slavic, Roman, Germanic). But seen from the outside there are important similarities, viz.,

- (almost all) Europeans are white, "Caucasians,"

- (almost all) Europeans are Christian,

- (almost all) Europeans talk Indo-European languages.

In addition the continent is small, meaning that for good and/or for bad there is a strong element of shared history, which implies shared or at least complementary myths. Europeans are condemned by space and time to high-level interdependence.

Added to this comes the shared image of the geopolitical context, meaning North Africa (Maghreb), East Mediterranean (Mashreq), Turkey and

Russia. What could be more convenient than grouping all of them together under the heading of the "Orient" as the negation of Europe, the place ruled by Oriental despotism, from Casablanca through Suez to Murmansk?[1]

Three times did the Orient invade Europe: the Omayyad Arabs after the coming of Islam, conquering Spain (the "caliphate of Cordoba"), their expansion halted by Charles Martel between Tours and Poitiers in 732; the Ottoman Turks conquering the Balkans, their expansion halted by a multi-national force under the Holy Roman Empire outside Vienna in 1683; and Communist Russians after the Second World War, their (imputed, but never proven) expansion halted by governmental policies (Marshall aid, socially-oriented capitalism and a military alliance – NATO) and popular forces (the dissident movement in Eastern Europe and the peace movement all over Europe) in 1989, in Warszawa–Budapest–Leipzig–Berlin.[2]

The counter-invasions should also be counted. The anti-Arab, anti-Islam crusades, called by Pope Urban II in 1095, took place ten times (if we count the Children's Crusade) and lasted two centuries, till 1291 (and the expulsion of Arabs from Spain in 1492). Action against the Turks was very slow in gaining momentum, but ultimately resulted in the dissolution of the Ottoman Empire in 1924 and in the firm establishment of Western imperialism in Mashreq (England in Palestine–Iraq after having annexed Kuwait as a protectorate out of the Ottoman Empire in 1898, in addition to their hold on Egypt; and France in Lebanon–Syria in addition to most of Maghreb).

But action against the Russians was a constant feature of European politics: Vikings, German Teutonic Knights, Wasa Swedes, Napoleon, the Kaiser, the interventionist wars, Hitler form a dense web in time, practically speaking without counter-action westwards.

The Russians, also expansionist Europeans, headed south and east; into their Orient, the "empty" Siberia, trans-Caucasia, Central Asia, even East Asia. Of course the Europeans developed peace plans that took the shape of alliances against the threat from the "Orient," sometimes the Turks, sometimes the Russians.[3] The plan by Abbé Pierre (1306) is archetypal [4]   and prefigures today's European Community/European Union.

EUROPE AND THE INNER DIALECTIC:
A MACRO-HISTORICAL IMAGE

There are many Europes, twenty-eight countries today not counting eight mini-states (Liechtenstein, San Marino, Monaco, Andorra, the Vatican State, Gibraltar, Faroe and Åland), one maxi-state (Greenland) and countries in the Soviet Union. A glance at history shows them to be intensely competitive, belligerent in all kinds of combinations, not necessarily uniting even under pressure from the outside.

In this dialectic two dividing lines are useful, at least as a guide to European macro-history. An East–West axis divides Europe in the cis-alpina South and the trans-alpina North (with Spain obviously in the former and the line possibly cutting France in two, the Occitanie in the South and the Ile-de-France with Paris obviously in the North). And a North–South axis divides Europe in the Slavic East and Roman-Germanic West, possibly placing Finland to the West, seeing Germany united as it should be according to a line that would follow the Oder-Neisse today, wondering about Hungary and not even trying to classify Albania (neither Christian nor Indo-European). Romania and Greece would probably be placed in the East given their belonging both to the Eastern Roman and the Ottoman Empires, and to the Orthodox churches. Obviously there is a grey zone for both dividing lines.[5]

However, one fact emerged about half a millennium ago: the overarching salience of the north-western corner of the European continent. A cultural-economic-political-military syndrome catapulted the North-West into prominence.

Protestantism liberated the individual from the Church, placing the Church under the King/State which in turn confiscated Church property but also rewarded the State faithful and promised human rights, democracy and a rule of law providing predictability for the economically liberated individual, the entrepreneur. New military technology and compulsory military service made the syndrome extremely powerful militarily, capable of colonial conquests beyond the Orient like Catholic Portugal and Spain had already done, and of economic penetration in Southern and Eastern Europe.

Of course there was a reaction, but it was slow in coming. Both Portugal and Spain had to have their *decadencia*. Napoleon was the single dictator capable of "opening" most of Europe to the influence of the North-West, although – or exactly because – he was beaten. All the social changes brought about went in the same direction: homogenization, and homologization of European society even as far as Egypt – which was one among several reasons why Egypt modernized (which means westernized), under Mohammed Ali and tended to be more "Western" than other countries in the region. But how did Europe South and East react?

Of course there was a reaction which ultimately took the form of rejection of north-western cultural-economic-political penetration. Evidently this meant harking back to one's own past, unadulterated by the north-west, economic self-reliance and political control, to impose all of this on the population and to guard against north-western counterattacks. In Catholic Southern Europe this general reaction took the form of *fascism* (Portugal, Spain, Italy, Croatia, Hungary) and in Orthodox Eastern Europe it took the form of *Stalinism* (Russia and other parts of the USSR), meaning that in south-eastern Europe, the Balkans, it took both forms, one after the other.[6]

THE SECOND WORLD WAR AND ITS AFTERMATH
THE GERMAN FACTOR

The position of Germany was, literally speaking, in-between. Ruling parts of Germany were Protestant, and there was certainly economic entrepreneurship and military strength. The weak point was political: Germany was lagging behind in human rights and democracy. However, this was hardly the main reason Germany in two wars was fighting for its position in the north-western club of "modern" nations, winning only by losing the second and most brutal of these wars.

Germany was fighting for a position at the top, not for an existence in a more or less well protected margin of a Europe operated by the North-West. The trans-Orient had already been colonized by the others (England, France, Netherlands and Belgium and to a much lesser extent by the Southern countries Portugal, Spain and Italy). Maghreb and Mashreq had been colonized (by England and France, and to a much lesser extent by Italy).

Obviously the only thing left was Russia, but instead of turning east together with the rest of the North-West in a crusade against Communism Hitler's hatred of the victors from the First World War made him enter a two-front war he could not possibly win. And in addition genocide against the other chosen people in Germany: the Jews!

The outcome of the Second World War was certainly not too good:

a) the German problem, seen as "barbarism in our midst";
b) de-colonization on the horizon;
c) Southern Europe, Portugal and Spain, still under fascism;
d) Eastern Europe more than ever under Communism.

In other words, four major threats to the north-western project of running Europe and having Europe run the world as its chosen centre!

THE EUROPEAN COMMUNITY AS THE CARRIER OF PROJECT NORTH-WEST

Let us now look into how these four problems were handled:

Problem a) Maybe French brilliance was needed to see the solution, although Churchill had similar visions. Two world wars had taught Western Europe to stand together against the Germans; two world wars had taught Western Europe that a new approach was needed to Germany. Associative rather than dissociative peace policies, the peace researcher would say;

---

linking parties in peaceful cooperation rather than freezing the conflict in the dangerous shape of opposed camps, turning into alliances, engaged in arms races and ultimately in war.

The history of the European Community does not have to be told here.[7] Suffice it only to say that even the first step, the European Coal and Steel Community (ECSC) linked Germany with five other north-Western countries in a community that was not only cooperative but also designed to make the production of steel, essential for the arms industry, less national and more multi-national. That way Germany was, supposedly, effectively contained; the European Atomic Energy Community (EURATOM) was the modernization of that concept.

Problem b) The colonial problem was handled by giving the colonies political independence, yet designing an economic formula that would retain them as markets and sources of raw materials; a military formula that would make intervention possible, even easy; and a cultural formula that would facilitate the continuation of cultural dominance by old colonial powers, at least in the elite. The general formula used was the set of Yaounde-Lome conventions, initiating an "outer market" in 1964, so far comprising 66 former colonies of the 9 out of the 12 EC members that were former colonial powers.

Problem c) The Southern European problem could only be handled when the fascist regimes collapsed. So they did in the mid-1970s, first in Portugal embroiled in a colonial war, then in Spain upon the death of the patriarch. Both of them made a giant leap in history by having the French revolution – in the sense of curtailing effectively the power of the offspring of the aristocracy, the landowners, the military and the church – almost two hundred years later.

Their EC membership became effective from 1986. For both of them, but particularly for Spain that had not been a member of NATO, acceptance in the EC as a club had the same significance as for Germany: we are *in*.

Problem d) The Eastern European problem, to the surprise of the EC countries, may be heading for the same kind of solution. The Communist regimes collapsed in autumn 1989,[8] almost all of them, leading to speculation as to how many and who could become members. The four freedoms of mobility for products and production factors – people, capital, goods and services – are incompatible with self-reliance policies, so the countries have to be watched closely: will their transition to the market economy be irreversible?

When not only unemployment but also poverty and direct misery strike large sectors of the society, fairly repressive regimes may emerge to make the *economic* transition irreversible – which means that *democracy* will not be irreversible.

Then the real question becomes: what has top priority – the four freedoms of the market economy, or the human rights embedded in the rule of law and in democracy as a social formation? Time will tell. Obvious is that, even for the EC, 110 million Eastern Europeans, not to mention 290 million Soviet citizens may be more than the system can handle. The former DDR is already highly problematic.

THE DEEPENING OF THE EUROPEAN COMMUNITY

Given the four problems of the North-West of Europe after the Second World War the subsequent 45 years, 40 years after the birth of the European Community as an idea May 9. 1950, have been remarkably successful. From the very beginning, however, the goal went beyond a community.[9] There was talk of a Western European Union although this particular name was to be used for the military coordination arrangement initiated by the Brussels Treaty in 1948 as a precursor to NATO, involving the six original EC members and Britain. But the European Union has long figured in the vision of leading EC politicians. And it is quite clear that what they have in mind is a *federation* and not a confederation, a *Bundesstaat* rather than a *Staatenbund*.

More concretely, this means four important political steps:

– *a common finance policy* with a Central Bank, a common currency, etc.;
– *a common foreign policy;*

– a common military/defense policy;
– irreversibility.
The last point is important because it means that there is no way back if a country wants to secede, except if the others agree with a sufficient majority.

A *confederation* has the opposite characteristics. Each country has its own central bank and currency and retains ultimate decision-making power over the key financial mechanisms, retains its own foreign policy, raises its own army, and can leave a cooperative arrangement, or at least lay down a veto when they think costs exceed the benefits. The EC has for a long time been in a process of development from one to the other.

Clearly, this move presupposes centralization. At the same time the coming European Union (EU), as a union of democratic countries, has to be built on democratic institutions, meaning an executive responsible to a parliament and a parliament responsible to the voters. Thus, the EC clearly has to move toward a legislature with power to introduce bills and to legislate, meaning that both the Commission as constituted today and the national legislatures will lose power to the European Parliament. Both moves are opposed by the French who probably are fighting a losing battle. The models are clearly the United States and the Federal Republic of Germany.

In short, a superpower is now not only in the making, but around the corner.[10] For Europe this is a sensation. For world geopolitics it is a major transformation. Yet the event passes without discussion as if the European Community were only an economic arrangement with a single inner market.

In Germany I would even go so far as to say that the EC/EU is one of the four tabooed issues in the German debate – together with the United States, Jews–Israel and, indeed, the German aspects of Germany. There may be many reasons for this. First, NATO was always controversial in Germany, yet it was one of the two vehicles through which Germany gained European legitimacy after the war, the EC being the other. Precisely because NATO was controversial, the EC is seen as beyond debate.

Second, the whole issue is wrought with a dilemma: either Germany becomes the *primus inter pares,* in which case Germans feel uneasy, or it does not, in which case Germans, possibly some other Germans, also feel uneasy.

And general uneasiness inspires taboos. The French and the British may have similar sentiments.

PROGNOSIS

Where does this lead us? Not to develop some reasonably well-founded ideas, but to continue reasoning about "Europe" as if a giant is not being born on its western flank on the basis of something held by many to be worse than irresponsibility, namely political blindness.

One way of approaching an answer would be to see it all as a late – twentieth and early twenty-first century – continuation of the last four, five hundred years of the project of North-Western Europe. More precisely, we would assume the following four effects even in the short term:

a) rapid emergence of some Third World characteristics in parts of the Southern European (and some other) EC members having to sell out to Centre industries and focus even more on tourism, etc.;

b) rapid emergence of the same economic characteristics in an Eastern Europe increasingly related to the EC/EU, whether as full or associated members, or through trade agreements;

c) deepening of the Third World nature of the Third World countries associated with the EC/EU through the Lomé system;

d) rivalry, possibly split among the central powers in the construction, meaning the Germany–France–England triangle.

The characteristics of the Third World economy we have in mind would appear through a division of labour with the periphery producing very unsophisticated goods, through the emergence of cooperative elites in the periphery, enjoying a living standard comparable to that of the centre and then, consequently, an increasing inequality and widespread misery in the

★ ★ ★ ★ ★

114

---

periphery. This syndrome tends to be deep-rooted and very hard to transform.

As mentioned above, a likely response to increasing inequities of periphery capitalism – a reality well masked by the catch-all phrase of "market economy," making no distinction between the centre and the periphery varieties – is to combine inequity with repression. This may make revolts more dramatic, and call for even more dramatic responses. A glance at European history shows what that likely response would be: military force, legitimized by the democratic organs of the EU and coordinated through a common defence policy.

However, the reaction will be tuned to the nature or perhaps rather location of the conflict manifestation. More particularly, "trouble" inside the EC/EU may be handled at the national level by police action; inside the inner periphery in Eastern/Central Europe and parts of the Soviet Union by European Peace-Keeping Forces (EPKF); and inside the outer periphery of the ACP system by European Rapid Deployment Forces (ERDF).

The rhetoric is not difficult to imagine. People who are downtrodden, exploited and/or repressed or in general have their backs against the wall do not always operate according to the best of manners. If the root of their problems is in the very EC/EU construction, then that would tend to be the last place the EC/EU will look for an explanation, given the sacrosanct nature of the four freedoms and democratic legitimation.

The blame will be put on those who break the law and the response could be as indicated. The system produces its own reasons: protection of investment and own rationale for a common military policy. The system becomes socio-politically self-sufficient. No institution can be eliminated: certainly not the military EPKF and ERDF capability.

The third setting for a military operation would be strong internal rivalry, in other words a European Civil War, something like the American Civil War of 1861–65. It should be remembered that the latter was primarily over keeping the Union (the US) together, not over slavery, although that became the dominant rhetoric to justify the large-scale manslaughter.

Thus, would a major split in the future, for instance between the two major parts of Western Europe, the Germanic-speaking and the Roman-speaking peoples seem so inconceivable? Of course not. The US broke up less than one hundred years after its creation based on entities then at most 250 years old; the European "entities" are four times that old and separated by language, religion and myths. Granted that German is likely to quickly become as important in the EC/EU as French and English, what will be the reaction of the French and the British to what for them will easily become an overdose of German?

With Germany by far the most efficient economy of the twelve, will the locomotive forever enjoy pulling the other eleven (or so) wagons, or will it demand some de-coupling for speedier access to coveted economic goals? What happens when German policies look increasingly like re-unification with Pommern-Schlesien (in Poland) through selective investment and plebiscite, and with Ost-Preussen (in Poland and the Soviet Union) through settlement of the Volga Germans and demand for a corridor? How about similar policies in the Sudeten, even if not necessarily intended to have such effects? Will the other parts of the European Union follow through, or will they demand caution, and what will then be the German reaction? How will Germany reward those who reward Germany? And punish those who do not?

And yet it is the fourth possibility that, after the Gulf War, looms largest: the revival of the old controversy with the "Orient." With Turkey and the Soviet Union somehow incorporated in the north-west project, but on its periphery, not in its centre, the Arab part of the Orient remains. There are 22 Arab countries with Palestine and about 200 million inhabitants, and the Muslim world counts about 45 countries and more than one billion people.

A pan-Arabic or pan-Islamic superpower is obviously on the cards although the level of integration is far below that of the coming European Union. But dialectically they are destined to emerge together by a history tying them together in space and time. The Gulf War may drive that dialectic further along that spiral of force and self-righteousness for which true believers in monotheistic religions can be relied upon.

In short, the logic of the federation as super-state is not that different from the logic of any strong state based on exploitation and/or repression except for one thing: the threat of a civil war among the constituent components.   This will lead to careful balancing and mixing of the components, like in the French–German brigade outside Stuttgart, reputed to speak French and German every second week. But such social engineering tricks need much time, generations, centuries, to take root. For a long period they will look artificial, imposed; and to reconstitute national armies will be an easy job once emotions are high. The whole topic of a possible civil war within the European Union will probably remain taboo, meaning that precautions to prevent major schisms from emerging and the possible use of force will not be discussed.

THE EC AND EU IN A PAN-EUROPEAN SETTING

Of course there is more to Europe than the European Community. But 340 million out of 540 million, not counting the Soviet Union, is a substantial proportion (63%). In addition, many of the remaining 200 million to the North and to the East of the present European Community are directing so much of their activity toward that major centre of gravity that we can safely go higher.

Maybe 75% is a more fair estimate of the significance of the European Community in today's Europe. Of course, adding the 290 million of the Soviet Union changes this picture. But then the Soviet Union is undergoing the opposite transformation, from federation to confederation, meaning that in due time the EC/EU can pick off one part after the other for trade agreements and/or associate membership (full membership being less likely for the time being).

In practice this means that the CSCE conceptualization of Europe with pan-European institutions is probably already an anachronism, in spite of – or because of – the very positive role it played as a necessary condition leading up to the ending of the Cold War. To talk about thirty-odd countries when twelve are integrating and one is disintegrating is an effort to turn back the clock; any agreement reached is bound to be unrealistic. If the Soviet Union managed to attain status as a confederacy and the European Community managed to remain one, then a dialogue between the two might be interesting although it would also be over the heads or backs of many smaller countries. For that reason the image given in the preceding section is probably closer to reality. If so, we need other measures than organizational architectonics.

More particularly, the economic infrastructure has to be addressed. The McKinsey consulting firm seems to have as its guidelines for economic activity in Eastern Europe: (1) no social aspects, only economic activity; (2) no complicated production, that the West does better; (3) be in the black or else. These are, of course, prescriptions for anti-development if we assume that development has to do with taking on challenges (making complicated products) and has a social dimension also at the micro-level of the firm. But this type of prescription goes very well with the extreme right-wing economics prescribed by such finance ministers as Balcerowicz in Poland and Klaus in Czechoslovakia.[11] Moreover, this is probably also what the majority of the population wants for the time being, operating on the assumption that if a communist economy was 100% wrong then a free market economy, with no such adjectives as "social" or "ecological," must be 100% right. However, if Marxism is 100% wrong, then a useful analytical tool for understanding what capitalism is about has been eliminated, meaning that the people will not know what has hit them.

As a consequence they will hit something else, like another ethnic group, employing the type of analysis entertained at the centre of the system about fundamentalism, ethnic conflict, and "Balkanization," meaning some kind of pre-Orient.

In summary, the future for the European system is bleak. The completion of the super-state configuration can be done already in the 1990s according to the communiqué from the Rome meeting in December 1990.[12]

The process is quick and decisive. Any counterprocess has to have the same qualities.

★ ★ ★ ★ ★

118

NOTES AND REFERENCES

1. This theme is developed by Mogens Trolle Larsen in Hans Boll-Johansen & Michael Harbsmeier, eds., *Europas Opdagelse*, Copenhagen: Ejlers, 1988, pp. 9–37.

2. See Johan Galtung, "Europe Fall 1989: What Happened, and Why," 1990, in several languages.

3. For a general survey of peace plans from Europe, see Johan Galtung, "Peace Concepts in the Occident," in ch. 15 in *Essays in Peace Research, Vol. V*, Copenhagen: Ejlers, 1980, pp. 415–27. The peace plans can be grouped under two headings, "Ingroup peace against the outgroup" projects and "Universalism with a Western centre" projects. The EC/EU tradition draws on the former, the UN as it was planned by the Allies on the latter.

4. Pierre du Bois, *De Recuperatione Terrae Sanctae*, written after the Crusades had been defeated, was a general peace plan in Christendom to re-conquer the Holy Land, with a clear anti-Islamic bias. The plan is often quoted in EC pamphlets.

5. For more details, see Johan Galtung, "Europe the contradictory: A macro-geographical and macro-historical overview," ch. 1 in *Europe in the Making*, New York: Taylor & Francis, 1989.

6. It is hardly by chance that fascism became the reaction of the Catholic South and communism the reaction of the Orthodox East to the challenge and pressure from the highly dynamic Protestant North-West. There is a basic compatibility between hierarchic Christianity and a fascism without any egalitarian pretensions, as there is between communist and Orthodox optimism, and the pretended equality of both.

7. For one analysis, see ch. 2, "Europe the contradiction-free: From community to superpower" in Galtung, 1989.

8. For an analysis of the collapse, see Galtung 1990.

9. Robert Schuman in *La declaration du 9 mai 1950: "La mise en commun des productions de charbon et d'acie est la première étape de la Féderation européene."* And Churchill called for a United States of Europe in his Zurich speech in 1946.

10. The title of my first book on the subject was *The European Community: a Superpower in the Making*, London: Allen & Unwin, 1973. For my own discussion of the book, see the chapter with the same title in *Essays in Peace Research, Vol. VI*, Copenhagen: Ejlers, 1988.

11. See *Der Spiegel*, no. 3, 1991, pp. 129–32, "Harte Zeiten nach der Wende" and "Prague gets the Chicago treatment," *The Nation*, December 10, 1990.

12. The Rome meeting took place on December 14–15, 1990. The key dates for the common financial policy are now 1994 (for the central bank) and 1997 (for the common currency). For the military union 1998, when the EC can take over the remaining defence functions of the WEU since the WEU Brussels treaty of 1948 expires in 1998. Even now some foreign policy issues can be decided by majority vote rather than by unanimity (John Palmer, *Guardian Weekly*, 2 December 1990). Not only the President of the Council of Ministers at the time, de Michelis, but also the chairman of the foreign affairs committee of the European Parliament, Willy de Clercq favours a European Army. And the WEU already served the important function of coordinating the navies of the member countries participating in the Gulf War.

6

Arms Control and Disarmament in Europe

Johan Galtung

THE TRANSFORMATION OF CONFLICT FORMATIONS

Europe, and the entire Cold War system including not only the Soviet Union but also the United States, has undergone a dramatic period of accelerated history. Only future generations will be in a position to appreciate fully the significance of a process affecting directly the lives of 275 million inhabitants in North America, 540 million in Europe – West and East, North and South, and Centre – and 290 million in the Soviet Union; all together well above 1.1 billion human beings, close to one-fifth of humanity. Obviously, there are also implications for the rest of the world, but they are less direct and immediate. What follows is an effort to spell out the significance in ten points.

Two major scourges of humankind are gone from Europe, and probably irreversibly so, in a process that started with the conclusion of the Final Act of Helsinki in 1975, and culminated in autumn 1989. The first is the totalitarian *Stalinism* of the Soviet Union, including the continuation and expansion of Russian imperialism within and outside the Soviet Union. The second is the genocidal *nuclearism* of the superpowers and their alliances planning for a credible and winnable nuclear war. With these two mutually reinforcing syndromes gone, the Cold War is over. There are good reasons to celebrate.

However, four new conflict formations are now taking shape, all of them complex and demanding our most creative attention.

First, the rapid disintegration of *pax sovietica*, a peace-keeping system under Moscow military control, which may or may not coincide with the political disintegration of the Soviet Union. There has been open fighting between Azerbaijanis and Armenians and in the Baltic states, and between Hungarians and Romanians. Disintegration of *pax americana* followed by, say, fighting between Greeks and Turks has not (yet) taken place. The process is asymmetric.

Second, the rapid transformation of some Eastern European economies from centrally planned socialism to peripheral capitalism with such Third World characteristics as vertical international division of labour, asymmetric investment, tight elite cooperation and increasing inequality and unemployment, even misery at the bottom of society. Central planning with immobilization of people and inability to deliver goods and services is gone for now. But the problems of capitalism are the same as before, with impressive centre growth at the expense of periphery depression and misery.

Third, there is the rapid unification process for two parts of pre-war Germany, BRD and DDR, posing the question of what will – in the long run – happen to the other four parts; now Polish, Soviet and Czech lands, and Austria. *Das Dritte Reich* occupied seventeen countries in Europe and caused the death of 26 million in the Soviet Union alone. The way unification is brought about by the 2+4 formula looks like Versailles in reverse. *Das Vierte Reich* taking shape?

Fourth, the rapid transformation of the European Community to a European Union, with not only cultural and economic, but also political and military integration, using the Western European Union.[1] With the unification of Germany, 340 of 540 million Europeans, or 63%, will live in the present twelve EC member states.

In short, we are witnessing two conflict transformations: from a *bipolar* Europe with two alliances confronting each other to a *unipolar* Europe with the hegemonic centre in Western Europe commanding tremendous military and economic resources; *and* from *military* to *economic* resources as the leading factor. Integration in the West, except for German unification, is nothing new in post-war history. It is the disintegration in the East that brings about the steepest West–East gradient in European history. Along this gradient all kinds of power are bound to flow, sooner or later.

Deploring this – warning of the consequences – implies no nostalgia for the Stalinist *pax sovietica,* nor for Cold War, nuclear confrontation with a non-zero probability of a hot nuclear war. Although there are still important military residues remaining from the Cold War the hard core of the conflict formation, the point of disagreement, disappeared when the fate of Eastern Europe was decided in Moscow's disfavour. Not only the population of the former Cold War system but also peoples in the Third world – who will no longer have the Cold War acted out hot, by proxies – can feel relieved.

The Europe taking shape bears a strong resemblance to Europe one century ago; but with power and integration more discrepant. Consequently, *security has to be redefined, rethought, re-searched.*

The Transformation in the East

In this process the Soviet Union and Eastern Europe have:

a) de-stalinized politically, working at it economically;
b) changed military doctrine, toward defensive/sufficient/non-provocative defence: more deeds now have to follow the words;
c) proposed total withdrawal of nuclear weapons, of Soviet troops by 1995–96 and of all foreign bases by the year 2000;
d) argued for the transformation of NATO and WTO from military–political to political alliances and, later, the dissolution of the WTO;
e) put forward imaginative proposals for a Common European Home based on the equality of all participating countries.

Much of this makes virtue of dire necessity, for economic and political change. But the thrust toward a New European Peace Order is clear. And the new virtue is preferable to the old vices.

THE NON-TRANSFORMATION IN THE WEST

In the same process the United States and Western Europe have:

a) declared their own system victorious with no self-criticism of the dark side of nuclear terror balance and capitalist economies;
b) kept a highly offensive military doctrine, entering the discourse of defensive defence only in a CFE context;
c) argued for short-range nuclear arms increases and for keeping 195,000 US troops in Central and 30,000 in Southern Europe regardless of what the Soviet Union does, and for European bases;
d) announced plans to expand NATO, admitting unified Germany;
e) put forward asymmetric, West-centred concepts for Europe;
f) conducted the Gulf War.

THE WESTERN EUROPEAN SUPERPOWER

At the same time the superpower character of the twelve-member (so far) European Community/Union is more clear, comprising[2]:

a) *economic integration*, with an inner market from 1993;
b) *political integration* from around 1995/96;

c) increasing argumentation for *military integration*, possibly based on the nine-member (out of the twelve) Western European Union;

d) a very high level of *cultural integration* based on shared history, Christianity/Enlightenment and similar languages;

e) a sense of *global mission* based on the sunny side of European culture and the dark colonial experience shared by nine EC members;

f) potentially continental size and a nine-digit *population* base;

g) an ongoing *nuclearization* with a deep-water navy with nuclear submarines, French and British nuclear forces independent of NATO, missiles, space satellites, etc.;

h) an inner *French–German friendship axis* combining French political vision since 1950 with solid German economic backing.

Of course there are problems in the EC/EU–Germany–US–NATO quadrangle, and some of them may have security implications. Thus, will the EC always remain pregnant with a baby the size of Germany, and if not, will the delivery be painless? Can Germany forever be "contained" in NATO, with foreign troops stationed there in what may look increasingly like occupation, even by six countries, rather than protection, now that the threat is gone?

We have already witnessed the US involve other NATO members in new confrontations in the Middle East – and it could happen in North Africa, too – now when the classical East–West conflict dissolves further. How will members and others react in the future?

PROGNOSIS: FROM BLOC-CONFRONTATION TO HEGEMONY

The major security problems both *in* and *of* Europe will from now on be variations over the general theme of Western hegemony. One hypothesis might view the Yalta and the Malta system as similar only in that the former

---

divided Europe and the latter the whole world in "spheres of interest." The US will exercise hegemony in the Western Hemisphere and the Middle East; the EC in the ACP system in general and in Africa in particular; Japan in East and South-East Asia, and the Soviet Union over itself, like India and China.

Thus, the US may involve the EC in the Middle East and the EC the US in Africa, both of them invoking the fight against, say, drugs and terrorism as major motives. But an unprovoked threat to the security *of* Europe from Africa or the Middle East is unlikely.

The consequences for security *in* Europe of the gradient from the Western peak to the Eastern trough will be considerable. *Western military superiority* derives from many factors: an intact alliance; the transfer of Eastern Germany from WTO to NATO; three nuclear powers in the West as against one in the East; a Western superpower whose territory falls outside the purview of the CFE whereas Soviet territory does not, and US sea-based missiles together with Star Wars strategic superiority – to mention just some of them.

Western political superiority derives from the five strong intergovernmental organizations: NATO in Brussels, WEU in Paris, EC in Brussels, OECD in Paris and Council of Europe in Strasbourg.

Western cultural superiority derives from free world dynamics as opposed to the backwaters of Stalinist cultural repression.

CASSANDRA'S SCENARIO

But the basic threat to security derives from Western economic superiority. Imagine the economic landscape of Eastern Europe/Soviet Union, devastated by Stalinist economics, invaded economically by heavy EC economic investment up to the Ural Mountains, with Japan also investing up to the Urals from the East.

With the Frankfurt Stock Exchange established in Volgograd and German and Japanese businessmen meeting in the Urals, World War II is over. Popular, including vulgar, Western culture with commercials and commercialism, junk food, junk news and junk entertainment will replace Stalinist scarcity and austerity. What happens then?

Using general knowledge of hegemonic, unipolar systems with economic superiority as the leading factor, for instance from the Western hemisphere or from the European (very recent) colonial past, this is *one image, painting the future Cassandra dark:*

a) there is heavy economic growth in Eastern Europe/Soviet Union around capital-, technology- and management-intensive poles; *and* increases in unemployment, even misery, and property crime;

b) consumerism as cultural invasion collides increasingly with old European values, already eroded in the West, with loss of identity, alcohol and drugs, violent crimes and suicide/homicide;

c) there is *tristesse*, even nostalgia for the socialist security and cultural identity of the past, even if jobs, food and shelter were inadequate and the identity and cultural creativity was a consequence of Stalinist oppression and may disappear with it;

d) as this unrest cannot be articulated in marxist-socialist terms although that discourse may be used as blackmail – "if you don't invest more we'll become communists again" – *ideological expressions* will probably take such right wing forms as nationalism, religious fundamentalism, even fascism, with governmental rule by decree;

e) this formula suits those who benefit from periphery capitalism while suppressing those who will not benefit;

f) class conflicts will be hitched onto the rich texture of ethnic conflicts, so far successfully hidden by *pax sovietica;*

g) *violent expressions,* such as terrorism, destruction of foreign enterprises, kidnapping of foreign nationals, etc., will be more than local police are able or willing to handle;

h) Western Europe then responds with European Peace-Keeping Forces (EPKF) to protect investment abroad; and European Rapid Deployment

---

forces (ERDF) to come to the rescue of its own nationals. Both will be by invitation of Eastern governments totally dependent on investment from the West, and will be referred to as self-defence;

i) a complication might be "most favoured economic treatment" to former German territories in Poland and RSFSR, leading to *de facto* economic integration and demands for political *Anschluss;*

j) US interests may separate from EC interests, like in Latin America, making US troops stationed in Germany and Japan look like occupation forces checking economic competitors;

k) German interests may also separate from EC interests in general, being more Eastern European, less ACP-oriented;

i) new alliances may take shape, and major violence may occur.

POLYANNA'S SCENARIO

There is no disagreement with the major and rather obvious premise that a transformation is taking place from bipolar to unipolar, and from military to economic, confrontation. Nevertheless, there are alternatives with more balance in Europe and more pan-European cooperation, in *a scenario painting the future Polyanna light:*

a) *economically* the weaker countries in Eastern Europe and the Soviet Union might produce as much as possible locally and nationally, cooperating among themselves, and trade more with the 33 million EFTA countries[3] in Western Europe (small, but the EC's largest trade partner) with solid welfare state traditions;

b) *culturally* the Eastern countries may find it to their advantage to preserve and develop further the rich Central/Eastern European culture, so important as a non-violent weapon against Stalinist repression, while being open to the rest of the world and not only the West;

c) *politically* the Eastern countries might insist, in all contexts, on pan-European decision-making, using fully the Conference for Security and Cooperation in Europe (CSCE) with the US and Canada (the Cold War system) to ensure that any *fait accompli* on major issues like German unification is not forced upon the Europeans;

d) *militarily* the Eastern countries may not only insist on the transformation of NATO and the WTO from military to political alliances, the dissolution of them or – as a minimum – on the transformation from offensive to defensive doctrines and postures, but also on *the creation of a UN Security Commission for Europe, SCE*[4] like the UN Economic Commission for Europe, and a permanent CSCE secretariat to monitor agreements and process complaints, possibly also with peacekeeping capacity.

A FUTURE BETWEEN CASSANDRA AND POLYANNA?

The near future will probably be closer to the Cassandra than the Polyanna scenario. If so an opportunity is being lost. Europe has rarely been so *plastic* as during autumn 1989. The Western leadership quickly understood this and skilfully shaped the raw material, a plastic Europe, to their advantage. They had been the spectators, taken entirely by surprise ("nobody could have predicted this").

True, *they* could not have predicted anything so far outside their discourse as Europe was liberated from the scourges of Stalinism/nuclearism essentially by an unlikely alliance[5] of the dissident movement in the East, the peace movement in the West, and Gorbachev.[6] This was a revolt from below, the signals being used by the leader of one of the superpowers only, the Soviet Union.

Using the *confederation* as the most effective general peace formula we know, combining cooperation within with separation of parliaments, governments and financial/foreign/military policy so as not to be provocative, even aggressive without, *five ideas* can be proposed for Europe,[7] some of them still feasible:

a) a *German confederation* of BRD, DDR and Berlin (West), as *Staatenbund*, not *Bundesstaat*, with neither *Mauer* nor *Zaun*, and free flow of ideas, persons, and production factors and products;
b) keeping the *European Community* as a confederation, not moving further toward financial/foreign policy/military unification;
c) creating a *Central and Eastern European Confederation;*
d) transforming the Soviet Union from a tsarist/Stalinist empire to a *Soviet Confederation*, with the present republics as members;
e) creating a *Common European Home, like a confederation*, with the CSCE as the supreme organ and the SCE as one secretariat.

COLD WAR RESIDUES

There are still residues to be dealt with, energetically and boldly "cleaning up the mess" left behind by the irrationality of the arms race of recent decades. When so doing it might be worth reflecting on one major point: neither the western, nor the eastern side has the proof that the other side ever seriously prepared an unprovoked attack. The Soviet Union had plans for massive invasions westward, and the West for massive (nuclear) bombardment eastward in case of an attack. But that is no proof of aggressive intent, only proof of offensive postures and doctrines and their provocative implications.[8]
Consequently:

a) under CSCE or UN auspices *an international conference* should be organized on military doctrines, requesting all CSCE countries to state explicitly their military doctrines with a view to moving the whole continent toward non-provocative doctrines and postures;

b) the CFE process of disarming offensive weapons systems – thereby *transarming Europe* toward conventional defensive defence – should be accelerated, focusing particularly on offensive armed vehicles;

c) the US position notwithstanding, timetables should be established for the removal of all foreign bases, weapons systems (particularly for mass destruction) and armed forces from Europe;

d) the Swiss referendum of November 26, 1989 with 35.6% voting in favour of the abolition of the Swiss Army by the year 2000 could be repeated in other countries. This could open a serious debate about what a future Europe without national armies might look like.

CONCLUSIONS

For a person used to the Cold War, Europe today is hard to recognize. This also has *implications for the neutral/non-aligned countries*. With the bipolar confrontation gone, neutrality in the sense of nonalignment makes no sense: who can be nonaligned when there is no major conflict with clearly conflicting parties to be aligned with?

But neutrality as a general foreign policy doctrine of non-participation in military conflicts is equally meaningful in a unipolar configuration. The pledge is made credible through defensive defence and would be very meaningful for unified Germany.

The ambiguity of unified Germany in NATO will remain as long as NATO is a military alliance: will NATO contain German revanchist/ expansionist forces or will these forces be able to persuade NATO to push eastward? A transformation of NATO to a political alliance would remove that objection to a unified Germany in NATO.

Stationing of Soviet troops in the eastern part of unified Germany as a *quid pro quo* for US troops in the western part would only preserve the status quo and serve to legitimize overstaying US troops. Fortunately the Soviet Union decided not to play that game.

But even German unification is overshadowed by the emergence of the (Western) European Union as a superpower. This is as deplorable as it was predictable from the early 1950s onwards. The EC relation to the inner periphery of Eastern Europe and the Soviet Union, and to the outer ACP periphery is loaded with tensions. But that is where the major security problem of Europe is located now. *In a world that badly needs fewer, not more superpowers.*

NOTES AND REFERENCES

** This chapter was the author's testimony for the Political Affairs Committee, European Parliament, in Brussels on March 20, 1990, published here with minor changes by the editor.*

1. The communique from the Meeting of the WEU Ministers of Foreign Affairs and Defence, Den Haag 26–27 October 1987 mentions (Preamble, 2) the determination to create the European Union and the conviction that this will be incomplete so long as integration does not also include security and defence.

2. See Johan Galtung, *The European Community: A Superpower in the Making*, London: Allen & Unwin, 1973 for an early discussion of this theme, and the follow-up in *Europe in the Making*, New York/London: Taylor & Francis, 1989, chapter 2, "Europe the contradiction-free: From community to superpower," pp. 22–36.

3. Nobody would deny the overpowering relevance of the EC countries for the neo-liberal regimes in Eastern Europe. But a deal with EFTA would create a community of close to 150 million people, with the Soviet Union 100 million

more than even the EC with the eastern part of Germany. A negotiation between two equals might bring about a better European Economic Space, EES. But the EC, at an early stage, had Monet and Schumann and the Soviet Union has Gorbachev. Eastern Europe and the Soviet Union have what EFTA does not have: charismatic leaders. But then they have other problems!

4. See Galtung, J. and Lodgaard, S., eds., *Cooperation in Europe*, Oslo: Norwegian Universities Press, 1970, chapter on security commissions. The research was done for the Council of Europe 1967.

5. They both came into being as mass movements around 1980, the dissident movement above all in Czechoslovakia and Poland and the peace movement above all in the Netherlands and Western Germany. Typically the dissident movement saw the peace movement as willing to compromise with the communist regimes if they showed moderation in the arms race; and the peace movement saw the dissident movement as willing to drive the world closer to war if that would help bring about the end of Stalinism. There was some truth to both perceptions, but frequent meetings between the two made the dissidents more peace-oriented and the peaceniks more human-rights-oriented through the first half of the 1980s.

6. See Johan Galtung, *"Europe Fall 1989: What Happened, and Why?,"* Honolulu, spring 1990; for many publications.

7. Except for the Soviet Confederation the reader will find these developed in *Europe in the Making*, particularly in the Introduction and the Conclusion.

8. Another, also important, consequence of this is that nuclear weapons did not deter a major war in Europe: there was nothing to deter. And they certainly did not deter Soviet aggression on Eastern Europe, particularly not in Hungary 1956 or in Czechoslovakia 1968; but then they were not intended to do so either. See Galtung, *op. cit.*, chapter 4, "The Structure of a Myth: Nuclear deterrence has preserved peace in Europe for 40 years" pp. 49–59.

7

Norden Rearticulated

Ole Wæver

HOW TO BE NORDIC IN A NEW EUROPE

What is Norden if Europe is a new low-tension region? In a certain sense the old arrangement was ideal: Norden was embedded in a stable European constellation, with Norden's own situation somewhat better than that of the others.

The meaning of 'Norden' in security terms was not something outside Europe, nor was it an arrangement that could in itself be an alternative. It meant 'a little better than the others.'

What appears as 'progressive' nowadays is the integrating, market-based, cooperative, sovereignty-neglecting *Europe*, not the distancing, Third Way, self-protecting, global and inward-oriented *Norden* of the sovereign states.

It is widely felt in the Nordic region that 'Norden' in the old sense is not a powerful instrument for handling the challenges of the closing twentieth century. Norden – as a concept, an answer – appears increasingly *irrelevant*.

What can be a timely meaning of Norden? What does it mean to be Nordic in an intregrated/integrating Europe of the 1990s and beyond?

To answer this question we will need first a brief look at the constituent elements of the existing Nordic identity. What are the cultural, political, geographical, historical and other elements? After that this chapter lists the main patterns of reaction and investigates finally one of these: the changing meaning of 'Norden' if a Baltic Sea orientation becomes a dominant element of Northern Europe.

NORDIC IDENTITIES

Searching through, for instance, culture, literature, language, history, humour, structure of industry, and intellectual style, one would find several traits which characterize one or all Nordic peoples, states and societies. It would also be possible to find instances where each of these was used by the people themselves as point of self-identification. However, we are interested here in those central meanings that constitute 'Norden' as a political category. These identities will be *differential* and *symbolic*.

As to identity cum *difference*, it is possible to point to important contrasts of an intra-Nordic form as well as of an extra-Nordic one. It is well known that the national identities of the Nordic countries have largely been developed against their (largely Nordic) neighbours. Sometimes different neighbours serve as contrast on different dimensions, as in Norway where the question of national, cultural identity is first and foremost defined in relation to Denmark and the Danish language for the very obvious reason that it was from the Danish culture, history and language the Norwegians had to disentangle their 'own'. As relates to direct 'actor-based' threats, the main contemporary challenge is Sweden, Swedes, and Swedish capital (which has bought up substantial parts of Norwegian industry). Thus the jokes and the other means to put off challengers are mainly directed against Swedes (there are far less Dane-jokes, whereas the culture-struggle has Denmark as the threat). In other cases different neighbours serve to reinforce the same self-understanding, as in the case of Denmark, where Germans and Swedes take the same position as the bureaucratic, hierarchic, self-important negation to the Danish (allegedly) informal, peoples-based, humorous culture. Who has the honour to play the main character, Sweden and Germany, is changing now and then. Also 'Norden' as such has been defined by differences, by what is not-Nordic. (Cohen, 1986: 2)

And why *symbolic?*

> The response [to the increasing similarity in the machinery of people's lives] – interpretation, meaning – is not mechanical, and frequently is not overt. It belongs to that realm of phenomena which anthropologists label the 'symbolic'. It is in the symbolic that we now look for people's sense of difference, and in symbolism, rather than structure, that we seek the boundaries of their worlds of identity and diversity. (Cohen 1986: 2)

We do not question that lots of concrete 'similarities' and points of connectedness will continue. The Nordic languages *are* closer to each other than to other languages. There are many common elements in their history and in everyday life. Thus, it is still very likely that when a dozen Europeans meet in Rome (or even Bruxelles), the Nordic participants will first talk with each other.

As argued in Chapter 1 there is a certain correspondence between the Europe/Norden constellation in security and socio-economics. The Nordic identity has been a not-fully-established *third point*. It was not as solid as the other two; it was always a derived third, one that for its interpretation depended on the two others, whereas they were defined in relation to each other, not in relation to the Nordic third.

Hence, the Nordic 'alternative' was never a real alternative in the sense of transcending the dualism it grew out of. It lived inside the East–West security order in Europe and existed inside a dualism of capitalism and socialism. For all practical purposes, Norden lived in the Western-capitalist part but *symbolically* signified the openness of the game. Norden was a dependent sub-

---

system, not an alternative order that could be realized in isolation, rather an addition. It was an accent in the European story.

What, then, was the meaning of 'Norden' in this context? 'Nordic' meant being part of Europe, but a little better (off) than the others: more peaceful, with more space for social solidarity as well as in the global perspective.

This system experienced various challenges during the 1980s. There were not only increasing external pressures; the internal mechanisms of the system showed signs of weakness in the mid-1980s. For instance, the position of Sweden as the regional great power was questioned, partly by the economic and military strengthening of Norway, and the success of Finland in handling the crisis of the 1970s, and partly by the increasing contradictions in the Swedish model of neutrality (Øberg, 1986).

Turning to the other main axis, the welfare societies, it can be claimed that the 'Swedish' and 'Nordic' models are alive and well,

> exactly because these concepts of models are retrospective, rear mirrors through which the present watches the past. The Swedish and the Nordic welfare states have not grown consciously or been formed as models. Even the word 'welfare state' has in Swedish a clear accent of academic research and intellectual debate. (Therborn 1987: 35)

Thus the models are with us, not necessarily due to the vitality of the processes. The 'Scandinavian/Swedish' model cannot be defined alone by being 'welfare states,' since these exist in several forms and are quite frequent in Europe. In Scandinavia one finds, however, the main examples of what Gösta Esping-Andersen sees as one out of three clearly discernible types of welfare states: *the social democratic one characterized by 'de-commodification' and universalistic social rights on a high level* (Esping-Andersen, 1990: 27f). At a more abstract level, the welfare models have reflected a self-conception - and a view by others - saying that the Swedish model was unusually *modern*, it was the future realized today, the transparent planning society.

If one believes that the crisis of the Scandinavian, or Swedish, model is a product only of the EC decision in 1985 on the Single Act and the project of 1992, and/or of the events in Eastern Europe 1989, and/or of the economic problems of Sweden in 1989–90, it is useful to re-read a brilliant essay by Arne

Ruth, which shows – by being printed in 1984 – that this is certainly not the case:

> Swedish political culture in the 1980s seems more fragile, less rooted in a firm conviction of its own values, than the culture of the neighboring countries. This may seem to contradict the traditional view of Sweden as a self-righteous model for the world. In fact, Sweden's vulnerability appears to some extent to be the unexpected consequence of the country's position as a model.
>
> In terms of social psychology, the sense of being admired by the world is the antithesis of the state of doubt that plagued Sweden's self-identity a hundred years ago. But the dialectics of history in this instance seem not to have provided for a synthesis. The basic uncertainty reemerges as the trajectory of Sweden as the embodiment of social progress goes into decline. Against this background, it seems clear that the case of Sweden cannot be explained simply in terms of a general 'Scandinavian' model, even though the Nordic countries are faced with similar social and economic problems. (Ruth, 1984: 54)

We could add that it is not possible to explain the general 'Scandinavian' crisis without understanding the peculiarities of the crisis in the core country, Sweden. The central elements of 'the social democratic century,' economic growth, equality, work, rationality, state, and internationalism "have also been pillars of the Nordic concept of political values" (Ruth 1984: 55).

Therefore, the changes "will not simply be a matter of concern for Nordic Social Democrats, but would go, rather, to the very core of national culture in the Nordic countries. The crisis of of social democracy would be a crisis of national identity as well, and...Sweden would be even harder hit than its neighbours," says Ruth.

The Nordic/Swedish model is hit by the general questioning of modernity and Enlightenment values. Sweden has been competing with the United States as the symbol of modernity. Sweden was a place you could travel to in order to experience the frontier of social modernity (Ruth, 1984: 88 and 66). The model – and especially the Swedish national identity – has been riding some curious contradictions: "a sense of common purpose as strong as

---

anything ever dreamt of by nineteenth century romantic nationalist, yet uncommitted, even hostile, to pre-industrial values. A rationalistic futurism replaced religion; social and technological change was felt to be not only unavoidable, but morally imperative. Antitraditionalism became, paradoxically, the dominant tradition" (Ruth, 1984: 92).

From the refugees in the 1930s through the configuration of the post-war system, Norden has represented the calmer corner, the benefit of distance.

> According to these refugees there was about Sweden of the 1930s an air of innocence. But they also saw an unbroken optimism and a strong belief in social and political planning. Sweden was becoming transformed into a very 'modern' state, and several exile-Europeans who would after the war become politically leading in their home countries received here a lasting impression of how the society of the future should be formed. (...) Sweden was a national who was seen to show the way out of the burden of historical tradition. Europe's future rested in a 'Scandinavization'. Swedish and Nordic identity should change the European heritage through a process of learning. (Karlsson, 1987: 5).

Thus, with a general crisis for the rational society, for planning, for the 'modern' society, the status of the Nordic model was destined to be questioned.

The third component relates to Norden–South relations. In the case of Sweden, Arne Ruth argues that it was during the fifties, that "the concern for the plight of the Third World" entered into Swedish popular consciousness as an additional aspect of the Swedish model (Ruth, 1984: 67). Since then, the image of a progressive Nordic role has increasingly become generally accepted, not only in Norden but also in the rest of 'North' and in the 'South.' Not only do the Nordic countries contribute an unusually high percentage of GNP to development assistance, they also take more interest than most others in the actual effects of the programmes – that they are not just prestige projects or (only) aid to the donor's own industry but (also) makes a sensible impact locally.

EUROPE' IS DOING BETTER

At least for the two first of the three dimensions it appears that the essence is: being better off, rather than being better. That is, it is seldom (openly) declared that we in the Nordic countries are better human beings, or more morally developed, but it is often claimed that we have – somehow – managed to create a society with a number of positive traits (welfare/low tension), and therefore we must a) preserve it against negative impulses from outside, and b) recognize that we do have something valuable in or with us since we have been able to produce this, and therefore we should also try to play a role in world politics.

The basis for expecting that we can play a positive role in the Third World (and sometimes in Europe) is not found in our nature, nor in our history/mission as such (like the United States, France and the Soviet Union that was), but rather in the societies we *have;* because they are removed from the harsh East–West struggles we can play a more independent role, and because they are domestically peaceful, social and rich, we can be an ideal and model for other countries.

An important effect of this type of identity is that in order to function as identity it has to function in reality – as actuality, as outcome, as status. We must be more able to display lower tension than central Europe, and we must live in a society with more solidarity, more justice and a comparatively high level of wealth.

This does not mean that the Nordic identities are immune to real-world developments. It means that Norden is going through a three-step process: 1) the identities are constructed as contrasts and comparisons between Norden and Europe; 2) but in a way that makes them dependent on an image of who is actually doing better; 3) this image is constructed by the way contemporary mega-trends are perceived and narrated as contemporary history.

What is the *meaning* of our times? It used to be an East–West conflict with the derived question of joining it or transcending it; now it is the 1989/1992 Europeanization with its key concepts being political freedom, rights, free markets, and integration. Suddenly the sources of the future are found on the continent.

Thus, when we measure (and perceive) the performance of the Nordic project we increasingly arrive at the conclusion that 'Europe' – not we, ourselves – is doing better in terms of peacefulness in international politics and the future-oriented model for domestic societies.

Some have argued that the 'Scandinavian model' ought to be on the agenda now as a solution for Eastern Europe. But not only does this not seem to be a widespread view in Eastern Europe; it also goes against the dominant perception in the West of the 'lessons' about socio-economic models.

There are at least two lessons: the Eastern one of the impossibility of a planned economy – which has spilled over to some extent into the debate in and about Sweden. Second, there is the Western lesson that the German economic model seems to be the preferable one; it has even confusingly been labelled a "third way" in-between the US model and the Swedish model.

Welfare is not off the agenda, but at present, in the European debates on economy and politics, it is defined in terms of a struggle between a) the *dirigisme* of France and the EC Commission, b) the *total free-market* orientation of Britain, and c) the – probably more powerful – *German well-functioning economy* based on high welfare but a 'smaller' state with less intervention and steering compared to the Scandinavian model (Schmidt, 1990).

Under these circumstances the Nordic societies cannot be allocated a prominent part in the concert. The overall change of the system of coordinates is unfortunate for Norden: the old system had two competing points by which distance led to the privilege of being a third way. The new system has one dominant centre, the EC, and thereby all distance to this it turned into simple peripheralism.

In security and political terms this European uni-polarity is decisive (see Chapter 3). In economy it is less unequivocal, since there is inside this dominant core, a competition of at least three sub-models. The Nordic countries will be able to join the 'best' (i.e., preferable *and* winning) one of these, the German, but they will not be able to set the agenda. It is thus grossly misleading when it is claimed that we will be able, when all Nordic states have joined the EC, to form a powerful coalition with Germany and

Holland for the Scandinavian model. Probably there will often be such a coalition – for the German model.

Thus, the conclusion is clear regarding the two first components of Nordic identity (low tension and welfare state): we are no longer better than Europe.

The third factor, the progressive role *vis-à-vis* the Third World might be doing slightly better. It should be observed, however, that this third dimension is both smaller than the two others (in the mind of most citizens) and derived from the two in the sense that the 'mission' in the Third World grew from the performance in one and two.

It is possible that the Nordic Third World profile has been blurred somewhat by the end of the Cold War; the Nordic voice was more necessary and unique in a bipolar world than in the present multi-polar one. Still, this Third World role survives better than the two other identity components, and it is frequently mentioned as that which must be safeguarded when some Nordism is saved in the process of Europeanization.

NORDIC 'NATIONALISM'

Nordism appears to be a kind of "collaborative nationalism" that places Norden morally above others. But are the Nordic peoples nationalist? Hardly in the sense of strong xenophobia and aggression – but in the form of believing strongly in the deep reality of nations. In an international perspective the Nordic states are some of the few that come close to the ideal of a nation-state; correspondance between state and nation, even taking into account the mutual Swedish–Finnish minorities and the Sami people. The format of the nation-state seems more self-evident and stable in this corner of the world than almost anywhere else.

Thus, when reality on a global scale displays a political order based on *sovereign territorial states* (which have existed in Europe for some 400 years)

---

which dress up as *nation-states* (which they started doing 200 years ago), the Nordic peoples tend to take rhetoric for reality, since they themselves are living in the realized rhetoric.

In Norway and Finland nationalism has, from time to time, been a mobilizing force and in Denmark and Sweden the national existence has not been threatened for a long period. In both cases, it appears as if an underlying 'nation' is 'there,' and building politics upon this is a guarantee of stability.

This contrasts strongly with the experience in other parts of Europe where attempts to fit politics to the map of 'real existing nations' led to disaster upon disaster (Germany, East Central Europe, the Balkans). To claim that the latter just did not succeed in being consistent and complete is of course a possible point of view that will be shared today by many Croats, Slovaks, and Lithuanians, but it is hardly destined to find a harmonious solution in the near future.

The innocence of the nation-state is a peculiar Nordic trait. The concerns about sovereignty and cultural identity which play such an important role in relation to the EC are not unique to this part of Europe, but when it takes such a stubborn form here it is *not* – as is often believed in these countries – because life in Norden is better and there are therefore more to defend, but because the existing, organizational framework is more stable and unquestioned due to the historically well established congruity of state and nation with an almost complete lack of regionalist secessionists and autonomists.

Naturally, the Nordic peoples have nationalist traits like everybody else, but they take a peculiar, inverted form. For instance, there is the Danish tendency to say that we are free from all chauvinism and megalomania – we are actually quite extraordinary in that we are *so* un-nationalistic (Østergard in *UNDR*, 1987). And there is the Swedish *internationalism* which performs as *Ersatz*-nationalism. Norwegian nationalism is comparatively more straightforward. And the Finnish one is even more complex and impenetrable for the outsider.

In conclusion, Nordism appears to be a "collaborative nationalism." This modern version of Nordism does not deviate much from the older (and at some points much stronger) forms of Scandinaviansm and Nordism, which have seldom served as a tool *against* the separate nationalisms, but rather a pooling of nationalisms.

CAN 'NORDEN' ACHIEVE A NEW MEANING?

The challenge now is whether 'Norden' can achieve a new meaning *in* Europe, as *a European accent*. Will Nordic increasingly be something one is *at the same time* as being national *and* European *and* holding an occupational, a social, a sexual and many other identities? Or is Nordic *qua* pooled nationalism still confronting 'Europe' as competitor – the same way that Britain and Europe are seen as opposites?

We witness a gradual change in the relative weight of internal-Nordic references and Nordic-European ones. Where stories about national characters and national culture were previously told in terms of contrasts among the Nordic countries, the tendency has been for the last 15-20 years to emphasize the relations to the other Nordic people in folklorist and familiar terms, whereas the 'real' dynamics have increasingly focused on 'Europe' and European ways.

The writings of the 1980s always end up dealing with the issue of being a European periphery (Karlsson, 1986, 1987; *UNDR*, 1988). This is most clearly the case with the two most continuous nation-states, Sweden and Denmark, whereas Norway and Finland are more actively defined by their liberation from the aforementioned co-Nordic states.

There are numerous fragments in the Nordic past that can be seen as early forewarnings of what was to come, but there are almost always other pre-histories as well. We do not have our present identities *because* of these historical predecessors, but we are *able* to articulate them today *because* they – *amongst others* – are found in our pool of past identities.

Thus, Nordic identity is nothing eternal or unavoidable. Nor can it be just *any* identity. The age-old patterns, however, are not the most important

---

ones. Rather, the system of meaning which emerged from the 1930s, especially in the post-war period, and ran into a crisis during the 1980s which culminated at the beginning of the 1990s, is what we have to understand ourselves by, live with, use and – change. Let us, finally, look at some possible identity changes.

POSSIBLE NEW NORDENS

1. Anti-European Nordism

The Nordic "card" has been used by the EC opponents in the EC debates in all the Nordic countries. Nordic values have been contrasted with the European market, and Nordic cooperation has been put forward as an alternative to European integration. Now the relationship has become a bit more complex. Nordism has increasingly also become an argument of the EC integrationists, since it can be claimed that the Nordic countries will only be more split if *some* stay outside the EC.

Still, the vision of Norden as an alternative lurks in the background, and if it should happen that one or more Nordic countries are blocked from joining either by an EC "no" or by the EC demanding a very long waiting period, it is likely that the Nordic option will be rediscovered as compensation/fall back option (Pertti Joenniemi 1991).

If Norden or the remaining part of Norden ends up building a Nordic community as an alternative or as compensation in relation to the European main-track, this Norden will most likely be constructed around a core of contrasts such as Norden versus Europe, welfare states versus market, neutralism versus European defence identity, South-policy versus Ostpolitik, Anglo-Saxon versus continental orientation.

2. An EC-Coordinating Norden - Or Even a Nordic Caucus in the EC

The future of Norden may well rest with the process of Europeanization, even the EC version of Europeanization. It is possible that the Nordic countries will be more united than ever, if they all become members of the EC. At least, the EC question would not divide them any more. And there will be plenty of occasions to discover – in EC internal policy-making – that the Nordic countries have more in common with each other than with the more southern Europeans. This perspective is much discussed today and, admittedly, there is a considerable element of tactical argument involved here. The 'Europeanizers' have suddenly turned Nordists, since the argument started to fit the integrationist rhetoric.

I believe that there *is* a solid basis for the argument that Europeanization will lead to regionalization, and of course it then seems natural to conclude that the region of Norden will be revitalized (Buzan et al., 1990: 219-23; Gleditsch et al., 1990: 185-87). However, it is not necessarily *Norden* that becomes the region of the region. It could well be imagined that the conceptual and geographical focus will be displaced – for instance to the Baltic (Wæver, 1991a). Logically, a 'Europe of regions' cannot possibly imply that *all* regions receive a new boost and vitality. We shall have to investigate carefully the dynamics of sub-regionalization and try to map the emerging units of a 'Europe of regions.'

So far I have only argued that one cannot (like Wæver and others started doing in 1990) claim that the process of integration/regionalization *automatically* strengthens Norden just because it is a subregion, but we will have to examine the more specific arguments in favour of the 'Norden via EC' thesis.

The arguments are at least four: 1) there will naturally be a Nordic sub-group inside the EC; 2) the Nordic countries do have common interests; 3) the Nordic countries will have to face similar challenges from the continuing process of integration and will therefore try to coordinate their responses/adaptation; and 4) on the way to full membership there will be a substantial need for mutual assistance among the countries who are at different stages.

First, when we look at the likelihood of a subgroup or caucus in the EC we acknowledge that the EC is not open to organized subgroups in the decision-making process. The Benelux cooperation was allowed, as stated clearly in the treaties, to retain its own process of more far-reaching integration, and new subgroups, like the Schengen-group, have emerged which push ahead of the general process.

But formal alliances inside the political process in the EC will definitely not be welcomed. Furthermore, there is the question of how the dynamics of the subgroup is actually influenced by joining the EC. Again, we could try to consult the Benelux experience: "No sooner had the dynamics of the EC come into play than the will of the three countries to work together was more or less paralyzed" (Tindemans, 1991: 58). It seems that, in the day-to-day politics of the EC, other coalitions often offer themselves as more important; also, and even more interesting, in the emerging 'Europe of regions' the Benelux format seems old-fashioned and will have to find ways to adapt to 'cooperation across borders' where the lower authorities are concerned, and draw in for instance the Lower Saxony and North Rhine Westphalia regions of Germany.

Will the same happen to 'Norden'? Will it open itself from being a state-based grouping to a cross-border region-of-regions including Northern Germany, and the border areas around the Baltic Sea?

The second argument involves more substantial issues of common interest. The heavy economic issues, and especially agriculture and fisheries, will most often send the Nordic countries into different competing coalitions. This is, after all, what the EC is all about. There should be no general geo-political alliances, but issue-specific coalitions at the substate and sometimes at the state level. In this perspective there is no guarantee, to say the least, that the Nordic countries will cooperate.

Hope is then invested in value-based issues like the environment, the welfare state and Third World policies. It is not unlikely that there will be a (largely Protestant) Northern European coalition around them. It will, however, not be labelled the 'Nordic' model, but the 'German' one.

Third, one would expect some attempt by the Nordic countries to assist each other in handling the challenges they face – the process of adaptation to the internal market and ever deeper integration in the future. It is possible that the Nordic countries will somehow link up their EC committees (*markedsudvalg*) in the Nordic parliaments, as pointed out by Sverre Jervell. That this should become a high profile 'Nordic' business is less convincing, and it is unlikely to form the basis of popular support for Nordic cooperation.

The fourth argument, however, is correct. For instance, the Nordic Council has started discussing security issues; there is the inter-ministry officials' study on a Nordic nuclear weapons free zone, and the foreign policy institutes of the Nordic countries havecooperated *for the first time ever* on a joint project – on "Norden in Europe."

Thus, we are likely to witness a certain revival of Nordism (especially in high politics) in the period of adaptation/transformation. But the pressure will decrease when all (or all minus Norway) have joined some time in the mid-to-late 1990s.

Since the three other arguments are at least doubtful, one could be tempted to write briefly and provocatively that "in the next five years there will be a revival of interest in *Norden*, and in formal Nordic cooperation - especially in High Politics. Then it is dead. Nordic cooperation, 1991–1996, will be a club for managing the difficult and painful transformation of Norden and entrance into Europe. Then Nordic cooperation will become unimportant" (Wæver, forthcoming).

Obviously, it is silly to predict dates, and of course Nordic cooperation will in many ways continue (as argued above). But it is not silly to focus on whether and to what extent Norden will be a reference point: will there be 'Nordic' projects, more 'Nordic' cooperation, a stronger feeling of Nordic identity?

The year 1996 *is* the next magic year after 1992. 1996 is the time when the treaties will have to be revised again and the decisive steps taken towards a Union with all issues included on equal basis (and not in three pillars as in the treaty being prepared for 1992). Furthermore, especially the WEU/EPC arrangements in defence will have to be redefined since 1996 is the year when France intends to cash in on the investments made in 1991 for the slow emergence of a European defence identity (Wæver, 1991b).

So the European train is likely to accelerate considerably in 1996. After all, 1972 was predominantly about the internal market; the political conclusions to be drawn from this will only partly be drawn in 1992, but to a large extent they will be clarified by 1996. Much of the EC debate in the Nordic countries is based on the premise that Sweden, Finland and Norway are considering whether to join the EC of 1972. But their choice will be whether or not to join the EC of the 1990s.

Then, the fourth factor will be out, and the first three (which will be further undermined by a Nordic split where some join and some not) are not powerful enough to sustain Nordic cooperation, and we are left with:

3. Baltic (and Possibly Also Arctic) Rearticulation of Norden

Today there is much talk about the emergence of 'Europe of the regions.' Why shouldn't there be such a region up here, one may ask? Probably there will, but *that* region will be the Baltic Sea Region!

Why Baltic? Is this region more real than Norden? No, on the contrary – Swedes and Lithuanians have very little in common. But the existence of identities is not a static question. When the nations were discovered or invented by intellectuals, historians and politicians, they did not exist, but after the projects of nation-building had been on for some time, they were very real indeed. *There are two reasons, why the Baltic project is more attractive than the Nordic.* (For a more elaborate version of this argument, see Wæver, 1991a.)

The first reason is that it is new. The Nordic belongs to the old Europe, the Baltic to the new. Or to put this differently: we are supposedly living in a 'new Europe' after 1989, but sometimes when I wake up in the morning it is difficult to feel it. What does it mean concretely to me? I need a concrete, local 'new Europe' to take part in, and that is why most of the new regions in Europe emerge along and across the old East–West border. Not because there are a great deal of tangible gains to be made, but because this cooperation used to be impossible, and therefore it is now interesting.

The second reason is that it takes the appropriate form for a European region: it is non-state based. It has to be. If it were to contain such enormous units as 'the Soviet Union' or 'the Federal Republic of Germany,' it would not be attractive to the small Nordic countries. But St Petersburg, Estonia, Schleswig-Holstein, etc., are just perfect. And most of it will be organized in a decentralized way with business, cultural initiatives, etc. This fits particularly well with the networks that emerge around Germany in the new Europe. Germany in the emerging Europe channels its energies into non-state forms to avoid reactions of fear among the other states. This fits nicely with Baltic cooperation. Nordic cooperation is a classical state-to-state cooperation.

Exactly because the Baltic Sea region is on the one hand a not-very-real identity at the moment, and is on the other hand a proto-region with a potential – but only in the form of non-state cooperation – it is hard to see how it will come to the fore. The states cannot do it, and it does not emerge as a 'natural' unit.

This is the reason it has started the way it has, with conferences, news reporting on conferences – just the way it happened with the nations: the intellectuals start out creating the image of what is 'natural.' And when it is in place and we all take it to be normal to cooperate in a Baltic frame, all kinds of business, political and cultural cooperation will naturally take this pattern, and the Baltic Sea region will be very real as a network and an identity.

Definitely, there is an intense interest in regions at present. There is a widespread feeling that the region has to find a reply to the European challenge. The mood is probably most clearly expressed by Herman Bang in the article 'Ten years of respite' ('Ti aars frist') from 1888. The Danish author argues that in the most fortunate case it will take 10 years before the North-East Sea Channel (today known as the Kieler channel) will be ready. "This respite is what Copenhagen is offered. The town has these ten years to guard its future, to arm against competition, and attempt to preserve thereby the country's economic position" (Bang, 1888).

This is the sentiment we live with till January 1, 1993. With the appearance of the internal market in the EC, the competition among regional growth centres in Europe will accelerate. Kiel and Hamburg will compete with Copenhagen and Stockholm, but what is more important, the whole region of Northern Europe – including Kiel, Hamburg, Copenhagen and Stockholm – will have to struggle to avoid the now likely fate of the periphery, of low-growth compared to southern Germany, northern Italy, etc.

In this context one is well advised to watch closely what is happening in business circles in Northern Europe. Social democrats, industrialists, and trade unionists headed by Bjørn Engholm and Pehr Gyllenhammar have joined forces in the so-called 'North European Club,' which works with various projects mainly relating to infrastructure but also for instance to an Environmental Academy. Business-based initiatives like the North European Club are aimed at drawing Northern Europe into the inner circle of the new Europe. Their core area, however, is Copenhagen–Skåne–Oslo–Kiel, and the Northern areas in Scandinavia fear that they will just be instrumentalized as resource regions for a growth project for southern Scandinavia.

This is but one configuration of Nordic–Baltic regionalism. But it is likely to be a part – an important part – of the emerging region. Other constellations will be:

a) The Baltic republics and their friends. The Baltic republics create a natural focus of interest and empathy. This draws cooperative projects all the way to Falster, Southern Jutland and Kiel. The Baltic republics constitute symbolically and emotionally the apex of the Baltic Sea region.

b) The Baltic Sea as such constitutes the focus of cooperation emerging around fisheries, environment and parts of the cultural initiatives. Only here do areas like Poland's Baltic coast, Kaliningrad and Mecklenburg-Vorpommern gain respectable positions.

THE FUTURE OF NORDISM AND BALTISM

We have witnessed an increasing awareness of new patterns of cooperation such as that along the Danube, the constellation of Catalonia, southern France and northern Italy; the eastern Alps (Alpe Adriatic); the western Alps (Arge Alp) and the Baltic Sea region. They are more often than not grounded in a combination of history and geography.

History is always a popular reference since it establishes something as 'natural' or 'original.' One can always find a period in history suiting whatever plan one wants to put forward today. Geography in itself tends to point out "natural" areas of cooperation – for instance, when pollution requires cooperation along lines that figured less prominently in the periods dominated by nation-states and power blocs.

During the 1980s, culture and history increasingly appeared as *objective* and *obligatory* guidelines for politics, a certain 'culturization' of politics (Knudsen, forthcoming) took place. The interest in Central Europe and in 'Europe' often took the form of advocating a particular policy because it was compatible with some deeper reality of true 'Europe' – deeper, that is, in our soul (culture), past (history) or ground (geography).

In some places we see old patterns being reactivated as cooperation among *countries* – for instance the "pentagonale" cooperation between the old Habsburg countries: Austria, Czechoslovakia, Hungary, parts of what is now former Yugoslavia and Italy. Such a cooperation is "regional" in the sense that it is a part-Europe and it does not follow extra-European definitions of economic or power blocs but reactivates pattern "from below." But it has nothing to do with regions *in* the states.

In other places we see *parts of states* cooperating with other part-states (for instance German *Länder*) across national boundaries. "Alpe Adriatic" in the eastern Alps consists of Friaul, Trentino–Southern Tirol, Venezia, Croatia, Slovenia, Kärnten, Upper Austria and Steiermark, with Bavaria and Salzburg as observers. Here we talk about regionalization in the dual sense of 'region in Europe' and independent politics by the regions in the countries.

Baltic cooperation has so far been discussed mostly at the state level: certain countries are defined as "Baltic" and they meet at conferences on the environment, fishing, etc. It is, however, evident that some towns, municipalities and counties are more Baltic than others, and several arguments in the emerging debate on the Baltic seem to assume this kind of cooperation. The difference between the two kinds has, so far, not been specified clearly. Pertti Joenniemi has noticed that one quality of the "Hansa" metaphor is that it signals a cooperation among towns, ports and communities, not states. Although we might witness a growing cooperation among *states* around the Baltic, the specific and valuable quality about a Baltic cooperation will, in the long run, rest with its truly (sub)regional perspective – i.e., when it develops along with regionalization *in* the states.

Regional cooperation among the states will be necessary in a number of specific fields, such as the environment. But the primary regional groupings at the state level will remain the "Nordic" (more or less expanded) and the EC (more or less expanded). *Mare Balticum* has its most important political–cultural promise at the non-state level, as a cooperation growing in numerous fields (environmental, cultural, economic) among actors simply searching out partners in this space without any formal or legal orders enforcing it.

In the current configuration, regionalization in the Baltic region is going to be part of a hidden, quiet German expansion – the growth of an informal *Mitteleuropa*. As pointed out elsewhere (Wæver, 1991a; Wæver et al., forthcoming), Germany's Europe is not about setting up institutions and actor-capable political units. *On the contrary, the German Europe is invisible.* Or at least it aspires to be so.

Unification is visible enough – although one tried to hold back formal, legal formulae until international recognition came through. Until then Kohl wanted "confederative structures" which means exactly very little, and therefore could trigger no four-power diplomatic reactions. Unification was carried out in the non-state form first and then transferred to the world of inter-state relations. Beyond this, the German Europe unfolds where borders lose their importance in the Centre of Europe. *Mitteleuropa* today becomes tied together by German capital, German historical relations, German tourists and the "regionalist" policies of the *Länder*.

The German state does absolutely *not* want to declare any projects here – no names, no official *Mitteleuropa*. The less talk (of politics), the more will happen when business people, economists, culture-intellectuals and grassroots talk.

In a pattern of regionalization, where northern Germany cooperates in the Baltic, and Badem-Württemberg cooperates with the other 'strong' regions (Barcelona, Lyon, Milano) and Sachsen, Oberfranken and Oberpfalz with Bohemia, in a new 'Regio Egrensis' (*Frankfurter Allgemeine Zeitung*, December 10, 1990: 3), the Germans have an obvious advantage being the only federal state in the EC. The German *Länder* are much stronger actors than part-state actors in the other countries.

Thus, to a large extent, the network process and 'regionalization of Europe' means the smooth and peaceful establishment of a larger zone around Germany which is *not dominated* by 'Germany' in any narrow sense. But it will be a zone organized around Germany, penetrated by networks largely of a German brand.

The Nordic countries should actually not be so unhappy about being part of a 'German zone.' *Remember, they are not heading for a Europe where Germany just grows and grows economically, and where this is the only thing happening.* Nor are the German sub-state processes the only ones unfolding. Inter-state relations continue to be important in the CSCE context and a meta-state is emerging in the form of the EC.

The interrelated character of these processes means that it probably does not make sense to oppose the EC with the goal of obtaining more CSCE. On the contrary, the EC should be seen in this broader context where the Nordic and Baltic states link up to a German, sub-state *Mitteleuropa*. One should probably only oppose this *benign hegemony* if one does not want the total package deal of the three Europes, i.e., if one prefers spheres of interests around medium-to-great European powers. The problem for some Nordic and Baltic states can be formulated this way: how can they become as much a part of the *other* Europes as of the German one?

It is positively certain Germany will not attempt to obtain a profile the way France does. Should Germany begin to strive for nation-state attributes or seek to instrumentalize the EC for its own purposes, the relationships of cooperation and trust would break down - in the East as well as the West. Some of us would end up in a German sphere anyway - but a less nice one.

The most peaceful, plural and cooperative vision is the illogical and complex mixture of *three Europes:*

– a classical inter-state cooperation in security – NATO and especially the CSCE;
– a meta-state, the EC, emerging to take on a number of state qualities without becoming a nation-state and therefore without resorting to the brutal tactics of homogenization known from the nation-states;

– sub-state and around-the-states structures emerging around the German *Länder* and other regions.

The new, emerging 'regional' patterns of sub-states have a particularly high concentration along the former East–West line. Does this mean that they were started as détente-like, anti-division projects? No, this does not seem to be the case. Rather, in the post-Cold War era there is a need for visions to embody concrete, operationalized answers to the question: *what is this 'new Europe' going to be like?* Such a vision, of course, has to be something *new* – it cannot be just 'Nordic Cooperation' since this existed all along. So cooperation is likely to emerge where it was previously not possible.

In order to avoid putting our own thinking back in East–West terms, it is important to view *the essence of these projects as novelty,* not 'East-West' cooperation as such. From the search for *novelty* follows then the search for *historical* reference, as well as for a functional logic of cooperation. 'Baltic cooperation' is not coming to the fore *because* it has a historical precedent, or *because* it is functionally the most rational.

Pertti Joenniemi has pointed out, correctly I believe, how the researchers interested in 'Baltic cooperation' in the mid- and late 1980s started out with some implicit idea of functional, economic rationality being the basis for it, whereas they (we) now see much more *the political play:* the uses of Baltic cooperation for the Nordic countries in relation to the EC and in relation to Soviet developments, to North Germany, to the Balts, and in relation to Russian domestic affairs, etc., (see Joenniemi, 1990).

* *Northern Germany* has an interest which has already been presented. In the process of German 'networking' it is important for each of the regions to find partners across borders. As the Northern *Länder* are among the economically less successful, it is important to find new networks through which all benefit. The new markets in the East, and the growth areas along the border to France and in relation to Italy – all this happens without much participation from Northern Germany. Thus, the new Hansa.

This is not only a material interest, it is also a way to redefine the meaning of being from and living in, let's say, Schleswig-Holstein or Hamburg. Instead of just meaning a poor farmer from the North, it could start reminding people of the 14th century, and of the active and interesting relationships to Leningrad.

* *The Balts*, of course, have the most obvious interest of all. The Baltic states are the route to Europe, an alternative to the economic 'union' called the Soviet Union. Another 'common market'? Certainly an identity which strengthens those of sovereign Baltic states today.

* *The Russians* – or some of them – might also be interested. The Baltic Sea is a traditional gate to the West; the Baltic states are known in the Soviet Union as the 'Soviet West'; and for those who strive for a Russian (re)turn to Europe, the Baltic road might be attractive. Furthermore, as Pertti Joenniemi has reminded us, there were strong Slavic elements in the Hansa; Novgorod was part of the Hansa. Today the Baltic is not a purely European affair; it is about linking Europe and the 'deep East.' Thus, Baltic cooperation is very much a matter of Russian interests.

* Even from a *Soviet* perspective, there *could* be something to gain. As I have argued elsewhere (Buzan et al., 1990: 219 ff; and Gleditsch et al., 1990: 170-73; see also Simon, 1990), it might be that the emergence of overlapping, multiple identities serves to defuse the unmanageable, polarized conflict between 'Russians'/The Soviet System and 'Balts' and the return to Europe. If a Baltic reality emerges in a form which is not in logical conflict with some kind of Soviet 'Union,' this could serve as a means to stabilize the situation. This is probably too late by now.

* *The Nordic factor* is probably the most complex, and the most interesting. There is probably a broad, a narrow and a very narrow logic at play.

The *very narrow logic* has to do with markets, and the like.

The *narrow* one has to do with the new dynamics in the EC and German unification. Fearing a shift towards the South or the centre, various very different groups sense a need to strengthen (in their particular field, and in general) some kind of counterweight. Some see this as an alternative to EC membership, others as a counterbalance *inside* the EC. It is anyway intended as a pull to the North.

The *broad* logic is based on the fact that the meaning of 'Norden' collapsed with the end of the Cold War. 'Norden' was defined in contrast to

Europe; as the modification ("low-tension") of the European confrontation; as a privileged area which nevertheless depended upon the stability of the overall European configuration.

What does this mean when the East–West conflict disappears? What if the meaning of East, West (and thereby of 'neutral') becomes blurred, and generally the North is far from privileged in terms of foreign military presence? To form a group inside or in relation to the EC is – in and of itself – not much of a new identity. A new meaning of *Norden* is hard to find in the old constellation of *Norden*-as-it-differs-from-Europe. *Norden* has to find its identity as *part of* Europe, as an element of the *new* European dynamics; and there the Baltic form seems to offer the possibility of a metaphoric relationship to general European development. Reaching across to the 'lost brothers' in the East, we repeat in miniature the European revolution of 1989.

Denmark does not have that close relations to the eastern shore of the Baltic. What is in it for Denmark? First, the possibility that the core of such a Baltic region will be a kind of borderless greater Copenhagen – sometimes referred to as 'Ørestad' – including first of all Malmö and Lund in Sweden. It has been claimed by the deputy director of the Danish chamber of commerce, Vagn Jensen, that because of Denmark's EC membership and the geographical structure of the Baltic region, Copenhagen could become the centre, the gate to the Baltic (Berlingske Tidende, August 28, 1990, p. 6 and II:6). This is a historical paradox: Copenhagen was founded as a countermove against the Hansa and might become the 'capital' of the new Hansa.

There is pressure from various sides, not least industrial interests in southern Sweden – to construct a bridge across the Sound (Øresund), and thereby make sure that the Copenhagen–Malmö area becomes one of the European growth centres. The Baltic ideology might be useful backing for such a project.

WHERE DO WE GO FROM HERE?

Exactly because Baltic cooperation is *not* based on state cooperation, we must try to answer a difficult question: how can we assist in developing it? Are we left with the option of waiting for it to grow 'naturally' or can we push it? Since it is not to be a centre-managed project but comes about through cooperation based on numerous, independent decisions, how can we all contribute to making it mature? The answer seems to be that we must focus our energies on creating the context for these numerous, independent decisions by influencing those points of reference used in the decisions.

In the case of non-state, network-type of cooperation, the important thing is that *a general image is in circulation* according to which 'this' is a natural and important context, the place of the future.

The first step, thus, will be to create the image that "The Baltic Region" exists. That will make it more natural for business, for political activists, for tourists, for students to follow this pattern and fill it with a meaningful content. In the case of the 'Baltic Sea Region' – the new Hansa – the very first step has been to set up a series of conferences, think tank reports, universities, traffic lines and articles in more or less scientific journals. The first steps were taken by intellectuals, to some extent by the cultural elites but in a more clearly political form. In the second phase these activities will serve as the backbone of frequent, numerous, independent economic, 'technical' and political decisions that, successively, are likely to weave the Baltic collage – or patchwork quilt.

In other words, I believe that – in this way – the future is with the Baltic project, not the Nordic project. I have often been met with the objection that this is too radical a conclusion and that it is not clear what it would and would not entail in its consequences.

Two responses deserves mention: 1) the old Nordic cooperation can and will continue for what it is worth. But 2) the local dynamism of the area will be the Baltic project. The reason is not that it is particularly 'logical' in the light of history, or social or political functions or economic rationality. The point is that it is something *new*: it is *our* new Europe here in the North. Norden can be rearticulated as a Baltic project. This has much more *Schwung* and can mobilize new energies.

Thus, there will still be lots of Nordic networks, lots of cooperation built on the similarities of languages, etc. But *politically* and *emotionally* the driving idea will not be *Nordism*. It has often been pointed out in studies of Nordic

---

cooperation that it is almost inexplicable without reference to the ideology of Nordism (Wiberg, 1986; Björklund, 1991). In this chapter it has been shown how and why this idea has lost much of its dynamism and mobilizing force.

Instead, the concept of Baltic Sea cooperation is on the rise. It is a matter of taste whether one chooses to phrase this as: Nordic cooperation has a bright future when Norden has taken a different shape, changed some of its core ideas and expanded eastwards; or one says Nordism is dead, long live Baltism![1] The content is the same. Regional cooperation in Northern Europe *does* have a future, but it will not be in the classical state-to-state form of the Nordic Council, it will increasingly be in a networking Baltic Sea.

As an interesting parallel, the Arctic is emerging as a point of identification. It shares many traits with Baltic Sea cooperation. It has a strong original impulse in that the Sea defines a natural eco-region; it shares the strong Nordic cooperative tradition while also giving it a new twist. One of the major differences might be that the material promise of the Arctic is in the long run far more important than that of the Baltic. At the same time, however, decentralized, 'spontaneous' cooperation is so much more difficult there (Archer, 1991; Osherenko & Young, 1989).

In a historical perspective, the reference points for 'natural regions' have changed several times. For many centuries the sea was a natural connecting factor because it was the most efficient means for transport (think of the Hansa, but also of the North Sea and the Mediterranean). "The Mediterranean is regarded as the cradle of civilization, the teeming meeting-ground of cultures from times immemorial. The Baltic by contrast is usually seen as a chilly, peripheral backwater on the very edge of the civilized world" (Kirby 1990: ix).

With romanticism a symbolic value was added; the sea was given images such as being the Mother, but it was also mysterious and dangerous. Mountains, in contrast, were hard, dividing and more impressive. For instance, at that time Europe's eastern border was fixed along the (rather unimpressive) mountains of the Urals instead of the various rivers that used to compete for that function.

With railroads the 'Columbian epoch' ended and land distance became decisive (Mackinder, 1904). Seas became walls rather than connections. The further evolution of technology and transportation has now reached the stage where neither land nor sea transport is most important. With planes and information technologies everything is instantly connected and we achieve an unprecedented freedom of choice in our lives and in frame of reference. The emotional, psychological and mythical dimensions obtain a much higher profile. And then seas again count. *They* are the prime mythic sources of identity.

REFERENCES

Bang, Herman, 1888, 'Ti aars frist' (Ten years of respite) in *Politiken*, January 1, 1888; reprinted in H. Bang, *Udenrigspolitisk journalistik,* ed. by V. Greene-Gantzberg, Copenhagen: Gyldendal 1990, pp. 71f.

Buzan, Barry, Morten Kelstrup, Pierre Lemaitre, Elzbieta Tromer & Ole Wæver, *The European Security Order Recast: Scenarios for the Post-Cold War Era*, Pinter Publishers, London 1990.

Cohen, Anthony P., "Of symbols and boundaries, or, does Erties greatcoat hold the key?", pp.1–20 in *Symbolising Boundaries: Identity and Diversity in British Cultures*, Manchester University Press 1986.

Esping-Andersen, Gösta, *The Three Worlds of Welfare Capitalism*, Polity Press, Cambridge 1990.

Gleditsch, Nils-Petter; Bjørn Møller, Håkan Wiberg and Ole Wæver, *Svaner på vildveje: Norden mellem supermagtsflåder og europæisk opbrud*, Vindrose forlag, Copenhagen 1990.

Hassner, Pierre, "Culture and Society" in *The International Spectator*, Vol. 26/1, pp. 136-153, 1991.

Ingemar Karlsson (ed.), *I kontinentens utkant*, 1st of 4 reports from the project 'Sweden and Europe' published by FRN–Framtidsstudier, Stockholm 1986.

Jervell, Sverre, in S. Jervell (ed.), *Norden i det nye Europa*, Oslo, forthcoming.

Joenniemi, Pertti and Ole Wæver, *Baltic Sea Politics*, 1992 in preparation.

Joenniemi, Pertti, "Regionalization in the Baltic Area: Actors and Policies" in P. Joenniemi (ed.), *Cooperation in the Baltic Sea Region: Needs and Prospects*, pp.147–166, Tampere 1991.

Johan Jørgen Holst, 1991, "From Arctic to Baltic: The Strategic Significance of Norway," in *NATO's Sixteen Nations*, Vol. 36/3, May/June, pp. 23–35, 1991.

Kirby, David, *Northern Europe in the Early Modern Period: The Baltic World 1492–1772*, Longman, London/New York, 1990.

Knudsen, Anne, "From Political Culture to Culture as Politics," in Ole Wæver (ed.) *European Identities* (forthcoming).

Mackinder, H.J., 'The Geographical Pivot of History,' *Geographical Journal*, Vol. 23, pp. 421–437, 1904.

Møller, Bjørn, *European Security Structures for the Nineties and Beyond: A Nordic Perspective*, AFES-PRESS Report no. 40, Mosbach 1991.

Northern European Club, Three position papers drafted by the staff of Minister president Engholm and Dr. Gyllenhammar, to serve as a background for the discussion about developing a programme for the North European Club; for a meeting 3 September 1990 in Stockholm, 1990.

Norton, Anne, *Reflections on Political Identity*, The Johns Hopkins Press, Baltimore 1988.

Petersen, Thomas, "EF-Unionen og det Øvrige Europa" i Sverre Jervell (ed.), *Norden i det nye Europa*, Oslo (forthcoming).

Ruth, Arne, "The Second New Nation: The Mythology of Modern Sweden," *Dædalus*, Vol. 113/12, pp. 53–96, 1984 (abbreviated translation with a postscript in *UNDR*, No. 52, 1988).

Schmidt, Manfred G., 'Die Politik des mittleren Weges: Besonderheiten der Staatstätigkeit in der Bundesrepublik Deutschland,' in *Aus Politik und Zeitgeschichte*, Band 9–10/90, February 23, pp. 23–31, 1990.

Stiftelsen for Industriudvikling i Norden, *Norden – en europæisk region: Et program for sterkere samarbeid* (Norden – a European region: Programme for stronger cooperation), unpublished. (Programme of the fund for industrial development in *Norden*, 1991.)

Therborn, Göran, "Den svenska välfärdsstatens särart och framtid," in Ingemar Karlsson (ed.), *Lycksalighetens halvö: Den svenska välfärdsmodellen och Europa*, 2nd of 4 reports from the project 'Sweden and Europe' published by FRN–Framtidsstudier, Stockholm 1987.

Tindemans, Leo, '(Bene)Luxuriant Inaction,' in *European Affairs*, Vol. 5, No. 2, pp. 58–62, April–May, 1991.

UNDR, special issue on "Nordic Borders" with articles by Trine Deichman-Sørensen, Pasi Falk, Uffe Østergård, Arne Ruth, and Gudbergur Bergsson; No. 52, 1988.

Vares, Peeter and Olga Zurjari-Ossipova, *Nordic and Baltic Countries*, in a collection of small works from the project 'Norden in Europe,' Oslo 1991.

Välfärdsmodellen och Europa, 2nd of 4 reports from the project 'Sweden and Europe' published by FRN–Framtidsstudier, pp. 13–44, Stockholm 1987.

★ ★ ★ ★ ★ ★ ★

164

Wæver, Ole, 1991a, 'Culture and Identity in the Baltic Sea Region,' in P. Joenniemi (ed.), *Cooperation in the Baltic Sea Region: Needs and Prospects*, pp. 79–111, Tampere 1991.

Wæver, Ole, 1991b, 'Europæisk Forsvar: Samarbejde i forsvars- og sikkerhedspolitik," in the *Danish Yearbook of European Affairs*, Copenhagen 1991.

Wæver, Ole, "Northern Europe on a new Continent," paper presented at the conference 'Region in the Making,' Tallin, Estonia, 28 May–1 June 1991; forthcoming in a volume edited by Mare Kukk and Sverre Jervell.

Øberg, Jan, 'Towards Understanding Common Nordic Security Alternatives,' in *Current Research on Peace and Violence*, Vol. 9, No. 1–2, pp. 74–94, Tampere 1986.

Østerud, Øyvind, "Nationalism och modernitet. Ett skandinavisk perspektiv" in Ingemar Karlsson (ed.), *Lycksalighetens halvö: Den svenska välfärdsmodellen och Europa*, 2nd of 4 reports from the project 'Sweden and Europe' published by FRN–Framtidsstudier, pp. 109–132, Stockholm 1987.

NOTE

1. The major impulses to the development of the present 'anti-Nordist' ideas about Europe/Norden, identity and community have come from my participation in the 'Europe' circle of the *'Nordic* Summer University,' where uncommonly free and experimenting academic discussions take place because of the common language and the probably less ancient common Nordic penchant for informal, playful style. I would like to emphasize that the Nordic countries do – and did – not have a problem-free relationship with the Baltic republics/states. At the CSCE conference in Paris in November 1990, only Denmark and Iceland protested against the (Soviet initiated) exclusion of the Baltic republics. The immediate neighbours were more cautious. At the meeting of the Nordic foreign ministers in Molde, Norway, on 12 Sept. 1990, the Norwegian and the Danish ministers wanted regular meetings with the foreign ministers of the Baltic republics; whereas the Swedish and Finnish foreign ministers were less enthusiastic and emphasized the importance of a more encompassing cooperation in the region also including the Soviet Union and Poland. (Berlingske Tidende, September 13, 1990, p. 8.) Meetings of all Nordic and Baltic foreign ministers eventually did take place, but the differences in Nordic attitudes to more 'provocative' policies of independence remained conspicuous until the Baltic republics were recognized as independent states; cf. Vares and Zurjari-Ossipova 1991.

Regionalization in the Baltic Area
Actors and Policies

Pertti Joenniemi

WINDS OF CHANGE

It is easy to understand that a discussion has emerged on new, regional opportunities in the area of the Baltic Sea. Essentially, there are two themes – one on the various opportunities that open up with the fading away of the rigidities of the Cold War, and the other on the danger of becoming a semi-periphery in the new, integrating Europe.

These two themes tend to overlap; thus, for instance in a recent report[1] from the think tank of Premier Björn Engholm both are emphasized.

On the one hand the study group agreed that the Baltic is a sea of opportunities; countries and regions located close to each other and with a considerable potential for cooperation have been deprived of opportunities due to the Cold War.

On the other hand it expressed the fear that the Baltic Sea region might become marginalized in the merging new Europe. It will fall behind the other parts of the continent unless countermeasures are taken. The reason given for such a negative prospect is that the focal points of European development are currently more in the South than in the North. In sum: there is both push and pull and needs as well as opportunities. But what are the prospects of regionalization in the Baltic Sea area? Which perspective is more realistic, the positive or the negative? Could the Baltic really provide, as one of the areas structuring Europe from the sea, a basis for a joint identity? And will it be able to develop a regional pattern of more intensive cooperation?

These are rather tricky questions. European developments are so uncertain and conjectural that firm answers cannot be offered. The Baltic Sea region is not in the forefront of the debate on the future architecture of Europe. Many factors conditioning a cooperative development of the region would have to change, and there is not much in the post-war record of the region that justifies an optimistic view.

The idea of a Baltic Sea region, as one major formation in the new Europe, has to compete with a number of other projects and lines of development which could turn out to be more promising and easy to realize. It could well be argued that the Nordic countries are better prepared for such a role because of their experiences over the last decades and, indeed, the basis for intensified Nordic cooperation is already in place. It is true that there is nothing natural or self-evident about the formation of the Baltic Sea area into one of the new regions in Europe. The field is competitive, and there has to be something especially attractive about the Baltic Sea area before such potentials are utilized. Functional arguments are not sufficient as such, neither is it persuasive to maintain that cooperation in the area is a recipe for automatic material growth. These are necessary but not sufficient conditions.

Although political and economic demands and a functionalist spirit seem to dominate the current debate, an intriguing set of underlying questions concerning identities and politico-cultural orientations have to be raised as well. In this light, we shall work here with the question: how likely is it that the idea of a Baltic Sea regionalization will work and provide an alternative in Northern Europe?

An Emerging Debate

The Baltic Sea area has been almost totally without an identity of its own since 1945 – a rather blank spot on the mental or metaphoric map of Europe.

Now this seems to be changing. Concepts such as an *Ostseeraum*, a Hansa-Europe, a Baltic Europe or a Scanno-Baltic political space have surfaced in the debate during the last couple of years. They are significant because they signal an interest in developing a latent potential within a larger setting of cooperation. It is a fact that there is not much of a network of cooperative relations in Northern Europe but this may very well change when the divisions and obstacles shaped by the Cold War disappear.

One of the first few to advocate a new Baltic Europe was Åke E. Andersson, director of the Stockholm Institute for Future Studies. In his view a Europe composed of horizontal networks is in the making, contrary to the previous vertical structures, and the Baltic Sea regions stands to gain from such a development. The Premier of Schleswig-Holstein and SPD chairman Björn Engholm, has presented ideas and proposals along the same lines.[2] The Finnish Board for Trade and Commerce, a non-governmental organization representing commercial life and business, took *Mare Balticum* for "Sea Area of Trade and Culture" in a specific publication investigating the prospects for cooperation in the Baltic Sea region.[3]

Later have followed numerous proposals, e.g., the one on establishing a Baltic Council to work on issues of trade, communication, tourism, culture, ecology, education and research. [4]

Another significant event was the high-level seminar – "The New Hansa" – with a number of top politicians from the Baltic area that took place in the summer of 1990 in Kotka, Finland. This and several other meetings have contributed more concretely than ever before to the formation of a joint identity – what Johannes Salminen has later on talked about as "the Kotka spirit."[5]

In the German debate the concept of *Ostseeraum*, a term with considerable geopolitical connotations, indicates a new aspiration to formulate policies towards the northern part of Europe, Scandinavia and the Baltic.[6]

It may also be observed that the idea of regionalization and building of a regime in the Baltic Sea region has attracted scholarly interest over recent years. An interesting example of this is a book edited by Arthur Westing and produced in cooperation between The Peace Research Institute in Oslo (PRIO) and the United Nations Environment Program (UNEP); it uses environmental concerns and solutions in the Baltic Sea area as a unifying theme.[7]

There is still a constant flow of articles on military development, weapons deployment and the like in the Baltic sphere, but also some studies of economic cooperation, trade, fishing and legal developments have appeared in recent years. These topics have been studied by a number of scholars, among them Carl-Einar Stålvant, Hannu Kyröläinen, Osmo Tuomi and Marja Lehto.[8] New in some of these contributions is an effort to develop comprehensive points of departure for arms control and disarmament in the Baltic Sea region. Before, the region was hardly singled out or given specific attention in such a context.[9]

The Baltic Sea region is an open concept. The definitions of the region as well as its content vary considerably. Its general focus, however, is on the countries and regions bordering the Baltic Sea – parts of northern Germany, the coastal part of Poland, the three Baltic states, the St Petersburg region, the autonomous region of Carelia, Finland, Sweden, Denmark and, to a certain extent, Norway. This coastal region comprises some 45 million people but a somewhat broader delineation gives a figure of 70 million inhabitants. A recent publication of the Finnish Board of Business and Commerce operates with the rough figure of 100 million inhabitants.[10]

The region of the *Mare Balticum* is not primarily seen as an alliance or formation between the *states* in the region – although the Ronneby meeting was clearly a meeting between these states. Instead, the communities, the municipalities, a cultural entity, a pattern or network of contacts connecting people, towns, enterprises and regional formations on territorial grounds are the focus of these debates.

The foreign trade inside this region is around 6% of world trade. However, the overall pattern lacks features of any distinct network in the sense of conducting specifically and systematically intense cooperation.[11] Only Finland and the German Federal Republic have been trading extensively in both directions. The other countries of the Baltic Sea region lean either towards the West or towards the East. For example, the export of Sweden, Norway or Denmark towards the previously socialist countries of the region has been only around 2-5% of their overall exports. [12]

Most of the participants in the debate have had a favourable attitude towards regionalization in Northern Europe and the prospects for more intense cooperation in the sphere of *Mare Balticum*. Most authors depart from the idea that there is considerable opportunity for progress and that an intensification of trade and contacts is on the cards. The hypothesis, simply, is that it is somehow self-evident that cooperation will develop and intensify once the division imposed by the Cold War disappears and the security considerations that have prevented contacts from being established are gone.

However, in this respect it cannot be ignored that there are also some reserved and critical views. There are many, particularly in the business community, who doubt that the opening of borders to the East represents any really attractive opportunity. They seem to think, rather, that it will present us with a series of new problems.

Rudolf Jalakas, a retired Swedish bank economist and a specialist on the economies of the Baltic republics, is one of them. He warns against perceiving the Baltic Sea area as a new prospective European power centre. Jalakas is critical towards images of prosperity and booming trade – the basic elements in the idea of some kind of a new Hanseatic period. The expectations of speedy economic recovery in the three Baltic republics – now states – that have figured in the debate are far too rosy, he maintains. Limiting his argument to cooperation among the three Baltic states and the Nordic countries, he predicts that it will take a long time before trade and other indicators will point sharply upwards.

Jalakas also points out that only 1% of Swedish foreign trade was conducted with the Baltic states before the Second World War when these three countries were still independent. The change of their status may not, after all, mean that much for these countries. "I have difficulties in imagining

---

that current developments could have any major impact on the economic-geographic balance in Europe," he concludes.[13]

TOWARDS GERMAN DOMINATION?

The concept of a Hansa-Europe has been used quite cautiously in the debate, as a thought-provoking image, a resource base in history or a metaphor. It does not signify any specific plan or project and neither is it a grand design which aims to elevate the North into an increasingly central position within the European setting.

What it conveys is a belief, perhaps, that the northern part of Europe could gain in importance and become one among many political, commercial and cultural centres in the new Europe. There is no reason that the North should be doomed to the position of a periphery despite the dynamism, magnetism and core position of the European Community and the rapid development particularly in Central and Southern Europe.

The concept has some unwarranted connotations which easily lead the debate astray. The Hansa League was a commercial, political and military formation based on North German towns that bloomed from the 12th to the 15th centuries. Lübeck, Bremen, Rostock, Köln and Danzig were among the key centres within the League. These cities had an influential position in a network of towns and regions within a relatively loose setting of trade and interaction. Decisions were taken at joint meetings and membership was voluntary. It was a hegemonic formation using trade to bolster its position, but it also resorted to naval power in safeguarding its influence and shipping routes.

The obvious Germanic connotations of the Hansa League is a burden on the concept. Some actually see it as the code for a new sophisticated German expansion into the North and it raises fears about Germany once again becoming dominant.

These fears seem to be exaggerated. There is no evidence of a German expansion towards Northern Europe. There is some interest in Schleswig-Holstein – and perhaps, eventually, in Mecklenburg-Vorpommern too – but this should hardly worry us. On the contrary, it should be seen as one of the preconditions for the Baltic Sea region to prosper and achieve an existence of its own on the new European map.

The German states – *Länder* – are not in a position to become hegemonic. They are searching for allies and alternatives to avoid becoming underdeveloped parts of Germany. With German unification, and interest turning more towards the North, their chances are improving. The interest of these German states is a necessary, although not sufficient, condition for multipolarity to emerge. Such a constellation with a number of centres is needed if the idea of the Baltic Sea region as a functioning entity is to have a chance to "take off."

The strength of the Hansa concept is its reference to primarily non-statist cooperation, to relations between towns, enterprises, communities, citizens, associations, etc. The states around the Baltic Basin might provide a general framework for cooperation, but its concrete content will be shaped by various non-statist actors. Some of the structures, traditions and identities of the Hansa period, like in the Free Hansa Town of Bremen, seem still to be there, and they may also provide a basis for a concrete start.

THE GERMAN–SOVIET/RUSSIAN RELATIONSHIP

Despite the multicentred nature of prospective Baltic Sea region cooperation, some actors are more important than others. During the post-war years it became a kind of substructure of the general East–West setting. Central Europe was the *Schwerpunkt* of confrontation between East and West. The conflicts causing concerns for security were, in this sense, extra-regional in their essence and origin. The Baltic Sea region was rather peripheral in this confrontation; it has been a side-show mostly characterized by low-tension.

But it is another Europe now. The impact of the extra-territorial conflict is no longer what it used to be. It is still true, of course, that major power relations are a crucial factor influencing developments in the Baltic Sea area, but *the key relationship in the constellation is now the one between Germany and the Soviet Union/Russia.*

This relationship seems likely now to develop into cooperation rather than tension, conflict and mutual deterrence. The treaty between Germany and the Soviet Union, with far-reaching concessions from both sides, is significant evidence. It essentially consists of a non-aggression pact including assurances that the parties are not to participate in hostile activities against each other. Such developments allow, if they continue, an intensification of Baltic Sea regional cooperation.

Moreover, within the new Germany the northern part seems to gain in importance. This tendency remedies the previous danger of too many interests floating towards the southern Germany. It is precisely the northern part of the country, Schleswig-Holstein, the Hamburg region and now presumably Mecklenburg-Vorpommern, that have shown an interest in developing an intense cooperative relationship towards Scandinavia and the Baltic.

Good relations between Germany and the Soviet Union/Russia are important for both. Cooperation pushes further back the fears both sides have had throughout modern history. The conflicts to take into account now are those located within the region, particularly those between Moscow and the Baltic states, and within the (former) Soviet Union. Moreover various non-military aspects of security are coming to the forefront. Instead of the bipolar confrontation system we get conceptualizations of human security in post-industrial societies – which emphasize that security is "political" and increasingly identical with successful "management" of change.

It will probably take quite some time, but there is a fair chance that the Soviet Union/Russia will perceive the states around the Baltic Sea in a new light of partnership. Likewise, the Baltic states' view of the Soviet Union and their neighbouring republics might change once historical injusticies have been sorted out and an understanding has been reached regulating the new relationships.

The images peoples and states have of each other do not change overnight. New institutions deemed necessary for independent states might cause constraints on the way, but it is not probable that these constraints will have major implications in the military field and thereby decrease drastically the prospects for regional cooperation around the Baltic Basin. Indeed, the idea of cooperation in new ways may serve as a bridgebuilder and successively develop new and more benevolent images.

The German–Soviet/Russian setting provides a certain guarantee that no one-sided, hegemonic structures emerge in the Baltic Sea region. These powers will balance each other. Some might say that the Soviet Union - or Russia and the emerging independent republics – is too weak to counterbalance the growing influence of a unified Germany, but that is not necessarily the case.

Objectively speaking, the Soviet leadership share with us a genuine interest in the emergence of more intense cooperation around the Baltic Sea. So, too, does Russia of course and here lies a potential conflict – part of the ongoing struggle for power in Moscow. None of them, however, have an interest in fueling intra-regional conflicts as these would weaken their own position. Thus, we do *not* say that conflicts are out of question, but it deserves mention that there are also good reasons – in the longer run, at least – to believe that the parties will try to avoid them, play them down and successively realize that all parties have something to gain from peaceful cooperation in and with this region.

Much is also dependent on the development of the St Petersburg region. It has almost 7 million inhabitants, considerable industrial and technological potential and old European roots. If Soviet/Russian reform policies turn out to work here under the leadership of progressive forces, the preconditions for a balanced development improve considerably.

Besides, the idea of a *Mare Balticum* has also emerged in the Polish debate. Poland, with its long Baltic cost and large potential human resources is a very important actor. The political, economic and cultural transformation of the country has only started but, if successful, the weight of Poland will grow considerably, and Polish development will contribute to the multipolarity of the Baltic Sea region. For the Poles, Baltic Sea cooperation involves its relations with Germany as well as the Soviet Union and its republics; this equation, of course, is not a simple one.

Another hindrance to a full-fledged debate and active policies might be the complicated history of the coastal regions and the concentration there of people of German descent. Whatever the reasons, the impression is that the topic of Baltic Sea regional cooperation is somewhat sensitive in the Polish debate.

THE ABSENCE OF NORDIC POLICIES

For the emergence of a multipolar Baltic Sea region a Nordic – and preferably a joint Nordic – contribution is needed. There surely must emerge a division of labour, and the Nordic countries, with their well-established patterns of cooperation, would have to think creatively about active policies that can help bring about a strong and co-operative Baltic Sea region.

The Nordic countries should try to steer themselves into a fairly central position; their initiatives and policies are less loaded and contentious than those of the Soviet Union/Russia or Germany. By employing a 'middle-of the-road' policy, the Nordic countries may equalize the regional constellation and prevent the emergence of any hegemonic actor.

Unfortunately, such a Nordic policy has yet to be formed. The Nordic countries do not have much of a policy *vis-à-vis* the nearby regions now going through rapid transformations. They have largely continued their previous policies towards the Soviet Union and taken on a very cautious attitude towards these changes. This also tends to explain why the policies of the three allied countries have been somewhat different from those of the two neutrals, Finland and Sweden.

At most the Nordic countries react to initiatives taken by others, but they are not the driving force they could be in developing the possibilities that have emerged in the wake of the Cold War. For example, Sweden urged in the 1970s that the Baltic Sea regions should be made free of nuclear weapons, but there has been little movement now that the prospects to really implement such a proposal have emerged. The Nordic countries always argued that favourable security developments in Central Europe were the *sine qua non* of security and disarmament initiatives pertaining to the northern regions. But strangely enough, we have not seen any substantial re-thinking in these fields of politics as a consequence of the very fundamental changes in Central European politics and East–West relations.

The nearby region has no specific identity or existence of its own in Nordic eyes, it seems. Confronted by various challenges, like the aspirations of the (then) Baltic republics to be seated at the table at the Paris CSCE conference together with the other participants, the Nordic countries chose different postures with little coordination among them.

Denmark and Norway signalled, without consulting the others, that they were prepared to support the Baltic republics and thereby confront Soviet policies. Finland and Sweden for a long time adopted a more reserved position.

Similarly, all Nordic parliamentarians in a delegation from the Nordic Council visiting Tallin were taken by surprise when the Baltic leaders proposed that the Baltic states be included in the efforts to form a nuclear weapons free zone in the region. The Nordic delegates declined to accept this idea. At the time, the matter was still under study by a Nordic government official group and the Nordic Council has traditionally been reluctant to engage in matters of foreign or security policy. In other words, Nordic cooperation has been intra-regional and the Nordic Council was unaccustomed and poorly equipped to handle challenges originating from a rapidly changing environment.

The discussion that took place in the wake of President Gorbachev's proposal made in Helsinki in autumn 1989 to send a Nordic Council delegation to Moscow and then to the Baltic republics is another case in point.

Some of the problems were undoubtedly caused by Moscow as well as by the strain in relations between Moscow and the Baltic capitals. However, it is also quite clear that there is confusion in Norden and that a joint Nordic determination – and political will – to deal with these challenges is not just around the corner.[14]

True, there has been increasing policy coordination and the Council agreed upon various assistance programmes and the setting up of Nordic information and cultural centres in Estonia, Latvia and Lithuania. But it was not part of a new world – or regional – view.

But in the critical phase, the Nordic countries largely pursued unilateral strategies and they remain therefore, to some extent, in competition with each other. This was exemplified, among other things, by the Swedish initiative (originally proposed by Poland) to convene a Prime Ministers' meeting on environmental problems in the Baltic Sea region. The meeting took place in Ronneby, Sweden, in September 1990, and it resulted in the approval of a joint declaration and the setting up of a task force to tackle environmental hazards in the Baltic Sea region. But it would have been better if the Nordic countries had hosted the meeting jointly.

One explanation for the difficulties that exist in Nordic policies seems to have established itself in the traumatic experiences at the beginning of the 1980s. A previously peripheral region became considerably more central in the confrontation between East and West: the maritime strategic buildup to the North and submarines to the East, to mention only two of several important features.

These rather negative experiences are still in the minds of many decision-makers and writers and prevent an understanding of the fact that the whole security agenda of the 1990s will be fundamentally different from that of the 1980s.

Norden is no longer what it used to be. The Cold War conflict between East and the West provided Norden with a distinct identity of its own. In an integrating and co-operative Europe the old identity and the policies flowing from it will no longer carry Norden through. The traditional Nordic policy profiles which yielded quite positive results for the Nordic countries after

1945 (discussed particularly in Chapters 1, 2 and 6) did not favour change in general, nor the development of regional, Baltic Sea area strategy in particular.

Intensification of regional cooperation would suggest closer relations both with Germany and the Soviet Union, and some distancing from the United States. This would be unwise according to traditional security establishment thinking. Within the old Nordic paradigm this would disturb the "stability" or balance of the region and send the wrong signals.

Baltic Sea area cooperation is also burdened by the past in the sense that the German Democratic Republic argued strongly for such a line in its campaign to be fully recognized as an independent state up to the 1970s. Furthermore, it was a major feature in the peace politics of the old Soviet Union that the Baltic region be turned into a "Sea of Peace", which makes the Nordic countries somewhat allergic to such conceptualizations even today.

All these reasons provide some background as to why the Nordic countries have been quite slow in revising their positions on *Mare Balticum*, and in establishing active, cooperative policies.

All the Nordic countries are now challenged to develop policies which will not only cover the Soviet Union at large but also the new nearby and regional players: Estonia, Latvia and Lithuania, Carelia and the Leningrad area, a unified Germany with some internal problems and a Poland with another set of problems.

The understanding of the situation in the newly independent Baltic states, as well as in Russia and the Soviet Union, should be improved and updated. There is a real need now for a new determination operationalized in consistent, coordinated policies and initiatives at various levels, in various spheres. There is a role for each of the Nordic countries to play, e.g., for Finland in Estonia and Sweden and Denmark in Latvia and Lithuania, but it should be in a coordinated manner.

The formation of new intellectual frameworks and policies is a formidable task. The basic concepts used in the discussion will probably have to change, security meaning something entirely different from five or ten years ago. We no longer live in a region or an era in which concepts such as bipolarity, power politics, alliances and blocs, deterrence, offensiveness, military balance and strength take the first place as basic conditions for peace and security.

These concepts have largely lost their relevance in a Europe no longer shaped by two antagonistic blocs and a clear division into 'them' and 'us.' Today's security is aimed at realizing common social and political aspirations and joint security interests, rather than aiming at stability.

More generally, there is no longer a need for a pocket-like Nordic existence, a balance between participation and isolation, and in this context, an aspiration for something of a third road. It is uncertain what *Norden* will mean and what role it will play in the changing Europe. But, no doubt, it can do better and use some of the opportunities that are opening up in post-Cold War Europe, and thereby actively counteract developments that threaten to marginalize Norden and turn it into a rather peripheral part of a new Europe.

For too long, the Nordic countries showed that walls can crumble in Central Europe while old thinking prevails to the North. New regional policies are urgently needed and they will have to be linked to more general changes in the foreign policy thinking of the Nordic countries.

A determined policy for the Baltic Sea region could serve as a platform for a new and exciting role in a changing Europe and present substantive evidence that new thinking *is* emerging.

REFERENCES

1. See the arguments of the Schleswig-Holstein "Denkfabrik," *Chancen einer stärkeren Einbindung Schleswig-Holsteins in der Ostseeraum*. Kiel 1990.

2. Åke E. Andersson, Europas framtid ligger i regionerna (Europe's future lies with the regions), *Framtider* (Bulletin of the Institute for Future Studies), No. 1, 1990, pp. 26–27, and Björn Engholm, Mare Balticum. *Nordrevy*, No. 1, pp. 57–58.

3. *Mare Balticum. Talouden ja kulttuurin meri* (Mare Balticum. The Sea of Trade and Culture). Elinkeinoelmn valtuuskunta 1990.

4. Mats Hällström, Skapa ett Östersjöråd, *Svenska Dagbladet*, 13 November 1990.

5. Johannes Salminen, Ruotsin salainen suurvaltahaave (The Secret Swedish Dream of Becoming a Major Power), *Helsingin Sanomat*, 21 October 1990. Salminen's main idea is that "the Kotka spirit" should not be allowed to develop into nostalgic dreaming of reproducing a heroic and war-prone past.

6. See for example, *Mare Balticum: Zusammenarbeit im Ostseeraum*. Der Landtag Schleswig-Holstein, Rendsburg 1989.

7. Arthur H. Westing (ed.), *Comprehensive Security for the Baltic: An Environmental Approach*, SAGE Publications, London 1989.

8. See Carl-Einar Stålvant, Reflektioner över politik och funktionellt samarbete i Östersjöområdet (Reflections on policy and functional cooperation in the Baltic Sea Area), in Pertti Joenniemi & Unto Vesa (eds.), *Säkerhetsutveckling i Östersjöområdet*, Tampere Peace Research Institute, TAPRI, Report No. 35, 1988, pp. 146–188; Hannu Kyröläinen, The Development of Trade Relations between the Baltic States 1945–1975, *Instant Research on Peace and Violence*, No. 3–4/1979; Marja Lehto, Itämeren turvallisuusjärjestelmä erityisesti oikeudellisen säännöstön kehityksen kannalta (The Security System in the Baltic Sea region seen especially from the viewpoint of a legal regulations), *Arnek*, A/3, 1986; and Osmo Tuomi, Itämeri ja sen lähialueet Varsovan liiton turvalisuusjärjestelmässä (The Place of the Baltic Sea and its Surroundings in the Security System of the Warsaw Treaty Organization), *Arnek*, A/4, 1986.

9. See Mikko Viitasalo, Pertti Joenniemi, Kari Möttölä, Itämeren turvallisuuspolitiikka ja Suomi. Itämeriprojektin loppuraportti (Security Policy in the Baltic Sea Region and Finland). *Aseidenriisunnan neuvottelukunta* 1988, and Gregor Putensen, *Vårt försvar*. No. 9–10/1989–90.

180

10. *Ibid.*

11. For a recent calculation, see Gerd Paul Radtke, Regional Effekte und Perspektiven des Guter- und Personwerkehrs in den schleswig-holsteinischen Ostseehäfen. *Beitrag*, No. 11, 1990, Institut für Regionalforschung, Kiel 1990.

12. For a long-term pattern, see Hannu Kyröläinen, The Development of Trade Relations among the Baltic States 1945–1975 in *Instant Research on Peace and Violence*, No. 3–4/1979, and for more recent figures, Chancen einer stärkeren Einbindung Schleswig-Holsteins in den Ostseeraum, *Abslussbericht der 2. Projektgruppe der Denkfabrik Schleswig-Holsteins*. Kiel 1990.

13. For an interview with Rudolf Jalakas, see Magnus Wreede, Betydligt intresse för regionala förbindelser med Baltikum. *Nordrevy*, No. 1, 1990, pp. 47–49.

14. The speech of the (then) Swedish Minister for Nordic Affairs, Mats Hällström in Kotka in July 1990, provides clues to this thinking. He confessed that Sweden has been unresponsive to the special security arrangements between the Soviet Union and the Nordic countries proposed by President Gorbachev in his speech in Helsinki. One reason behind this scepticism and reluctance to enter into regional security arrangements, he stated, was the need to maintain the status of the Baltic as an open sea. The Soviet Union was seen as a global power, and consequently it can only be balanced by another similar power, and in a global context. This thinking implies that there is no room to manoeuvre for the Nordic countries with the Soviet Union unless also the United Stated is linked, in one way or another, to regional solutions in the Baltic Sea area.

9

The Environmental Option for Norden

Clive Archer

NORDEN – A QUIET CORNER WITH AN ENVIRONMENTAL POLICY POTENTIAL

The events of 1989 and 1990 in Europe marked a post-war breakpoint for many of the states on the Continent. This was seen most obviously in Eastern Europe where the political system forced upon the area between 1945 and 1948 was swept away in a matter of months. The process of German unification represented a major political development not only for the former two German states, but also for the neighbours of the new state.

The Intergovernmental Conferences of the member governments of the European Communities (EC) can be seen as part of the somewhat uncertain move towards closer integration of the EC in the political as well as economic field. Even the Iraqi invasion of Kuwait provided the opportunity for some European states to demonstrate their willingness to cooperate on security matters to a higher level than previously in the Western European Union (WEU), as well as through NATO and the process of European

---

Political Co-operation (EPC) of the EC states. (However, such common diplomatic action did not translate directly into united military activity.)

The London Communiqué of the NATO countries demonstrated further change in Europe: the Soviet Union was no longer to be regarded as an enemy; a dialogue would be opened with the Soviet government; disarmament was to be undertaken, and the Conference on Security and Co-operation in Europe (CSCE) process was taken up as an appropriate forum for a new security order in Europe.

In short, economic integration in Europe has continued; political change has taken place at a pace rarely experienced since 1945; the security map of the Continent has changed radically; new bonds of cooperation have been forged. Opportunities have arisen in rapid succession. Some – such as German unification – have been carried through; others – such as a monetary system for the EC – are still being debated; whilst a number – including the prospect of a federal Europe – seem to have been missed or postponed.

In this vast sea of change, one area of Europe has appeared calm, even sedate. Not the most directly affected region by the revolutions of Eastern Europe; scarcely heard on the question of German unity; on the periphery for most EC issues; welcoming of the disarmament moves in Central Europe but nervous of any collateral effect; outside the WEU system: all this suggests that *the Nordic region – 'the quiet corner of Europe'*– has been marginalized to an even greater extent than before by the events of 1989–1990.

This, of course, may not matter. There are advantages in not being at the hub of things and not having to respond immediately to a series of dizzying events. However, if the governments and peoples of the Nordic states wish to be more closely involved in international relations in Europe – especially where they themselves are directly affected – can they take initiatives that will produce useful returns?

It is the contention of this chapter that the Nordic region could most usefully expend their political resources and time in the post-Cold War period by placing greater emphasis on environmental policies. Of course, the Nordic governments – or at least some of them – have already been noted for their relative activism in this area. The Swedes initiated and hosted the 1972 United Nations Conference on the Human Environment, and Norway has provided the leadership of the World Commission on Environment and Development (1987).

First, an examination of the existing priorities in the external policies of the Nordic states should be undertaken before any assessment can be made as to the change in values as expressed by these policies.

THE CURRENT SITUATION: THE CENTRALITY OF SECURITY POLITICS

It is difficult accurately to evaluate the priorities in the present external policies of the Nordic states because of the lack of satisfactory indicators that can clearly demonstrate the functional preferences of the policy-makers.

What is meant here by 'functional preferences' is the relative amount of time and trouble devoted to issue areas such as security questions, economic issues, development problems, energy and human rights. Even the existence of these as distinct functional policy areas can be challenged (McLaren, 1985: 141–43) though with the exception of the last named, it is precisely these subjects that make up the functional 'desks' in the ministries for foreign affairs in West European countries.

A standard work on Nordic foreign policy identified security policy, international economic policy, Third World policy and neighbourhood (i.e., Nordic) policy as the four 'dimensions of the foreign policy behavior of the North European countries' (Sundelius, 1982: 6). Since this chapter aims at dealing with the Nordic states as a group as well as individually, the neighbourhood dimension can be set aside.

Energy policy can be seen as a subset of international economic policy, but it is one that has taken on an importance of its own, especially for Norway (Stoltenberg 1989: 24–36). Especially when seen in the context of the growing importance of the CSCE process, it can be argued that a separate heading for human rights is nowadays justified in the foreign policies of the Nordic states.

So part of the problem in deciding such preference structures is the overlapping nature of such broad functional terms as 'security' and 'economic.' However, it can be taken for granted that, as government ministries manage to divide responsibility for these issues, there does exist a core area for each one, though it should be remembered that the areas merge both in reality and in their treatment by government agencies (as seen either in interdepartmental cooperation or in ministerial rivalry on subjects).

It is the contention here that, since the Second World War, the security aspect has dominated the external policies of the Nordic states. The reasons for this are a combination of a response to the international environment, the wide definition of 'international security' used by Nordic governments, and bureaucratic factors.

Governments of the five Nordic countries have since 1945 found that the question of international security has impinged on them because of the growing strategic importance of the Nordic region.

An area called 'the quiet corner of Europe' which was able to remain neutral during the First World War, soon found itself embroiled in the conflict of the Second World War. Even Iceland, that had felt itself so isolated during the inter-war period that it had not bothered to join the League of Nations, was occupied. The aeroplane and the submarine had changed the strategic significance of the Nordic states. In the post-war world, these countries were quickly involved in the Cold War, especially as the region lay directly on the polar route between Moscow and Washington.

The fact that the five Nordic states were unable to create a single security response to the international situation of 1948 to 1949 demonstrated how the outside world had impinged on the northern part of Europe.

During the next forty years each of the five countries adopted measures to try to limit the presence of the superpowers in the Nordic region, but these efforts often flagged in the face of the 'strategic necessity' of either one or both of the alliances (Archer 1990: 22–26). The Norwegian and Danish 'base and ban' policies had to contend with the growth of the Soviet military presence on the neighbouring Kola Peninsula, the rise of the US Maritime Strategy and the 'neither confirm nor deny' policy of Britain and the United States for their warships visiting Danish and Norwegian ports.

Ries has identified three main priorities for Soviet strategy in the north-western part of the Soviet Union: a) maintaining its strategic weapons; b) regional military support operations; and c) theatre-level ground forces – with the latter two 'leading to problems for the regional states in preserving the strategic stability of their environment' (Ries, 1988: 132). Other semi-official publications have outlined the growth of the Soviet presence on the Kola, stressing its basic strategic nature while accepting that this has important implications for the Nordic states (Olsen 1989: 163–200). The Soviet Union has not been the only superpower with interests in the Nordic region. The United States has, particularly since the mid-1970s, 'rediscovered' the Northern Flank of NATO (Tamnes 1985: 40–56). In particular the advent of the United States' Maritime Strategy had importance consequences for the strategic significance of the Nordic region as it indicated not only an American interest in the area, but a willingness to include the area in plans, deployment and exercises (Børresen, 1985; Melby, 1985; Miller, 1988). Furthermore, Tunander makes the point that the Maritime Strategy, and more generally the US–Soviet competition in Northern Europe, has affected the Nordic region as a whole, turning it from 'a peripheral flank to a possibly independent front' (Tunander, 1989: 122), and has even affected Sweden's position in what could be considered a negative fashion (pp. 124–33).

Another reason for the dominance of security issues in the external policies of the Nordic states has been the wide definition of the term 'international security' by the governments of those states. Especially since the experience of the Second World War, the Nordic countries have accepted that a security policy involves more than just military defence. They have therefore developed the formula that their security policies are a result of a combination of defence policy, foreign policy and certain aspects of economic policy (Seidenfaden, 1970: 11). A foreign policy that encourages the use of international organizations and promotes arms control and disarmament is one that serves the security needs of small states such as Sweden and Denmark, it is argued. Aid to Third World states is likewise seen as a contribution to a more equitable, and therefore safer, world. Even

---

defence policy is defined as 'Total Defence,' which includes not only military defence but also civil defence, civil emergency planning and police activity. (Christensen, 1979: 5).

The third reason for the dominance of security issues can broadly be described as 'bureaucratic' factors. This arises from the importance attached to international security for the reasons given above. Four of the five Nordic states – Iceland is the exception – have ministries of defence which also have staffs and budgets in order to implement the most overt part of the countries' security policies, their defence policies. It is even known what part of the Gross National Product is spent by this sector of government: Denmark 2.1%; Finland 1.4%; Norway 3.3%; and Sweden 3.0% (Olsen, 1989: 142-43, the figures are for 1987). Also the foreign ministries of these countries (and of Iceland) have departments that deal with security issues and the prime ministers' offices normally have advisers on international security questions. While this bureaucratic involvement reflects the importance attached to the issue area, it also helps to entrench the treatment of international security as being one of the essential tasks of the state.

A TIME FOR CHANGE – BUT CAN THEY?

Will the situation described above change or will it endure into the first decade of the next century? Much will depend on the relative security importance of the Nordic region. So the question is whether the changes in Europe have brought – or will bring – about a lessening of the strategic importance of the Nordic region. There seems to be two sides to this coin.

On the one hand, because the military value of the area – as outlined above – has very much been associated with *strategic* weapons, the conclusion of European regional arms control agreements such as the INF treaty and the Conventional Forces in Europe (CFE) agreement is unlikely to affect their relevance for the northern region.

On the other hand, should the relationship between the two superpowers improve considerably, we are likely to see more arms control and disarmament agreements and the tension will go out of the superpower military involvement in the Nordic area.

Furthermore, even if one considered only the developments in Europe, it would seem clear that the strategic significance of the Nordic states has changed. The Soviet military dominance in the Baltic has faded, and Denmark is no longer a 'front-line state.' And with the three Baltic republics of Estonia, Latvia and Lithuania now independent, the Soviet/Russian presence in the area could be severely curtailed.

However, there is some Norwegian concern that the military might of the Soviet Union has been reduced in Central Europe but that some of it has also been redistributed to the north of Europe. This notion has been dubbed the 'sausage effect,' referring to the way that the meat in a sausage retreats to the sides when the middle is squeezed. In January 1991, Norwegian Minister of Defence, J. J. Holst, admonished the Soviets for planning their largest ever military exercise close to the Soviet–Norwegian border, for transferring air-landing divisions to the KGB and a motorized infantry division in Archangel to the navy (thus avoiding inclusion in the CFE arrangements) and providing other incorrect information (*Norinform*, January 15, 1991: 1–2).

A Finnish writer noted how, in the wake of the CFE treaty, both sides – NATO and the Soviet Union – had shuffled their better military equipment around in Europe to avoid it being scrapped. He claimed that this might represent "a more modern application of qualitative sausage theory, with, after deep cuts in the numbers of weapons systems, the quality of the remaining systems radically improved on the alliances' flanks" (Järvanpää, 1990: 132).

Given these suspicions – and the Nordic foreign-policy makers' familiarity with the security system of the last forty years which is often referred to as the 'Nordic Balance' – it is not surprising that the Nordic governments have not rushed to change their security policies in response to the European upheavals of 1989–90. Indeed, the Danish Defence Commission's Report, coming a few months after the opening of the Berlin Wall, represented a typically cautious approach (Forsvarskommissionen

---

1990, especially Vol. I, Part 1), an approach also reflected in the title of one of Pertti Joenniemi's works: "Europe Changes: the Nordic System Remains" (Joenniemi, 1990).

Perhaps the relevant question here is not whether the Nordic states *have* changed their security policies but the extent to which these policies *can* change?

Even within the bounds of cautiousness, the Finnish government has already repealed important elements of the 1947 Treaty of Paris and the 1948 Treaty of Friendship, Cooperation and Mutual Assistance, and the Swedish government has applied for full membership of the European Community. Furthermore, both Denmark and Norway became embroiled – albeit modestly – in the Gulf War against Iraq. Certainly the developments in Europe that are typified by the expression 'the end of the Cold War, provide an opportunity for change by the Nordic governments.

During the last years of transformation and turbulence in the Soviet Union and the increasingly independent republics, suspicions have grown as to how far the Soviet Union – or what may remain of it – and the republics can become members of the 'Common European Home,' but, in the end, the revolutions in Eastern Europe and the disarmament and arms control agreements in Europe have produced an entirely new menu of *opportunities* for decision-makers in the continent.

It is perhaps wise for the Nordic decision-makers to consider not just the existing situation (with all its dangers and uncertainties) but also the possible future with its potential.

NEW PRIORITIES – MAKING USE OF THE STRONG SIDES OF NORDEN

How might priorities change? Clearly the best impetus would be the easing of the security situation in Europe and between the superpowers so that the five Nordic states no longer feel themselves under such intense pressure to allow military and strategic considerations to dominate their external policies.

Any assumption of such a future must be optimistic, particularly as the ability of the Nordic states to effect such an outcome must be severely limited. However, what marks out the beginning of the 1990s is the new sense of movement and change in the international system. In other words, the weakening of strategic factors is part of a *possible* future.

Furthermore, in a period of movement there will be opportunities for the Nordic states to shape their policy priorities. A re-examination of the instrumentalities of their security policies could lead to certain adjustments.

In the first place, the 'end of the Cold War' could mean that the Nordic states can co-operate more closely on security matters. Even during the Cold War there was some common action in the context of UN peacekeeping operations, but this was quite limited. Discussion of a Nordic nuclear-weapon free zone 'has been to bury the issue rather than to promote it' (Joenniemi, 1990, p. 211).

Perhaps rather than starting in this very sensitive area, the Nordic governments should consider areas of foreign policy that they could run jointly?

To a certain extent this has been done at the UN (where there is close consultation between delegations), in diplomatic representations to some Third World states and with some development projects. Even in dealing with the Baltic republics, there was a certain amount of common action by the Nordic states – for example in meetings with the 'foreign ministers' of the three Baltic republics. This could well continue and be expanded now they are independent states.

Denmark is already part of the European Political Cooperation (EPC) system of the twelve members of the European Communities. In the past, Norway has tried to involve itself more closely with this process but has had limited success as it is not an EC member. However, with the prospect of Norway and possibly Sweden and Finland becoming members of an extended European Community by the start of the next century, *it may be wise for the Nordic states to start a formal process of closer external policy cooperation between themselves so that they may act more effectively as a group within EPC.*

Such a move has been suggested during the last couple of years by a number of senior Nordic politicians including the present prime minister of Sweden, Carl Bildt (*Nordisk Kontakt*, 18/90: 11–12).

After all, the major differences in foreign policy among the five states are those determined by their security policies, and if the factor that has shaped those policies – the Cold War – *does* melt away, then there is *a greater potential in the Nordic region* for, at first, *coordination*, then *cooperation*, and perhaps finally *common policies* in certain distinct foreign policy areas.

If such a change is undertaken, then it may be the opportunity for the Nordic governments to reconsider the resources that they use for their external policies. Such a new environment – and increased common action – would suggest the need for fewer resources to be devoted to international security issues. If this were the case, how should the five countries decide on the reallocation of their policy resources?

The criteria might be those of placing emphasis on the functional areas in which the Nordic states have particular expertise and experience, where the best returns can be assured and where those countries seem to have an advantage comparative to other states. These factors are difficult to operationalize but preliminary evidence might be considered.

The experience and expertise of the Nordic states is that of small developed, democratic, rich, social welfare countries. As such they offer attractive models, especially for the newly emerging democracies and economies of Eastern and Central Europe. However, in the rush – either side of the old Iron Curtain – to make judgement on the events in these ex-Communist-run states, the prime reference seems to be 'the market economy' and even to 'Thatcherism.'

Yet there is enough evidence – and reason – to believe that the needs of the populations of those states are not for capitalism 'red in tooth and claw' but something more along the lines of the social-welfare state of the Nordic countries. The problem is that this comes at a time when 'social democracy is exhausted' and the model is more likely to be the social market economy founded by Ludwig Erhard in the Federal Republic of Germany (Dahrendorf, 1990: 71 and 88). It did not go unnoticed that at a time when the East Europeans were struggling free of their chains, the Nordic states were also in economic and political turmoil, albeit in more luxurious surroundings (Vulliamy, 1990).

The expertise of the Nordic states in other areas of external policy – such as in energy questions and economic development – is varied. The main problem concerning the Nordic countries placing greater emphasis on energy matters in their external affairs is that the five countries have such vastly differing interests in this area.

Norway is an important exporter of oil and gas, while the other five states are net importers. Also the mix of energy sources is varied: Finland and Sweden both have important nuclear energy contributions to their energy production and Denmark imports a significant amount of solid fuel. Though there is intra-Nordic cooperation in the production and supply of electrical energy through the NORDEL system (Nordic Statistical Secretariat, 1990: 144), the extension of this network is bound to be modest as long as the Nordic states (with the exception of Norway) look outwards for their energy sources and as long as schemes for the Nordic participation in the Norwegian offshore effort come to nothing.

In the case of the Nordic states' development policy, it can be seen that three of them – Denmark, Norway and Sweden – have since the late 1970s achieved the UN target for official development assistance (0.7 per cent of their GNP) and that Finland is approaching that figure (Nordic Statistical Secretariat 1990: 295 and 299). Nordic assistance to the Third World is concentrated on a number of countries and there is an increased tendency for the five Nordic governments to cooperate in this area.

Joint Nordic efforts started in 1962 and there is now the Committee of Civil Servants on Assistance Matters that helps with the planning and administration of Nordic projects such as those to Tanzania, Mozambique and, more generally, to the Southern African Development Coordination Conference (SADCC) (ibid: 297–8). This relationship with Third World states also includes trade matters, an area that would come under the general remit of the Lomé Convention should the other Nordic states join the European Community. However, it does seem that, so far, the Nordic states have positive elements in their donor policies that are not noticeable in other western countries (Kiljunen, 1987: 153–67; Elgström, 1989: 216–20), though perhaps its enlightened nature sometimes slips (Stokke, 1985: 142–43) and reports suggest that it is not always as effective as intended (*Nordisk Kontakt*, 18/90: 56).

EXISTING ENVIRONMENTAL EFFORTS

Before examining the case for an increased share of the Nordic external policy effort being devoted to environmental matters, some estimate should be made of the current activities in this sphere. Raw indicators demonstrate the growth in the attention shown towards ecological issues in the external relations of the Nordic countries over the past 25 years. The first major entry of any of the Nordic states into 'environmental diplomacy' was that of Sweden in proposing and hosting the first United Nations Conference on the Human Environment, held in 1972. Since then, the involvement of the Nordic governments in this policy area has been increasing and, for states with such small populations, notable.

All five Nordic states have ministries of the environment which have been well-established for some years. For example, the first Danish Environment Minister was appointed in September 1973 (Helge Nielsen), though from October 1971 the Minister for Public Works – Jens Kampmann – had also been responsible for pollution control (Hvidt, 1984: 316-8). Although the foreign ministries take the lead in external affairs including international negotiations and conferences, the environment ministries undertake much of the practical and negotiating work on international agreements though, as in other countries, there is sometimes conflict between ministries about an appropriate response to environmental issues at the international level.

A better view of the existing effort by the five countries in international environmental affairs can be obtained by examining Nordic activities. In the Helsinki Treaty of Cooperation which elaborated on already existing Nordic cooperation, environmental matters were added to the areas covered by the work of the Nordic Council. Article 30 exhorted the Nordic states to 'put the environmental interest of the other Contracting Parties on a par with their own in their national legislation and in the application of the latter.' The Nordic countries, in Article 31, sought 'to harmonize their environmental protection rules' to attain 'the greatest possible similarity in standards and guiding principles relating to the discharge of pollutants, the use of toxins ... and other disturbances of the environment' (Nordic Council, 1978: 11). As a result, the Social Committee of the Nordic Council became the Social and Environmental Committee.

Furthermore the five Nordic governments signed a Convention on the Protection of the Environment on February 19, 1974 which sought to bring into the calculation the permissibility of environmentally harmful activities in one Nordic state and consideration of their effects on any of the other Nordic countries, allowing this to be a factor in cases coming before each of the states' national courts (Nordic Council, 1978 :47–51).

There now exists a Nordic Committee of Senior Officials for Environmental Affairs, which also has attached to it one group, three contact groups, an *ad hoc* group and eight working groups on subjects such as environmental economy, data, air pollution and chemicals (Nordiska Rådet, 1990: 94–95). The Nordic Council of Ministers have also prepared five-year environmental cooperation programmes, the third running from 1983 to 1987. The follow-up programme was more ambitious than its three predecessors, taking 'a multi-sectoral approach, presupposing co-operation across administrative and national boundaries' (NU, 1988–4E: 109), and was therefore only ready in January 1989 (NU, 1989–3). The Council of Ministers has also acted in more limited environmental fields, for example by taking a decision to produce a Common Nordic Plan against Marine Pollution in February 1987. The joint Nordic budget for environmental cooperation in 1988 was about Dkr 13 million (NU, 1988–4E: 109).

The Nordic Council very quickly embraced its new competence in environmental co-operation: in 1978 one-third of the Council's recommendations concerned the environment, and during that year's session the Social and Environmental Committee recommended to the Nordic Council of Ministers that a working group be established on the effect on the ozone layer of chlorine-fluoride methane compounds. By the mid-1980s the Council was concerning itself with air pollution, and the Nordic states led a campaign to reduce sulphur dioxide emissions by 30% by 1993 and were using the Nordic Council to advance this cause and place joint pressure on the United Kingdom to subscribe to the target (Nordic Council, 1985: 64; Nordic Council, 1987: 44; Nordic Council, 1988: 30).

In November 1988 an extra session of the Council was held in Elsinore to discuss environmental matters, and it was at this that the 1989 environmental cooperation programme was advanced. The Council of Ministers also adopted the Nordic Action Plan against Pollution of the Marine Environment at the Helsinki meeting of environment ministers in January 1989 (NU, 1989–2).

Nordic involvement in wider environmental diplomacy has continued apace since the early 1970s. First, the Nordic governments have worked persistently – and closely together – in the various United Nations agencies addressing environmental matters, including the United Nations Environment Programme (UNEP), UNESCO, the FAO and the WHO. Within Europe they have given particular assistance to the Committee of Senior Advisers on Environmental Problems of the UN Economic Commission for Europe and have been one of the leading advocates of the ECE's Convention on Long-Range Transboundary Air Pollution. They have also worked with the OECD's Environment Committee and within the Council of Europe, which in recent years has paid more attention to environmental matters, although it has always had an interest in heritage and nature conservation issues, the latter being one given particular priority by the Nordic states.

The second "basket" of the Conference on Security and Cooperation in Europe has provisions on environmental cooperation and the Nordic states have advanced proposals to the various CSCE follow-up conferences on transboundary air pollution, the marine environment and the ozone layer (NU, 1988-4E:,112–14).

On a more regional basis in Europe, the Nordic countries have also been in the vanguard of environmental politics and diplomacy. Denmark, as a member of the European Communities, has pressed for the adoption of the highest possible environmental standards within the EC, and it was partly because of Danish pressure that the Single European Act – which introduced the environmental aspect into the Treaty of Rome – allowed states to maintain environmental measures higher than those agreed on a Community-wide basis (Article 130T).

Though EFTA is not seen as a major instrument of environmental co-operation by the non-EC Nordic states, environmental issues have been an area of discussion between the EC and EFTA, and the environment ministers of the two organizations met for the first time in October 1987. Also an ad hoc group has been established within the Nordic Committee of Senior Officials for Environmental Affairs for matters which are of common concern between the EC and the Nordic states. Denmark, Finland and Sweden are also members of another regional organization – that of the Baltic Marine Environment Protection Commission (the Helsinki Convention), established in 1973 to protect the Baltic Sea from all forms of pollution. Its activities have taken on particular meaning since the unity of Germany and the movement of Poland towards democracy on the southern borders of the Sea.

The Nordic states are also active in the work carried out under other conventions, for example the Oslo Convention on the dumping of wastes at sea and covering the North Sea, the North Atlantic, Skagerak and Kattegat; the Paris Convention covering land-based sources of pollution in the same seas; and the Bonn Agreement between the North Sea states on oil and chemical spills. Finally, the Nordic countries have played an active part in environmental cooperation in the Arctic, giving full support to the Finnish Initiative of 1989 for an intergovernmental meeting on the Arctic environment.

In summary, the effort of the Nordic countries in the field of environmental diplomacy, both individually and collectively, can be described as thorough, far-reaching and with an effect out of proportion to the small population size of these five states.

THE FUTURE CHOICE

Even from the above brief description, it does seem that the area of environmental diplomacy and policy is one where the Nordic states have a particular expertise and experience. It is also perhaps the functional area that can bring the best returns for a relatively small diplomatic 'investment'. The Swedish initiative in raising the environmental issue at the United Nations in the late 1960s and in hosting the UN Conference on the Human Environment laid the ground for the creation of UNEP. Danish insistence on its own high environmental standards within the European Communities was an important factor in the inclusion of Article 130T in the Treaty of Rome.

The Norwegians have been instrumental in keeping the issue of acid rain on the European agenda. Furthermore, the Finnish government managed to bring together the Arctic governments for their first ever inter-governmental meeting – on environmental matters. The Nordic neutrals, in particular, can claim a good 'strike rate' with their diplomatic moves on international security matters such as helping along the CSCE process and the Stockholm agreements on Confidence and Security-Building Measures. However, with the end of the division of Europe into two hostile blocs, perhaps this "go-between" role is not needed so greatly.

The Nordic countries also seem to have an advantage in the area of environmental matters compared to other states. They have an interested and supportive public and, with some notable exceptions, have few heavy polluting industries. They have advanced laws on environmental matters and strong Nordic cooperation on such matters. Finally, they have a developed bureaucratic structure: ministries of the environment and government-supported research establishments.

Furthermore in the New Europe – one no longer divided East–West but one dominated by the EC – environmental matters are taking on a heightened saliency, whereas traditional security concerns no longer seem to dominate the political agenda. Indeed, the attainment of *environmental security as a contribution to the strengthening of comprehensive security* has already been recognized (World Commission on Environment and Development, 1987:

Chapter 11; Westing, 1989: 129–32; Holst, 1989: 123-28). Likewise the link has been made between environmental protection and economic development both in the Brundtland Report and in the title and draft agenda of the next world environmental meeting, the United Nations Conference on Environment and Development. Indeed, the Nordic states have added an environmental element to their aid-giving policies in the Third World. So a more active environmental policy need not exclude a consideration of security and development policies.

The Nordic Council's Committee on International Cooperation reported in 1988 that 'there has not been any real strategy or programme to develop Nordic participation in international environmental co-operation'. (NU, 1988–4E: 120). It saw the makings of such a strategy in the new Nordic environment plan and asked for the Nordic Council of Ministers to be given a greater role especially in information exchanges, though it doubted whether this could be done on existing resources. (ibid.: 121). It thus called for the Council of Ministers and the relevant Senior Officials' Committee to meet more often. It considered that the Nordic countries 'should endeavour to make a greater commitment to its environmental activities' and suggested more binding agreements, more research and increased activity in the international organizations (ibid.: 121-23).

The report was a demonstration at a high political level of the need for the Nordic states to do more in the environmental field. But perhaps its recommendations did not go far enough.

In this new Europe it might be better for the Nordic states to place more resources in the field of environmental policy. However, *to be effective the Nordic states will have to act as one* – whether inside the European Communities or not. Has the time come for them to work towards a *Nordic* Ministry of the Environment that could act on their collective behalf?

To start with this may just mean further and deeper cooperation and co-ordination through the present structure of the Nordic Council. Eventually this might develop into a confederal Nordic Ministry with inputs from all five countries but with – in most cases – one policy output. The 1992 UNCED Rio meeting might be a catalyst. Just as the Nordic states had one negotiator

★ ★ ★ ★ ★ ★ ★ ★ ★

198

---

in the GATT Kennedy Round of the 1960s, might it not be possible to have one spokesperson (or perhaps a panel of spokespersons) at UNCED?

It is vital that the more enlightened environmental policies of the Nordic states are heard and felt. And it is not only vital for the people of the Nordic region.

REFERENCES

Archer, Clive, 'The North as a Multidimensional Strategic Area' in *The Annals of the American Academy of Political and Social Science*, Vol. 512 (The Nordic Region), November 1990, pp. 22–32.

Beretning fra Forsvarskommissionen, *Forsvaret i 90'erne,* Copenhagen, Statens Informationstjeneste, 1990.

Børresen, Jacob, 'USA-marinens operasjoner i Nord Atlanten og Norskehavet' in *Internasjonal Politikk*, Thematic issue 2, 1985, pp. 109–162.

Christensen, Ivan, *Total Defence*, Copenhagen, The Information and Welfare Service of the Danish Defence, Copenhagen 1979.

Dahrendorf, Ralf, *Reflections on the Revolution in Europe*, Chatto & Windus, London 1990.

Elgström, Ole, 'Book review' in *Cooperation and Conflict*, No. 24/3–4, 1989, pp. 216–220.

Holst, Johan Jørgen, 'Security and the Environment: A Preliminary Exploration' in *Bulletin of Peace Proposals*, Vol. 20, No. 2, 1989, Oslo, pp. 123–128.

Hvidt, Kristian, *Folketingets Håndbog efter Valget den 10. januar*, J. H. Schultz, Copenhagen 1984.

Järvenpää, Pauli, 'Finland: An Image of Continuity in a Turbulent Europe' in *The Annals of the American Academy of Political Science*, Volume 512, 1990, pp. 125–139.

Joenniemi, Pertti, 'Europe Changes: the Nordic System Remains', in *Bulletin of Peace Proposals*, Vol. 21, No. 2, 1990, Oslo, pp. 205–218.

Kiljunen, Kimmo, 'Nordic SADCC Cooperation' in *Cooperation and Conflict*, Vol. 22, No. 3, September 1987, pp. 153–167.

McLaren, Robert I., 'Mitranian Functionalism: Possible or Impossible?' in *Review of International Studies*, Vol. 11, No. 2, 1985, pp. 139–152.

Melby, Svein, 'Norskehavet i amerikansk marinestrategi' i *Internasjonal politikk*, Thematic issue 2, pp. 57–89.

Miller, Steven, 'Maritime Strategy and Geo-Politics in the High North' in Clive Archer (ed.), *The Soviet Union and Northern Waters*, Routledge, London 1988, pp. 205–238.

Nordic Council, *Cooperation Agreements Between the Nordic Countries*, The Nordic Council and the Nordic Council of Ministers, Stockholm 1978.

Nordic Council, *Nordic Council 33rd Session*, Reykjavik, March 1985, Nordic Council Secretariat, Stockholm 1985.

Nordic Council, *Nordic Council 36th Session*, Helsinki, 23–27 February 1987, Nordic Council Secretariat, Stockholm 1987.

Nordic Council, *Nordic Council 35th Session*, Oslo 7–11 March 1988, Nordic Council Secretariat, Stockholm 1988.

Nordiska Rådet, *Nordiska Rådet Extra Session* i Helsingør den 16 november 1988, Nordic Council Secretariat, Stockholm 1988.

Nordic Statistical Secretariat, *Yearbook of Nordic Statistics*, Nordic Council of Ministers and the Nordic Statistical Secretariat, Copenhagen 1990.

Nordisk Kontakt, 'Norsk u-hjelp i søkelyset,' No. 18, 1990, p. 56.

Nordisk Kontakt, 'NPS, et formalisert utenrikspoltisk samarbeid i Norden,' No. 18, p. 12.

Nordisk Råd, *Nordiska samarbetsorgan 1990*, Stockholm 1990.

NU 1988–E4, *The Nordic Council and International Cooperation*. Report of the Nordic Council's Committee on International Cooperation, The Nordic Council, Stockholm 1988.

NU 1989–2, *Nordisk åtgärdsplan mot förorening av den marina miljön*, The Nordic Council, the Nordic Council of Ministers, Stockholm and Copenhagen 1989.

NU 1989–3, *Nordisk miljöprogram*, The Nordic Council, the Nordic Council of Ministers, Stockholm and Copenhagen 1989.

Olsen, Jan A., *Militärbalansen 1989–90*, DNAK, Oslo 1989.

Ries, Tomas, 'Soviet Military Strategy and Northern Waters' in Clive Archer (ed.), *The Soviet Union and Northern Waters*, Routledge, London 1988, pp. 90–133.

Seidenfaden Report, *Problemer omkring dansk sikkerhedspolitik*, Regeringsudvalget vedrørende Danmarks sikkerhedspolitik, Copenhagen 1970.

Stoltenberg, Thorvald, 'Norwegian Energy Policy in a Foreign Policy Perspective' in Ole Gunnar Austvik (ed.), *Norwegian Oil and Foreign Policy*, for the Norwegian Institute of International Affairs, Sandvika, Vett & Viten, 1989.

Sundelius, Bengt (ed.), *Foreign Policy of Northern Europe*, Westview Press, Boulder, Colorado 1982.

Tunander, Ola, *Cold Water Politics: Maritime Strategy and Geopolitics of the Northern Front*, Sage Publications, London 1989.

Vulliamy, Ed, 'Sad Death of a Swedish Model' in the *Guardian*, February 16, 1990, p. 21.

Westing, Arthur, 'The Environmental Component of Comprehensive Security' in *Bulletin of Peace Proposals*, Vol. 20, No. 2, Oslo, pp. 129–134.

World Commission on Environment and Development, *Our Common Future*, Oxford University Press, Oxford 1987.

10

The Dilemma of Periphery and Centre in the North

Jyrki Käkönen

CHOOSING A PERSPECTIVE

In analysing the future of the northern parts of Europe there seem to be two contradictory options and they are based on three different theoretical and interrelated approaches. The first approach focuses on choices of social actors. The subjects can either adapt themselves to the existing realities provided by the external forces or they can choose to be a subject in and for themselves. In the first case the subject attempts to find the best method for adapting to the external conditions. In the foreign policy analysis this has been called the subordinating adaptation strategy (McGowan & Gottwald, 1975: 170). In the latter case the actor has to adopt an active and conscientious policy – an advancing adaptive strategy (McGowan & Gottwald, 1975: 172).

The second approach focuses on the dichotomy of centre and periphery. In a historical perspective the centre of the world system has been Western

---

Europe, which has expanded geographically, economically, culturally and politically into new regions and new continents (Wallerstein, 1974, 1980). The resources of the periphery have been used by the centre for its own economic and political development. In this historical process the periphery has mainly chosen the strategy of subordinating adaptation. Very seldom has the periphery implemented a policy of self-reliance, i.e., an active policy for itself (Hettne, 1982, 77-84).

The third approach is based on the relation between the civil society and the nation-state. The so-called civilization process of the Western world leads to the nation-state system (Gong, 1984). Modernization, development, urbanization and militarization are phenomena which cannot be understood without the concept of the nation-state. Nation-states have also been the leading force in the process which created the Eurocentric world system as well as stagnating peripheries (Wallerstein, 1974, 1980).

In this context the two alternatives for the northern periphery are the following ones:

1. The continuing peripherization.

In this perspective the Nordic countries are looking at Western European integration and especially the situation after the magical year of 1992. If we emphasise integration as the only alternative and take for granted international competition in the economic sphere, there will be fewer resources used in the peripheries. The population of the peripheries has to move into the centre and the periphery will be utilized in the interests of the centre. In a way this kind of development is deterministic and one might call it *trend development.*

2. Self-reliance-oriented development.

This alternative implies that the periphery has to embrace the role of an autonomous subject. The Nordkalott needs inter-regional cooperation, which might run counter to the interests of the nation-states. But there will be space for both the European integration process and regional integration in the North. One can even say that the latter process is likely to become a necessity. This development strategy includes a variety of alternative policy choices and we might term it *goal-oriented development.*

In what follows, the northern periphery, first, means the Nordkalott in the wider Arctic context. The whole Arctic is the northern periphery of the world system. In the geographical sense both the Arctic and the Nordkalott are regions or subregions. But in the economic or political sense it is difficult to understand them as regions with strong internal links. Still, we choose to describe the Arctic and the Nordkalott as regions. One of our aims is to try to define the preconditions for the development of a peripheral northern region. Another is to show that the future development of the region depends largely on its ability to develop regional cooperation.

It should be emphasised at the outset that the North is a periphery mainly when we talk about current economic and political realities. But if we look at defence and strategic realities, the North has increasingly become a center – or a front, rather – in the global strategy of the great powers due to the changes in military policy of the so-called superpowers as well as the development of maritime technology.

In the 1970s, the High North was still a strategic periphery. But since the early 1980s, it has become a focal point on the maps of the military planners of the USA and the USSR (Tunander, 1989, Jalonen, 1988). In spite of the political and military changes in the Soviet Union, the military importance of the Arctic is not likely to decrease soon. However, the Arctic waters will be the last area where strategic nuclear weapons are deployed as long as other, less vulnerable alternatives can be found (Miller, 1990).

Up to the present, the Arctic has mostly been economically utilized by indigenous people. This means that economic activities have maintained their traditional character (Polar Regions Atlas, 1979) and that, therefore, economic utilization has taken place largely in balance with the environment. Northern peoples still largely base their living on a subsistence economy. However, the share of modern industry in the GNP of the Arctic region is considerable and the Soviet Arctic has a long industrial history. Most of the so-called modern economic activities are – and have been – concentrated on fishing and the fishing industry. The only major exception is the Kola peninsula in the USSR, which is highly industrialized and modernized (Polar Regions Atlas, 1979: 17–22).

★ ★ ★ ★ ★ ★ ★ ★ ★ ★ ★

206

ARCTIC ENERGY

There are huge concentrations of natural resources in the Arctic, but technological development has only recently provided the means for their large-scale utilization. Mineral resources have been exploited mostly in the Soviet Arctic. The drilling of oil resources is the only modern economic activity found in the whole Arctic region (Polar Regions Atlas, 1979: 24). In the present situation natural gas and oil are the most important resources of the Arctic. It has been projected that those resources will be in extensive use from about the year 2000 (Jumppanen, 1990: 81). The effects of the 1990–91 Persian Gulf crisis and war will further support this kind of development. *This means that in the existing world system the economic role of the whole Arctic region will become more important.*

From the Soviet – or Russian – viewpoint the Arctic region has a significant role already. This was indicated in President Gorbachev's Murmansk speech in 1987. No doubt, an intensified utilization of Arctic resources is one of the preconditions for future economic development and the success of perestroika and general societal transformation (Vartanov, 1989). Arctic oil and gas resources are central in the Soviet (Russian) energy policy (Jumppanen, 1990: 75) since other sources, i.e., those in the Caucasus, are almost exhausted. Today Siberia produces the major part of Soviet oil and gas, either domestically consumed or exported. Many international analyses point to the fact that by the late 1990s the USSR – or whatever it will be called – will be an oil system (Georgiou, 1987: 305). This means that energy-saving production methods will not be enough for the Soviet economy for maintaining self-sufficiency in energy production.

The Arctic energy resources have an important position in the world economy as well. In international surveys it was already estimated in the late 1980s that the era of cheap oil will be over by the early 1990s (OECD Review, 1986: 15 and 31; Georgiou, 1987: 296 and 305). There are at least three main reasons for this unexpected trend:

a) The North Sea oil was one of the factors which turned down the price curve of oil in the early 1980s. The output of the production units there started to decline in 1986. It has been estimated that the resources of the North Sea region will be exhausted some time during the 1990s.

b) Also, some other sources will be exhausted before the end of this century (e.g., Nigeria). After the year 2000, oil will still be drilled in the Middle East, but it seems to be a fact that very few countries will supply oil for the world markets beyond the year 2000.

c) Then there is the concentration of the oil companies. It has been expected that by the late 1990s there might well be only four major oil companies left operating on the world oil markets. These companies will most probably be Exxon, Shell, Saudi-Arabian and Kuwaiti national oil companies.

These three factors together indicate that in the not so distant future it will be difficult to get oil from the free markets. Therefore it is most likely that oil market competition will intensify considerably. At the same time we have to acknowledge that there are very few, if any, signs that oil would be replaced by nuclear power or coal soon. Oil will probably maintain its share in world energy production and consumption well into the next century (Georgiou, 1987: 303; OECD Review, 1986: 42).

And, perhaps, we have to calculate in the future with one more factor that might push oil prices upwards. The Iraqi annexation of Kuwait and what followed demonstrated that the actions of one sovereign state can bring instability and affect the availability and the price of oil.

TREND DEVELOPMENTS

The West European integration process is a logical continuation of the historical development of a Eurocentric world system. From an economic point of view one central precondition for the survival of the capitalist mode of production has been the growth of production units, the concentration of

---

production and the internationalization of the entire economy (Wallerstein, 1979). Seen in a long-term perspective it seems as if there were no other options for the market economies; now, too, we witness that former centrally planned economies have no choice – or see no alternatives – but to make the transition into capitalist world market system.

A basic characteristic of this is that it displays cycles of changing hegemony and the expansion of the centre(s) into new peripheries (Käkönen 1988: 45–67). This pertains first to the economic and political centres of the Nordic countries which are interested in the integration project for economic reasons. Second, the centre means Western and Central Europe, where the integration is deepening.

The future or the Arctic periphery is, from this angle, not necessarily a bright or promising one. Peripheries have consistently been integrated into the economy of the centre. Up to the twentieth century the hegemony was in Europe. In principle it moved over the Atlantic Ocean as early as the beginning of this century (Käkönen, 1988: 61–67). For all practical purposes, the United States began to behave like a hegemonic power only after 1945.

In the 1970s the hegemony of the USA began to decline and its legitimacy was no longer accepted by all the actors in the world system. The challengers of US hegemony were Japan and the EC. One of the functions of the EC has been to increase the economic as well as the political capacity of Western Europe *vis-à-vis* the United States and Japan. This is also a necessity for the European economy, since the other alternative would be peripherization; i.e., to become a periphery of the Atlantic- and successively Pacific-centred world system.

There are experts who, today, insist that "Europe," i.e., the EC, has the potential to become a hegemonic power in the existing world system. Japan does not (yet) have the military potential or political will to take over the hegemony from the United States. The USSR is disintegrating and whatever comes out of its restructuring, the economy of that area is unlikely to permit a leadership role in world affairs although it will remain as a – or develop into a more – impressive military power(s).

The United States has difficulties in its own backyard and with the "domestic order," which means that soon it is likely to concentrate more on the problems of the western hemisphere and its domestic social, economic and environmental problems.

The war against Iraq might even strengthen the chances of the EC of becoming a new hegemony. The United States and its allies conducted a hegemonic war which will bind and consume tremendous resources one way and another; interventionism could well become a part of the "new international order" if lifestyles are not changed domestically in the rich world but remain fundamentally non-sustainable in the future. This, indeed, is an expensive way of keeping the world system operating, and the peripheries will pay one type of price while the centres will increasingly pay another.

The EC has, so far, committed itself much less to the Persian Gulf and has not – again, so far – developed an EC actor-capacity for such policies. But to realize a hegemonic dream, the EC will need constant economic growth and that growth is impossible without new resources, new markets and exploitative exchanges with various peripheries.

If we keep in mind the theoretical premises presented at the beginning of this chapter, there are reasons to assume that European integration and the growth process will increasingly lead to an expansion of the EC economy into the Arctic. Arctic resources could be one of several bases for a new European role in the world system. The other bases are in Eastern Europe and the former Soviet Union regions. And that might have a greater importance for the EC than the North. Thus, it remains an option for Northern Europe to be left as a periphery.

Be this as it may, the integration of Northern Europe into the centre will bring the Arctic resources inside the EC, the Soviet resources naturally excluded. Within the framework of the existing economic models, those new resources will be utilized to the benefit of the centre (i.e., national centres and the European centre). It will lead to an "Arctic boom" of course but one that implies more intensive peripherization. The northern regions of Europe will be preserved as natural parks for the people living in the urban centres of the centre.

In this respect it is not important whether the EC has a conscious Arctic policy or not. Today, the EC does not have any explicitly defined Arctic programme, although individual EC members have a strong interest in the

---

Arctic. The important point is that Arctic resources provide the EC with one among several bases for economic growth and expansion. On the other hand, the Northern European green belt has already been mentioned as a recreation ground for the whole of Europe. But the realization of this idea requires a policy of conservation of the nature in the North – a policy that will affect the wood and pulp industries of the northern countries.

Overall integration may have serious consequences for a country such as Finland. We already know that more Finnish capital flows out than international capital flows in. Finnish enterprises buy foreign companies in order to extend their share in the world markets, and thereby produce less in Finland. They will also export less than they have up till now, one result of which will be increasing unemployment. No doubt, the peripherization of the North will be more extensive in the future.

It seems inevitable that, during the period of adaptation to the integration and internationalization of Finland's economy and society, we will see more social problems, not fewer. There is likely to be less potential and less political will to take care of such problems.

To promote the internationalization of the economy, states and governments will cut their spending in sectors where they have traditionally subsidized their domestic peripheries. In other words, services and infrastructures will weaken in the periphery since this kind of spending does not add much, if at all, to competitiveness on the world market.

Northern realities easily support such arguments. The Nordkalott as well as the whole Arctic has been and remains sparsely populated. Consequently, it has been extremely difficult to build a sufficient infrastructure there; this, in its turn, has contributed to delaying the necessary economic and social modernization of the Arctic.

There are only two major exceptions to this: the infrastructure that is needed to extract Arctic resources, and the various projects and facilities built in the name of national security. In these cases states or governments have allocated financial resources to invest in northern development. This type of support does not strengthen the development of the local economies – the inflow of money being something very different from genuine local development.

Information and communication may serve as another example of peripherization as part of world (and European) market integration. The power over information will also concentrate into still fewer hands; foreign companies will own the media of the peripheries. Periodicals and magazines will still be published in Finnish, Norwegian or other languages, but news and information in general will be produced in the centres, not in the peripheries. Much less information and news will be given about local events while more, filtered through the eyes of a few centres, will be available.

What we have here called trend development gives rise to a contradiction, a dialectic of development and destruction. Arctic resources will be exploited in the near future, but this does not mean economic and social development for the northern periphery. From a theoretical point of view it is certainly possible to speak about industrialization and modernization. But they fit in only with the development needs of centres.

Thus, Arctic resources will be extracted and utilized by the enterprises from the South and by a labor force also from the South. Workers will work in the plants for short periods. Their holiday period between the shifts will be as long as their working period. And the holiday will be spent in the regions they come from. This is the system used, for example, by the companies operating in the Prudhoe Bay oil and gas fields and the Finnish company Outokumpu in northern Norway. This holds no promise of true development for the local communities or for the regions at large. Rather, it is more true to say that it supports further peripherization. The imported labour will be expensive and goods and services will, consequently, also be expensive for the local people. At the same time the traditional economies and modes of living will wither away, slowly but surely. In summary, trend development will be *maldevelopment* for the peripheries.

GOAL-ORIENTED DEVELOPMENT

Thus, the adaptive strategy is not very promising for the Nordkalott or the whole Arctic region. To avoid the continuing peripherization, the region itself

---

will have to play a much more active role. The region has to be transformed into a subject or actor by and for itself.

Western European integration is not the only alternative. It is not a result of unchanging natural or social laws, but a product of human decisions. An alternative to the periphery is a consistent policy aiming at self-reliance (cf. Hettne, 1990: 172–78). From a regional point of view it means horizontal cross-border cooperation in the Arctic and especially in the Nordkalott, i.e., *regional* integration.

Economic and social facts support this strategy. In the 1980s the small non-EC Scandinavian countries have done better than the EC countries due to their relative autonomy. The rates of unemployment and inflation have been lower in Norway, Sweden and Finland than in the EC (Andersson 1988: 393–407). Andersson argues that integration implies a loss of autonomy and consequently leads to a limited management capacity in rapidly changing situations.

The northern periphery must try to increase its regional autonomy rather than limit it, and exploit its comparative advantages in a variety of ways. If it applies the strategy consistently it can develop its management capacity and utilize the Arctic resources to the benefit of the peripheral regions – for instance, by building horizontal networks and cooperative structures. Whatever the operationalization of this philosophy, a more integrated Northern Europe or Calotte will be a stronger actor in the EC than individual states trying to express their national interests.

There can be little doubt that autonomous regional policies would offer opportunities to use Arctic resources in the interests of the region. Regional economic cooperation will enlarge the economic space needed for a growth-oriented economy. This will also serve as a base for expansion into the world markets. Regional joint ventures offer more possibilities for the survival of local enterprises and they strengthen the competitiveness of the region on the international markets. In other words, regional collective self-reliance is a precondition for participation in international cooperation.

Some may argue that this kind of alternative looks like a utopia. Does peripheral horizontal integration make any sense in an increasingly interdependent world? True, development in the Arctic is heavily dependent on external factors and it requires technology as well as capital from the centre. There is a scarcity of capital, and only a few local, advanced enterprises are potential competitors on international markets. It is also true that the national borders in the Nordkalott have become increasingly closed during the last 150 years.

From another point of view, the internationalization of production and the general tendency towards globalization provide a new space for local and regional production and new identities. We know that in the future, consumption will be more individual, less influenced by the "mass society." This means that some kinds of local production will find markets. It is also reasonable to suppose that, in the globalizing world, people will gradually need points of identification well below the level of the nation-state. Specific features, cultural characteristics and work with solving the particular problems of the Arctic region might, successively, develop a regional identity – unity in diversity, rather than in conformity. And when this kind of an identity becomes reality it will further support regional economic activities.

In the Nordkalott, borders have been a reality for only a short historical period. Therefore it is possible to imagine that the role of the borders can also decrease. In general, there seems to be a clear tendency towards such a regionalization which reaches across the existing national borders (Alger, 1988: 141–44). In the Nordkalott, the doors are open for a new kind of regional cooperation. In Helsinki President Gorbachev invited the Nordic Council to establish direct contacts with the Baltic republics, the Soviet Carelia and Kola regions, and even if this takes some time, the cooperative potential is considerable.

Energy production is the sector that offers the largest realistic basis for regional collective self-reliance and for participation in the international economy. As pointed out above, Arctic energy resources could well play a significant role beyond the year 2000. Therefore the very same resources are of crucial importance for the Nordkalott and the whole Arctic region and not only for the nation-states with sovereign rights to the resources inside their national boundaries and the so-called exclusive economic zones.

One way of striking a compromise between national and regional interests is to use a certain percentage of the future oil and gas incomes for development funds. The role of the funds would be to finance local economic and social development in the Nordkalott – funds that are controlled by the local population (Pretes 1989).

Finally, it is time to discuss what the concept of *civil society* means in the Arctic. In this chapter, we have connected it closely with the increasing autonomy and self-management in the dependent northern periphery. It is also important to see the Arctic as a region, as a region for the people who live there. Simultaneously, regarding the Arctic as a region might encourage Arctic nations to self-management, which in its turn further expands the base for increasing autonomy.

Struggling for Arctic autonomy, likewise, could strengthen the centres of political and economic power. If that happens, it will bring to the fore the positive self-reinforcing role of civil society, and that will – successively – limit the traditional power of the nation-states. Altogether, local traditions and knowledge will be better utilized and local human and social needs will be better satisfied in the future than at present. In the longer run, everybody will win – which is certainly not the case with trend development, as we have argued (Hettne, 1982: 172–74).

THE ARCTIC NEEDS GREATER POLITICAL AND ECONOMIC AUTONOMY

What we have done here is to show that the concept of the civil society itself is also a strategy. It embodies a vision of the future in which the northern periphery must – and can actually – adopt an active role in and take responsibility for its own development. It is a local mobilization process – not autarchy or self-isolationism but, rather, a self-reliant mutual reinforcement permitting variety among regions and between centres and peripheries. By mobilizing its own development, the regional political will affect both international development and the development of nation-states.

Now is the time for a conscious and active regional policy. The Arctic oil and gas are still a bit too expensive to be explored properly, still less exploited. Therefore, it is important to find and create activities which support future energy production in the Arctic. It is reasonable to assume that this will become successively more attractive as big corporations as well as states search for alternative energy production areas and a secure supply of energy.

During the next 10–15 years there will be a rush into the North. In the long-term perspective the Gulf War might emphasise the need to utilize the European Arctic oil resources. The EC has an obvious interest in reducing its dependence on the Gulf. The Soviet oil reserves in the Arctic are a potential alternative supply source. Therefore, it will be difficult later on to find an active role for small actors like the Nordkalott region unless they have been in the forefront. The rush has already begun. The Finnish companies of Wärtsil, IVO and Neste together with Soviet, American and Norwegian enterprises are jointly going to utilize a gas field in the Barents Sea. It is estimated that this field alone contains enough natural gas to satisfy Finland's natural gas needs at the present consumption level for 1,000 years.

This theoretical evaluation leads to two different conclusions: *either* the Nordkalott adapts the strategy of trend development, *or* it consciously chooses a goal-oriented development.

In the first case international structures and processes are the subjects of politics. In the latter case a relevant social actor for a policy of northern self-reliance has to be found. Possible candidates are the Inuit Circumpolar Conference (ICC), the Sami council, the Nordkalott Committee. In fact, a close cooperation between all these actors would be ideal. We are convinced that greater political autonomy for the Nordkalott is needed and that the role of local people has to increase in order – everywhere, that is – to create a basis for sustainable peripheral development.

REFERENCES

Alger, Chadwick, Effective Participation in World Society: Some Implications of the Columbus Study, in Michael Banks (ed.), *Conflict in World Society: A New Perspective on International Relations*. Harvester Press, Brighton, 1988.

Andersson, Jan-Otto, Integration – öde eller vilja? *Finsk Tidskrift* 7-8, 1988, pp. 393–407.

Georgiou, George C., Oil Market Instability and New OPEC. *World Policy Journal*, 1987.

Gong, Gerrit W., *The Standard of 'Civilization' in International Society*. Clarendon Press, Oxford, 1984.

Hettne, Björn, *Development Theory and the Third World*. SAREC Report, R2: 1982. Swedish Agency for Research Cooperation with Developing Countries, Helsingborg, 1982.

Hettne, Björn, *Development Theory and the Three Worlds*. Longman, Essex, 1990.

Jalonen, Olli-Pekka, The Strategic Significance of the Arctic, in Kari Möttölä (ed.), *The Arctic Challenge: Nordic and Canadian Approaches to Security and Cooperation in an Emerging International Region*. Westview Press, Boulder & London, 1988.

Jumppanen, Pauli, Environmental Aspects of the Exploitation of Arctic Oil and Gas Reserves, in Lassi Heininen (ed.), *Arctic Environmental Problems*. Occasional Papers, No. 41. Tampere Peace Research Institute, Tampere, 1990.

Käkönen, Jyrki, *Natural Resources and Conflicts in the Changing International System: Three Studies on Imperialism*. Avebury, Aldershot, 1988.

McGowan, Patrick J. & Gottwald, Klaus-Peter, Small States Foreign Policies, in *International Studies Quarterly*, Vol. 19, No. 4, 1975.

Miller, Steven, Oral presentations in The Kuhmo Summer Academy, Finland, 30 July –2 August 1990 and The Conference of the Northern Regions, Anchorage, Alaska, 19–22 September 1990.

OECD Review 1986 Energy Policies and Programmes of IEA Countries, OECD, Paris, 1987.

Polar Regions Atlas. Central Intelligence Agency, Washington, DC, 1979.

Pretes, Michael and Robinson, Michael, Beyond boom and bust: a strategy for sustainable development in the North. *Polar Record,* No. 25, 1989, Great Britain.

Tunander, Ola, *Cold Water Politics: The Maritime Strategy and Geopolitics of the Northern Front.* SAGE Publications, London, 1989.

Vartanov, Raphael, An oral presentation in the Arctic Seminar organized by Tampere Peace Research Institute in Aberdeen, Scotland, June 9–11, 1990.

Wallerstein, Immanuel, *The Capitalist World Economy.* Cambridge University Press, 1979.

Wallerstein, Immanuel, *The Modern World System, Vol. I and Vol. II.* Academic Press, New York and San Francisco, 1974 and 1980.

11

Arctic Cooperation

Clive Archer

THE BACKGROUND[1]

A pioneering social science work on the Arctic was published only twelve years ago, entitled *The Circumpolar North: A Political and Economic Geography of the Arctic and the Sub-Arctic*[2] and, as well as giving a very thorough account of the human geography of the region in the mid-1970s, it indicated the paucity of international relations in the Arctic at that time.

Such international agreements that existed for the area were mainly those covering fisheries in the North Atlantic and North Pacific (such as the North East Atlantic Fisheries Convention – NEAFC; the International Convention for the Northwest Atlantic Fisheries – ICNAF; and the International Convention for the High Seas Fisheries of the North Pacific). There were a few conservation agreements such as the Interim Convention for the Protection of North Pacific Fur Seal of 1957, renewed in 1969 (but which lapsed in 1984), and the work of the Polar Bear Specialists Group within the International Union for the Conservation of Nature and Natural Resources from 1965 which led to the Polar Bear Agreement of 1973.[3]

The first meeting in 1977 of a new international non-governmental organization, the Inuit Circumpolar Conference (ICC), was registered, as was the role of the multinational corporations in the burgeoning development of the Arctic's petroleum resources. There was also an international understanding on air transport in the North Polar region. However, by far the most dominant international interaction seemed to be that between the NATO states – especially the United States, Canada and Greenland – on defence matters, but on this there was, understandably, little cooperation with the Soviet Union.[4]

Indeed, the great strategic significance of the North and the exclusion of western visitors from the whole of the northern area of the Soviet Union was given as one reason for the lack of international scientific collaboration in the Arctic.[5] Despite an honourable history of Polar scientific cooperation – the International Polar Year of 1882–83, the Second International Polar Year of 1932–3 and the International Geophysical Year of 1957–8 with its Polex studies – much of the exchanges of scientific information and researchers was bilateral in the Arctic and there was no northern equivalent of the Scientific Committee on Antarctic Research (SCAR).[6]

The authors of *The Circumpolar North* remarked that 'The Soviet Union has had the fewest political relations and links with other northern countries,' that 'Greenland has not had close links with her North American neighbours; in fact, there has been no contact at all,' and that 'There is a negative aspect in the case of the Canada–United States link.' However, they noted the 'strong links in the Scandinavian north and between Alaska and the Yukon Territory' and the 'very high level of United States investment in the Canadian north.'[7] They expressed the hope that cooperation might spread into other fields such as scientific activity and the prevention of pollution.[8]

Such was the situation in 1978, on the eve of a major increase in the price of petroleum – that was to see a rise in resource exploration activities in the Arctic region – and just before the advent of what became known as the New Cold War, which involved increased hostility between the two superpowers and a greater interest in the military use of the Arctic region. The 1977 meeting of the ICC was an indication of the heightened awareness of the indigenous Arctic populations concerning their rights, which was perhaps most obviously seen in the achievement of Greenlandic Home Rule in May 1979.[9]

Taking into account these changes – and others that have affected the Arctic region – what now is the state of international cooperation there? The rest of this chapter will outline the main areas of international cooperation and the reasons for the development of Arctic collaboration in the past few years.

PRESENT INTERNATIONAL COOPERATION

Since the rather negative report on political links made in *The Circumpolar North* in 1978 (cited above), there has been a growth of contact between the societies and states there. This has necessitated an extension of the means of cooperation, however basic some of these remain. Renewed interaction between the Alaskan and Siberian Yuit was noticeable in the late 1980s after border restrictions across the Bering Straits had been eased by the Soviet Union in 1988. Furthermore, *trade and commerce* in the Arctic region have grown.

The US–Canadian free trade agreement of January 1988 should mean a 'reinforcement of trends towards continental strategies for the development of natural resources' in North America and less restriction on Canadian hydrocarbons being exported to the USA.[10] While Greenlandic trade with Canada has been somewhat erratic during much of the 1980s,[11] the commercial links with Iceland have grown considerably. The value of Icelandic exports to Greenland leapt from $280,000 in 1984 to $6.4 million in 1988, the greatest expansion being in machinery and transport equipment.[12]

Trade and links between people across frontiers in the Nordkalott area – the part of Scandinavia north of or intersected by the Polar Circle – have been encouraged on a multilateral basis since 1977 by the Nordkalott Committee (NKK). This has dealt in particular with labour market questions and

---

regional policy, has improved transverse traffic services, telecommunications and postal services and has coordinated efforts in education, technology, tourism, trade and industry.[13]

Soviet commercial relations with the other Arctic states have been somewhat more problematic. A 'fish for oil' trade grew up between Iceland and the USSR during the 1950s, but by 1988 Icelandic exports to the Soviet Union were a mere 3.5% and imports 3.6%.[14] Finland provides machinery and expertise for the Soviet exploitation of its Arctic areas, both onshore and offshore[15] and the Soviet government has been encouraging joint ventures with Nordic companies to develop the area.

In 1985 the Soviet State Committee on Science and Technology signed an agreement with the Norwegian firm, Boconor, for technical cooperation on offshore operations in the Barents Sea, and in October 1988 a Soviet–Finnish joint venture, representing a further Finnish involvement in 'Kola Projects,' was announced.[16] Further economic cooperation is constrained by Western concern over the commercial conditions for investment, by the COCOM restrictions on western advanced technology sales to the USSR, and by the lack of a Soviet-Norwegian demarcation line for the Barents Sea, which has adversely affected oil exploration there. Despite the disagreement about the division of the Barents Sea, the Soviet Union and Norway have had annual agreements since 1978 that have regulated fishing in an area overlapping some of the disputed boundary area.

As well as the growth in trade and commerce, there has been an extension in the Arctic region of *bilateral agreements and activity* in other functional areas. This Arctic scientific cooperation has become more formalized in the late 1980s. A Protocol on Canadian–Soviet Consultations on the Development of a Programme of Scientific and Technical Cooperation in the Arctic and the North was agreed in 1984, with a programme of projects in four main areas: geoscience and Arctic petroleum, the northern environment, Northern construction, and ethnography and education. An extension of the protocol in 1987 expanded the number of topics covered by the four areas from 18 to 30.[17] The Soviet Union and the USA had a scientific cooperation agreement dating back to détente in the early 1970s, but it was not specific to the Arctic and was adversely affected by the 'New Cold War' of the late 1970s and early 1980s.

In January 1988 a new five-year agreement was signed between the US National Academy of Sciences and the USSR Academy and the two institutions subsequently held a joint seminar on Arctic research. Also a number of bilateral agreements have been signed: the USSR–Norwegian agreement on Arctic science cooperation in January 1988, and the USSR and Finnish Academies of Sciences' protocol of April 1988 being examples.[18] Furthermore, Canada and the United States have a Memorandum of Understanding dating back to June 1970 dealing with research and development in transportation and in 1981 a R&D programme for the Arctic inland and coastal waters was added. A further agreement that included vessel testing of the US Coast Guard's *Polar Sea* was made in 1985.[19]

Bilateral environmental protection agreements for the Arctic have also been expanded in the late 1980s, with the Soviet Union as an active participant. As seen, the northern environment was one of four projects of the 1984 Protocol on Canadian–Soviet Consultations. This joint activity was extended by the April 1988 Canadian–Soviet protocol on atmospheric monitoring and environmental protection signed in April 1988.[20] A wide range of activity relevant to the Arctic was allowed by the 1972 US–USSR Agreement on Cooperation in Environmental Protection and it had a section covering Arctic and Sub-Arctic ecology which was revived in 1988 as a response to Gorbachev's Murmansk speech.[21]

The Soviet Union signed an extensive environmental accord with Norway in 1988, by which a Joint Commission was established to coordinate activities and make recommendations. A similar agreement was signed with Sweden in 1989 and joint environmental protection efforts with Finland in the Kola region were increased.[22]

More generally many *multilateral agreements* have a particular relevance for the Arctic, especially in certain fields of cooperation. Indeed, some two-thirds of the 36 treaties in the field of the environment and conservation that are relevant to the Arctic and to which the Soviet Union is party are multilateral, whereas 10 out of the 18 equivalent treaties on security and arms control are multilateral, and most of those in the fields of industry, commerce, science and culture are bilateral.[23]

The 1982 United Nations Law of the Sea Convention's (UNLOSC's) Arctic 234 deals with ice-covered areas, though its interpretation is controversial. The International Maritime Organization (IMO) has five conventions of relevance for Arctic shipping: that on the Prevention of Pollution from Ships (1973) and the 1978 Protocol (MARPOL); the International Convention for the Safety of Life at Sea (1974) and the 1974 Protocol (SOLAS); the Convention of the International Convention on Standards of Training, Certification, and Watchkeeping for Seafarers (1978); and the International Convention on Maritime Search and Rescue (1979).[24] UNLOSC's Part XII covers the protection and preservation of the marine environment, including regional cooperation in this area.

The 1972 UN Conference on the Human Environment adopted an Action Plan for the Human Environment which has relevance for the Arctic area, and the International Union for the Conservation of Nature and Natural Resources had declared the Arctic Ocean a 'priority sea' in its World Conservation Strategy.[25] Other relevant international environmental agreements include the 1973 Agreement on the Conservation of Polar Bears and the 1985 Montreal Protocol on Substances that Deplete the Ozone Layer. Multilateral scientific activities in the Arctic include the US–Canadian–Norwegian Arctic Ocean Buoy Programme, the Marginal Ice Zone Experiment (MIZEX), and the Programme for International Polar Ocean Research (PIPOR).

Conferences are a multilateral way of increasing international collaboration on a wide range of issues, and are sometimes precursors of international organizations. Intergovernmental conferences such as the Third United Nations Conference on the Law of the Sea (UNCLOS III) have covered topics relevance for the Arctic region,[26] though it has been the non-governmental meetings that, so far, have concentrated on the region itself. Examples are the Tampere Peace Research Institute's (TAPRI's) Arctic workshop, the meetings of the Working Group on Arctic International Relations, and the gatherings of Arctic scientists, such as that held in Leningrad in December 1988.

Conferences have often produced more enduring institutions (e.g., UNCLOS III led to the Law of the Sea Convention) or prepared the way for international organizations, as in the case with the Arctic scientists' meeting leading to the proposed International Arctic Science Committee (IASC).

The Arctic states have common membership of a number of *international organizations*. Though in most cases the Arctic is of marginal interest to their main activities, there are now developing a number of organizations with a strong Arctic dimension.

Of the Arctic-related *international non-governmental organization* (INGOs), the Inuit Circumpolar Conference (ICC) is the most outstanding.[27] It is a forum for Inuit opinion and as a political instrument for Inuit representatives in their various campaigns – against the Arctic Pilot Project, for an Arctic nuclear-free zone and for greater control over the resources of the Arctic. The Soviet Inuit were finally associated with the ICC in 1989 and this should increase its importance as, more than perhaps any other INGO, it will have access to at least the leadership of the Soviet Inuit – and maybe a wider audience – without many of the official constraints exercised previously.

Other relevant INGOs include the Arctic Ocean Sciences Board which has members from Canada, Denmark, the Federal Republic of Germany, Finland, Iceland, Norway, Sweden, the United Kingdom and the United States; the International Permafrost Association with its membership drawn from 17 states; the looser-formed Polar Science Network of the European Science Foundation; and the International Union for Circumpolar Health, founded by the American Society for Circumpolar Health, the Canadian Society for Circumpolar Health, the Nordic Council for Arctic Medical Research and the Siberian Branch of the USSR Academy of Medical Sciences.[28]

The emergence of the International Arctic Science Committee is a major development in Arctic international organizations. It is not the first purely transarctic organization; ICC has that claim. Nor is it the first functional organization dealing with Arctic matters – the Polar Sub-Programme of the World Climate Research Programme and the Arctic Ocean Science Board have prior claims here. But it is a scientific institution with both non-governmental and quasi-governmental representatives.

The original proposal for IASC came from a working group established by a meeting of scientists from the eight Arctic states, held in Oslo on February 13, 1987. The recommendation was for the establishment of a 'non-governmental scientific committee' to promote international cooperation in scientific research in Arctic areas; and for an Intergovernmental Forum on Arctic Science Issues made up of the representatives of Arctic nations meeting to discuss and make liaisons on Arctic science matters.[29] Later on, the idea of an Intergovernmental Forum was dropped and governmental interest in IASC became stronger.

The establishment of an International Arctic Science Committee took longer than expected as a result of governmental involvement in the negotiations.[30] One controversial issue has been the standing in the organization of representatives from non-Arctic states that nevertheless have strong Arctic research programmes.

In the RRT report, the importance of the contribution of non-Arctic countries was recognized:

• non-Arctic countries that have a tradition or expertise in polar science ..... may be in a better position to play a leading role in research with specific national or political Arctic responsibilities.[31]

Consequent to this, the report recommended that the organizational structure of IASC should involve

• a Board responsible for the day-to-day running of the institution and consisting of five to seven persons, of whom more than half should come from the Arctic states;
• a Council that would be 'the main operating and decision-making body of the Committee, responsible for its programme, policies, formation of Working Groups, etc.' and which would consist of a 'national representative of each country adhering to the Committee by virtue of active involvement in research in Arctic regions' plus the chairmen of the working groups;

• Working Groups of leading researchers in specialist areas identified by the Council as important for Arctic research, and nominated by national bodies for their expertise;

• a Secretariat, based in an Arctic country, to carry out administrative duties.[32]

It later became clear that the cost of Soviet acceptance of all the Nordic states being considered as Arctic states was a more exclusivist institutional framework whereby the representatives of the scientific organizations of only Arctic states (the five Nordic countries, the USSR, the USA and Canada) would be on the main decision-making Council.

This would deny decision-making powers to the non-Arctic states that may, however, have a greater interest and capability in Arctic science than some of the 'Arctic' countries. This was resisted by such non-Arctic states as the United Kingdom, France, the Netherlands and the Federal Republic of Germany, and it seemed to be one of the reasons for the continuation of the work of the more independent, more open, Arctic non-governmental scientific forum, the Commité Arctique International.[33]

The Founding Articles of IASC, signed at Resolute Bay, Canada, on August 28, 1990, represented a compromise. IASC is composed of the Council, the Regional Board, Working Groups, the Arctic Science Conference and a Secretariat.

The Council aims, *inter alia*, to develop policies and guidelines for co-operative scientific research concerned with the Arctic, and its membership consists of the representatives of the scientific organizations of the eight Arctic states and those of any other countries 'during such time as those countries are engaged in significant Arctic research' (Founding Articles, C2 ii).

The Regional Board is to 'consider general regional problems and other questions which affect the common interests of the Arctic countries' (*ibid.*, D1) and consists of the representatives of the relevant national organizations of the eight Arctic countries. The Arctic Science Conference is a review by and an advisory meeting of the scientific community involved in Arctic research (*ibid.*, F2), and the Secretariat, headed by an Executive Secretary, is based in Oslo. At the first regular meeting of the IASC, the United Kingdom,

---

Germany, Japan, France, the Netherlands and Poland were accepted as full members.

Although the RRT report's idea of an Intergovernmental Forum on Arctic Science Issues was never taken up by the relevant governments, there has been a parallel development in the field of environmental cooperation. At the end of 1988 the Finnish government contacted the other governments of the 'Arctic Eight' to garner support for a framework treaty on the Arctic environment which could later have more specific protocols attached to it. As a result, governmental representatives of the Eight attended a Consultative Meeting on the Protection of the Arctic Environment in Rovaniemi, Finland, in September 1989, the first such intergovernmental gathering of the Arctic states.

Working groups were established, one reviewing the state of the environment in the Arctic and the need for further action, another to consider existing legal instruments for the protection of the Arctic environment and the organization of future cooperation. The threats to the fragile and vulnerable Arctic environment mean that urgent action and special measures were needed to protect it, and none of the delegates thought the existing system of legal measures adequate. Further work on particular issues of concern (e.g., organic contaminants, acids, oil) is being spearheaded by a lead country for each topic drawn from the eight Arctic states with the exception of Iceland and the United States.

A Consultative Meeting in Spring 1990 in Canada, followed by one in Kiruna in January 1991, and a planned Ministerial Conference – to be held in Finland later in 1991 – on the protection of the Arctic Environment represent a continued institutionalization of this process.[34] In a speech in Finland in October 1989, President Gorbachev backed the Finnish initiative and welcomed the Arctic Environmental Conference, hoping it would discuss a common environmental programme, cooperation to develop more nature-protecting technology and the standardization of the norms and procedures of controlling the state of the environment.[35] If further intergovernmental meetings of the 'Arctic Eight' embark on this ambitious programme, this could lead to the *de facto* creation of an Intergovernmental Forum on Arctic

Environmental Issues. Low-level, functional cooperation could also usefully feed off some of the scientific work of IASC.

Suggestions for the continued institutional development of Arctic cooperation have been forthcoming from a number of academic sources. It has been proposed that an international Arctic organization be set up as a focal point for states' policies 'in the Arctic, a body for a long-term planning of the development of resources, use of vast expanses and preservation of the fragile ecosystem of the region.' [36]

A Canadian–Soviet meeting advanced the idea of a Conference on Arctic Security and Cooperation that would cover a wide range of issues from international security, indigenous peoples' affairs, scientific cooperation, economic and cultural development, constitutional development and environmental studies.[37] Others have suggested an Arctic Convention dealing with navigation and environmental issues[38] and an Arctic Resources Council that would help with 'conflict resolution' in this area.[39]

THE CONDITIONS FOR INTERNATIONAL COOPERATION

The above account of the state of international cooperation in the Arctic demonstrates a number of points. First, the level of international cooperation has increased, even since 1978. This has been especially true in the area of scientific study and environmental protection where multilateral contact has been established. Secondly, international cooperation has become increasingly institutionalized with a variety of activities such as international non-governmental organizations (e.g., The Nordic Sami Council, ICC), regular conferences (for example, those of Arctic scientists), and inter-governmental forums like the Consultative Meeting on the Protection of the Arctic Environment.

Thirdly, despite these developments, the level of activity – commercial, governmental, personal – across the Arctic international frontiers is small and

---

localized compared to the north–south transactions within the Arctic states. Many of the lines of transport – and of trade and commerce – run from the Arctic areas to their metropolitan hinterlands south of the Arctic Circle.

Nevertheless, Arctic international cooperation has grown over the past decade. Why has this been the case? The answer lies partly in the increased opportunities for cooperation and the greater willingness of those active in the Arctic scene to participate in cooperative activities.

Opportunities have been opened up by three sets of events: petroleum extraction in the Arctic region, changes in the Law of the Sea, and strategic developments in the area.

With the discovery of the Samotlor giant oil field in West Siberia in 1965 and that of the Prudhoe Bay field in North Slope, Alaska, in 1968, it became clear that the Arctic could become a major source of *petroleum production*. Today, Prudhoe Bay represents the largest United States' field, and Siberian oil and gas provides the main share of the Soviet Union's energy resources. Added to this have been the move north of the Arctic Circle of Norwegian offshore exploration and the discovery of less commercial reserves in the Canadian Beaufort Sea region and along Greenland's east coast.

In theory such an extension of economic activity to the north should provide opportunities for international cooperation. There has certainly been plenty of activity by the transnational corporations that permeate national frontiers.[40] Beyond this, there is little evidence that the discovery of petroleum reserves in the Arctic has led to greater international cooperation to exploit these resources. Indeed, attempts to build an Alaskan Highway Natural Gas Transportation pipeline system that might have served Canadian needs as well, and the Arctic Pilot Project (APP) have not been judged commercial.[41] In the case of the APP, the proponents had to face the opposition of the Greenlandic Home Rule Government and the ICC.

The one major case where there has been international cooperation over the exploitation of the petrocarbon resources of the Arctic is that of the development of the Urengoi gas field, whereby six West European countries were to receive natural gas from that Siberian field through pipelines constructed with West European technology.[42]

Perhaps the two areas where the opening up of the Arctic oil and gas fields has led to increased international cooperation are those of scientific research and environmental protection. While petroleum exploration has not been *the* major impetus for either activity, it has provided a stimulus. Drilling and exploitation have required geological and other scientific studies as well as environmental impact estimates and schemes for pollution protection, much of which has been undertaken by the major oil multinationals.[43]

Oil and gas activity can be seen as being responsible for the pollution control agreements between Canada and the United States of 1982 and of Canada and Denmark of 1983, for research cooperation between Canada and the United States in 1985, and for important elements in the Canadian–Soviet Union, United States–Soviet Union agreements on scientific and technical cooperation,[44] as well as in similar Norwegian–Soviet collaboration.[45]

The changes in the *Law of the Sea* codified in the Law of the Sea Convention of 1982[46] and presaged by the declaration by the Arctic littoral states of Exclusive Fisheries Zones (EFZ) or Exclusive Economic Zones (EEZ) from 1977 onwards, has provided a new set of opportunities for cooperation in the region. It also undermined some existing cooperative efforts, such as NEAFC, and created the possibility of new conflicts, especially over the delineation of maritime zones.

Article 56 of the Law of the Sea Convention allows coastal states to claim a 200-mile Exclusive Economic Zone within which it has 'sovereign rights for the purpose of exploring and exploiting, conserving and managing' the natural resources of the seabed and subsoil and the superjacent waters. Of the Arctic states, Iceland, Norway, the USSR and the USA have claimed a 200-mile EEZ, and Canada and Denmark (for Greenland) have claimed a 200-mile EFZ. This has a number of consequences.

First, delineation disputes have arisen where bordering zones have overlapped. Secondly, offshore resources, including fish, have been taken under the jurisdiction of national governments, meaning that other governments wishing to obtain access to those resources for their own citizens will have to come to an agreement with the relevant coastal state authorities. Thirdly, the Law of the Sea Convention requires the coastal state to give its consent for sea and seabed research in the waters of its EEZ (and to some extent its continental shelf beyond). This has even further narrowed down those areas in the Arctic where scientific research may be conducted without the permission of the Arctic states' governments.

As a consequence of the development of the Law of the Sea, delimitation disputes *have* arisen in the Arctic.[47] As mentioned above, a number of these have been solved by international agreement, though in others a solution is still outstanding. Of the latter category, perhaps the most serious disputes are those between Norway and the Soviet Union over the Barents Sea, the question of the status of the waters surrounding Svalbard,[48] and Canada's claim to include its Arctic islands in its internal waters.[49]

In a sense, the dividing up of the waters within the Arctic Circle has placed a premium on cooperation between states, as failure to agree can not only lead to possible conflict reminiscent of the 'Cod Wars' between Iceland and the United Kingdom, but can also prevent the utilization of resources in disputed zones. It is noticeable that even when the Soviets and the Norwegians failed to agree on the division of the Barents Sea, both sides were prepared to reach a series of temporary agreements concerning fishing in part of the disputed zone.[50]

The third development that has shifted the balance with regard to opportunities for international cooperation in the Arctic is that in *international strategy*. Since the mid-1970s, there have been a number of important changes in the security configuration of the region.

First, during the latter part of the 1970s until well into the 1990s, the Soviet Union's Northern Fleet expanded and became active out in the North Atlantic. It seems that the main strategic missions of this Fleet had more to do with the overall Soviet–United States balance than with any security aims in the Arctic area as such, or indeed with the Nordic region.[51] However, it did make one of the main approaches to the Arctic Ocean – the Greenland–Iceland–Norway Gap – more strategically important.

Furthermore, the United States' Maritime Strategy, which became prominent in the Reagan presidency, was partly a response to the feeling that the Soviet navy was placing North Norway, as well as a large part of Northern Waters, within its theatre of operations. The emphasis in the Maritime Strategy was to place US Navy forces forward in order to match the power of the Soviet maritime presence and to put at risk its home ports in the Kola peninsula.[52]

As a result of improvements in missile technology, it is now no longer necessary for Soviet strategic submarines to deploy off the coast of the United States in order to target major American cities and installations. Increasingly since 1982, the latest Soviet strategic submarines – *Delta IV* and *Typhoon* – have delivery systems that can reach the mainland United States while sitting off the northern coast of the Soviet Union.[53]

This has lessened the need for Soviet maritime forces to push out into the North Atlantic and, indeed, there are signs that the number of Soviet naval exercises there dropped during the latter half of the 1980s.[54] It has also meant that the Soviets have placed their strategic submarines in 'bastions' in the Barents Sea and Arctic Ocean, and possibly in the Greenland and Kara Seas, where they might be comparatively safe from Western anti-submarine activity.[55]

A final development has been the increase over the past decade in the number of cruise missiles at sea in Northern Waters, both in surface ships and in submarines.[56] These weapons pose a particular threat as they blur both the distinction between strategic and tactical missiles and that between conventional and nuclear weapons.

All these changes have given a new strategic significance to the Arctic region, including the Arctic Ocean.[57]

The above three sets of changes have often been moulded by technological advance. Improvements in ice-breaking capabilities and in drilling and working in northern regions have allowed oil and gas exploration to move north of the Arctic Circle. Technological change has also made possible sub-sea drilling to much greater depths than before and encouraged the extension out of coastal jurisdiction as seen in the Law of the Sea Convention. This was also made necessary by greater efficiency in fishing methods that began to strip the High Seas areas off fishing nations (such as Iceland) of their stocks. Finally, the improvement in targeting and missile technology and, to a certain extent, submarine design has led to a number of the strategic developments mentioned above.

RESPONSE TO THE NEW OPPORTUNITIES

Clearly, as far as Arctic international cooperation is concerned, the changes have not always been positive. For example, the increase in the number of sea-launched cruise missiles (SLCMs) in Northern Waters has offered a greater risk of conflict. Furthermore, the extension of coastal state jurisdiction has led to a number of delimitation disputes. However, there have been a number of positive responses to developments in the Arctic.

By far the most important initiative – because of its source and because it covered a wide range of issues – was taken by President Mikhail Gorbachev in his speech at Murmansk on October 1, 1987. [58]   In this he proposed talks with the West to transform relations in the Arctic and northern areas from the confrontational to the cooperative. He suggested a reduction in military activity, restrictions on the actions of navies and air forces, and a series of confidence-building measures to apply to maritime forces in the region. He reiterated Soviet proposals on a Nordic nuclear weapon free zone. He called for help from western companies in developing the Soviet Arctic and cooperation in environmental protection.

He wanted an exchange of scientific information and the establishment of a joint Arctic research council. A study of the problems and prospects of indigenous peoples was seen as an area of particular interest. Finally, the question of western access to the Northern Sea Route – from Murmansk along the Siberian coastline of the Arctic Ocean to Vladivostok – was brought up.[59]

The Murmansk Initiative was an example of President Gorbachev applying his *new thinking* in international relations to the Arctic region.[60] The actual contents of the speech are somewhat eclectic and were probably drawn from a number of western as well as Soviet sources. They were doubtless responding to Soviet requirements in the area, not least those brought about by the three major changes outlined above and by the growing concern within the Soviet Union about environmental problems.[61]

In the area of military security, while most of the proposals appeared to serve Soviet strategic interests, there was at least an emphasis on discussion with the West and on flexibility concerning any outcome. Perhaps most important, the *new thinking* has allowed the Soviets to disaggregate the subjects of environmental, scientific and economic cooperation from that of the military relationship.

As had been noted by the authors of the *The Circumpolar North* in the case of scientific cooperation, it had previously been the case that progress on the former had been smothered by the blanket domination of the security factor in Soviet considerations. The Murmansk speech suggested that, in Willy Östreng's terms, Gorbachev was taking a disintegrated view of security which was then reduced to the 'solely military-strategic conditions.' [62]

The willingness of the West to respond to Gorbachev's Murmansk Initiative and its follow-up has varied according to country and functional topic. Generally, the response has been more favourable in the areas of scientific and environmental cooperation where western scientists and environmentalist had already been active. Economic activity has been mixed and, on the whole, there has been a negative reply to the security proposals, especially from the NATO states.[63]

The creating of IASC and the consultative Meeting on the Protection of the Arctic Environment have demonstrated that the Soviet Union and western countries have interests in common in the Arctic. The changes wrought by Mr Gorbachev have allowed Soviet scientists, environmentalists and diplomats to explore a common agenda with their western counterparts. One implication is that this level of cooperation will only continue – and flourish – as long as the Soviet leadership is prepared to disaggregate security and non-strategic issues in the Arctic and as long as general East–West relations are relaxed and no longer feel the chill winds of the Cold War.

★ ★ ★ ★ ★ ★ ★ ★ ★ ★ ★ ★

236

NOTES AND REFERENCES

1. This article is part of a wider study on 'New Approaches in Soviet Arctic Policies and Consequences for the West' supported by the Economic and Social Research Council (UK) under Award No. R00231249. The author is grateful for assistance from David Scrivener, and thanks are due to Major Erkki Nordberg for translating Finnish material.

2. Terence Armstrong, George Rogers & Graham Rowley, *The Circumpolar North. A Political and Economic Geography of the Soviet Arctic and Sub-Arctic*, Methuen, London 1978.

3. *Ibid.*, pp. 241 & 257.

4. *Ibid.*, p. 263.

5. *Ibid.*, p. 268.

6. *Ibid.*, pp. 267–8.

7. *Ibid.*, p. 262.

8. *Ibid.*, pp. 277 & 265.

9. For an account of Greenland's autonomy see Jakob Janussen (ed.), *1. maj 1979. Grønlands hjemmestyre*, Nordiske Landes bogforlag, Copenhagen 1979; and Lars Toft Rasmussen, 'Greenlandic and Danish Attitudes to Canadian Arctic Shipping,' in Franklyn Griffiths (ed.), *Politics of the Northwest Passage*, McGill–Queen's University Press, Kingston & Montreal 1987, pp. 134–35.

10. John Merritt, 'Factors Influencing Canadian Interest in Greater Non-Military Cooperation in the Arctic' in K. Möttölä (ed.), *The Arctic Challenge*, Westview Press, Boulder & London 1988, pp. 286–7.

11. *Ibid.*, p. 299.

12. Nordic Statistical Secretariat (ed.), *Yearbook of Nordic Statistics 1985*, The Nordic Council Secretariat of the Presidium & Nordic Statistical Secretariat, Stockholm and Copenhagen 1986, Table 133; Nordic Statistical Secretariat (ed..), *Yearbook of Nordic Statistics 1989/90*, The Nordic Council Secretariat of the Presidium & Nordic Statistical Secretariat, Stockholm & Copenhagen 1989, Table 129.

13. *Yearbook of Nordic Statistics 1989/90* as note 12, pp. 386–7.

14. *Ibid.*, tables 118 & 119.

15. Richard M. Levine, *Mineral Development on the Kola Peninsula: Present Conditions and Future Prospects*, DNAK, Security Policy Library No. 9, Oslo 1989, pp. 17–18; Arild Moe, 'Soviet Petroleum Activities in the Barents Sea: Potential for Cooperation' in Möttölä, as note 10, pp. 277–8.

16. David Scrivener, *Gorbachev's Murmansk Speech: The Soviet Initiative and Western Response*, DNAK, Oslo 1989, pp. 37 & 43.

17. John Hannigan, 'New Dimensions in Canadian–Soviet Arctic Relations,' *CIIPS Points of View 6*, Canadian Institute for International Peace and Security, Ottawa, November 1988, p. 2.

18. Scrivener, as note 16, p. 56.

19. Cynthia Lamson, 'Arctic shipping, marine safety and environmental protection,' *Marine Policy*, January 1987, Vol. 11, No. 1, p. 7.

20. *UNESCO–MAB Northern Science Network Newsletter* November 1988, pp. 7–8 & 14; Alexei Roginko, 'Arctic Environmental Cooperation: Prospects and Possibilities,' paper for the International Studies Association Convention, London, March 1989, p. 6.

21. Scrivener, as note 16, p. 56.

22. 'Overenskomst Mellom Kongeriket Norges Regjering og Unionen Av Sovjetiske Sosialistiske Republikkers Regjering om Samarbeid På Miljovernområdet,' Oslo, 15 January 1988; 'Agreement between the Swedish and Soviet

governments in the area of environmental protection' (unofficial translation), 28 April 1989; information from Finnish diplomatic sources.

23. Gail Osherenko 'Environmental Cooperation in the Arctic: Will the Soviets Participate?', *International Environmental Affairs*, Vol. 1, 1989, no. 3, pp. 204 & 220.

24. Lamson, as note 19, pp. 4–6.

25. Roginko, as note 20, p. 8.

26. Bo Johnson Theutenberg, *The Evolution of the Law of the Sea: A Study of Resources and Strategy with Special Regard to the Polar Areas*, Tycooly, Dublin 1984.

27. Peter Jull, 'Inuit Politics and the Arctic Seas' in Franklyn Griffiths (editor), *Politics of the Nortwest Passage*, McGill–Queens, Montreal 1987, pp. 46–63.

28. *CAI: Commentary*, Lillestrom, Norway: Commité Arctique International, February 1990, pp. 4 & 19.

29. E. F. Roots, O. Rogne and J. Taagholt, *International Communications and Co-ordination in Arctic Science: A Proposal for Action*, 17 November 1987, mimeo, pp. 16–17. This became known as the RRT report after the initials of its authors.

30. Gail Osherenko, on page 204 in the article cited in note 23, stated that the eight Arctic countries were prepared to sign the agreement establishing IASC in June 1989.

31. As note 29, pp. 5–6.

32. *Ibid.*, pp. 18–19.

33. *CAI: Commentary*, Lillestrom, Norway: Comité Arctique International, May 1989, p. 3.

34. Information from Finnish diplomatic sources.

35. *Kansan Uutiset*, 27 October 1989, pp. 10–11.

36. Artemi Sagiryan, 'The Arctic Coordination of Approaches or a Common Policy,' paper given to Conference on Arctic Cooperation, Ivalo, November 1988, p. 8.

37. David Cox & Tariq Rauf, 'Security Cooperation in the Arctic: A Canadian Response to Gorbachev's Murmansk Initiative,' paper for Canadian–USSR Conference on Canadian–Soviet Arctic Cooperation, Ottawa, October 24, 1989, p. 25.

38. Lamson, as note 19, p. 14.

39. Rudiger Wolfrum, 'The Polar Regions: Legal Aspects' in Lucius Caflisch & Fred Tanner (editors), *The Polar Regions and their Strategic Significance*, Graduate Institute of International Studies, PSIS Special Studies, Geneva 1989, 2/1989, p. 13.

40. Gail Osherenko and Oran Young, *The Age of the Arctic: Hot Conflicts and Cold Realities*, Cambridge University Press, Cambridge 1989, pp. 60–2.

41. David VanderZwaag, 'Canadian Marine Resource Development' in Clive Archer & David Scrivener (editors), *Northern Waters: Security and Resource Issues*, Croom Helm for the Royal Institute of International Affairs, London 1986, p. 127.

42. Stan Woods, *Pipeline Politics*, Centre for Defence Studies, Centrepiece 5, Aberdeen, Spring 1983, pp. 6–13.

43. See Geoffrey Larminie, 'The Impact of Industrial Development on the Arctic Environment' and Richard A. W. Hoos, 'Beaufort Sea Energy Production and Environmental Protection,' both in Louis Rey (editor), *Arctic Energy Resources*, Elsevier, Amsterdam 1983, pp. 299–302 and pp. 303–312.

44. VanderZwaag, as note 41, p. 141.

45. Scrivener, as note 16, p. 44.

46. The United States did not sign the Convention and it has not yet come into force. However, it contains much that is accepted as customary international law.

★ ★ ★ ★ ★ ★ ★ ★ ★ ★ ★ ★

240

---

47. See Patricia Birnie, 'The Law of the Sea and Northern Waters' in Archer & Scrivener, as note 41, pp. 34–7; and Robin Churchill, *Marine Resource Exploitation in the Arctic: A Review of the Jurisdictional Issues*, paper to the International Studies Association Convention, London, March 1989, pp. 11–16.

48. See Robin Churchill, 'The Soviet Union and Jurisdictional Disputes in Northern Waters', and Uwe Jenisch, 'The Maritime Policy and Practices of the Soviet Union after UNCLOS III, with Special Reference to Northern Waters', both in Clive Archer (editor), *The Soviet Union and Northern Waters,* Routledge for the Royal Institute of International Affairs, London 1988, pp. 44–61 and 62–75.

49. VanderZwaag, as note 41, pp. 138–9.

50. David Scrivener, 'Soviet Fisheries and Offshore Exploration in the Barents Sea' in Archer, as note 48, pp. 76–9.

51. Tomas Ries, 'Soviet Military Strategy and Northern Waters' in Archer, as note 48, p. 115.

52. For an exposition of the Maritime Strategy, see Douglas Norton, 'Responding to the Soviet Presence in Northern Waters: an American Naval View' and for a critique see Steven Miller, 'The Maritime Strategy and Geopolitics in the High North,' in Archer, as note 48, pp. 179–204 and 205–238 respectively.

53. Jan Olsen (editor), *Militærbalansen 1989–1990*, IISS/DNAK, Oslo 1990, p. 163.

54. Albert Jonsson, *Iceland, NATO and the Keflavik Base*, Icelandic Commission on Security and International Affairs, Reykjavik, pp. 54–5.

55. Olsen, as note 53, p. 163; and Ries, as note 51, p. 117.

56. Olsen, as note 53, p. 191; David S. Yost, 'Controlling SLCMs: The Most Difficult Question,' *US Naval Institute Proceedings*, September 1989, Vol. 115/9, pp. 60–70.

57. George Lindsey, *Strategic Stability in the Arctic*, Brassey's for the IISS, Adelphi Papers 241, London, Summer 1989.

58. David Scrivener, as note 16.

59. 'Gorbachev – Speech in Murmansk,' Novosti Press Agency Release, 2 October 1987, pp. 5–10.

60. Thomas Trout, 'New Political Thinking and Soviet Strategy: A Perspective on Gorbachev's Arctic Initiatives,' paper to International Studies Association Convention, March 1989.

61. See Scrivener, as note 16, pp. 7–26.

62. Willy Östreng, 'Political–Military Relations among the Ice States. The Conceptual Basis of State Behaviour,' paper to International Conference on Arctic Cooperation, Toronto, 26–28 October 1988, p. 1.

63. Clive Archer, *Western Responses to the Murmansk Initiative*, Centre for Defence Studies, Centrepiece 14, pp. 10–31, Aberdeen, Spring 1989.

12

An Alternative Scenario: Dissolution of Norden

Håkan Wiberg

Håkan Wiberg

NORDEN AS A POSITIVE IDENTITY

Among the possible futures of Norden, one can be summarized as: no future at all. In this chapter we shall take closer look at this scenario.

To start with, what do we mean by "Norden" and "Nordic identity" in this context? There are several components in this identity, both "soft" and "hard" ones. The former have to do with culture and perceptions, the latter with interaction patterns and common interests, in particular economic and strategic ones.

There are some "objective" bases for a positive Nordic identity. We find common culture in terms of religion, language, etc. – and, of course, geographical contiguity. If we look closer at these bases, however, there are several question marks. Norden is only a subregion of the Protestant – or for that matter Lutheran – part of Europe, and is in any case fairly secularized. Among the Scandinavian languages, Swedish, Danish and Norwegian are – with some good will – mutually understandable. Icelanders, however, must learn one of these languages in order to participate, and the same is true for the vast Finnish-speaking majority in Finland, whose language is completely unrelated to the Scandinavian ones, having the relation of mutual understandability with Estonian, and with no other language. As for geographical contiguity, Norway and Sweden are the only Nordic countries whose boundaries are primarily with other Nordic countries.

These "objective" factors are neither necessary, nor in themselves sufficient to forge a common identity. There has to be a uniting ideology to make Norden appear a "natural" unit. This ideology was provided by "Scandinavianism" from the 1830s, initiated by some academic teachers and students to do away with the old Danish–Swedish enmity. Its social basis was then rapidly expanded to wider bourgeois groups and later even further. Its object was also expanded to include at least also Norway and to some extent the Swedish stratum in Finland (which was then under Russian rule). It suffered a considerable weakening when Denmark was attacked by Prussia and Austria in 1863, and Sweden/Norway did not come to its aid, except for individual volunteers. Still, it remained powerful enough to be an important factor in preventing a war when Norway seceded from Sweden in 1905. In the twentieth century, it was enlarged to "Nordism," making independent Finland in its entirety a part of this community. (One result of this is the frequent dilemma in Nordic contexts: whether to speak Scandinavian languages for identity reasons or English for easier communication.)

Both as an ideology and in terms of its relation to political realities, "Nordism" has some similarities to "Europeanism" and "Arabism." It means considerably less that one would be led to believe from some of the exalted speeches – but the cynic writing them off as "rhetorics only" would be equally misleading.

It is less easy to pinpoint the positive content of this Nordic identity. It seems have one component of "peaceful small nations with a warlike and heroic past," one component containing some central Protestant/Puritan values (in their religious or secularized versions), and one component of "welfare societies." It should be underlined that we are speaking about self-images, not necessarily about realities. There is, for example, a strong tendency to overestimate the Nordic specificity (historically and today) of the welfare society – and in addition, all the Nordic countries have lately seen widespread political (right-wing or Manchester liberal) revolts against it.

NORDEN AS A NEGATIVE IDENTITY

That leads us to look at the "negative" side of identity: how the Nordic identity is defined in terms of contrast. Here, we have to look at regional identity, since the national identities are to a large extent results of contrasting against each other. Thus, "Swedishness" was to some extent a product of wars with Denmark, Norwegian identity has been forged under Danish and later Swedish overlords, and Icelandic identity developed as an ideology of emancipation from Denmark.

Finnish identity was largely created in the nineteenth century with a Swedish-speaking upper class – and with Russian rulers. Denmark is culturally closer to Germany than the others, at the same time as its identity contains more of a contrast to Germany. These contrasts bring us over to the regional identity that sets Norden in its entirety off from a threatening environment by a notion of "we are not like them."

One identity element of contrast character is "Norden as a peaceful low tension area," as different from the perpetually warring Central Europeans and the militant superpowers. A different but related element is what we may call an "internationalist ideology," manifested both in strong verbal support for the United Nations (and previously for the League of Nations) and, e.g., in the Nordic countries, spending a higher percentage of GNP on international aid than practically all other Europeans or industrial nations. Still another part of Nordic self-image is that of being particularly democratic in contrast (for long periods) with the closest neighbours.

NORDEN AS AN AREA OF INTERACTION DENSITY

Norden is not built on ideology alone. There is also an encompassing substratum of high interaction of many kinds: trade, tourism, intermarriages,

---

regional NGOs and inter-state organizations, cooperation agreements, etc. In many of these cases, this "high" should be understood in relative rather than absolute terms. For example, all the Nordic countries trade much more outside than inside Norden – but the 20–25 % of their foreign trade that goes to other Nordic countries is much more than what is normal for a group of small neighbours.

There are several factors behind this interaction density. Some of it can be accounted for in terms of sheer geographical contiguity. There is also a clear element of mutual preferences, whether due to language similarity, ideology or long-standing habits; and this element both reinforces and is reinforced by the ideological sides of "Nordicness."

NORDEN AS AN AREA WITH COMMON INTERESTS

There is a tradition of "acting Nordic" *vis-à-vis* the external world. In many international contexts, especially the United Nations system, the five Nordic countries form a consultative caucus. They often act and vote together, whether or not in coalition with some larger group of "like-minded nations." This pattern has its limits, and the correlation between them is far from perfect. For example, the fact that they have different arrangements for national security often makes them vote differently, and the same is true for some economic issues. In fact, all the "grand schemes" have failed, like plans for Nordic defence alliances, customs unions or economic unions. This should serve as a reminder that the communality of interests is far from total. Different countries have traditions for seeing different primary security threats, and their most important extra-Nordic trading partners have traditionally also been somewhat different.

Let us now consider how Norden and "Nordicness" might be threatened. The four points above are also four potentially weak ones. The positive identity may be weakened by the decline of its bases. The negative identity may be weakened by disappearing contrasts or by competing identities. The interaction pattern may be weakened as a result of extra-Nordic changes. The constellation of interests may diverge even more than now. Let us spell out all this in more detail.

THREATS TO THE NORDIC IDENTITY: THE SOFT TYPE

At least some of the basic elements of the *positive* identity are waning. We have already mentioned the secularization – but then, some of the values have been rather easily transformed from religious to secular ones. The factor of geographical contiguity should also be expected to weaken: physical geography remains the same, but transportation and communication technology does not.

The language factor has also been reduced: two generations ago, the minorities with secondary or higher education had German as a common language, and one generation ago, they had English. Their being minorities added another reason for speaking Scandinavian languages at Nordic meetings to the symbolic one: the desire to avoid elitism. Today, many find it easier to understand English than to understand another of the regional languages. This has reduced the anti-elitism ground for speaking Scandinavian languages only.

The *negative* identity is also threatened in several ways. One of them consists in better knowledge of the surrounding world undermining some of the more mythical parts of this identity, and another has to do with change in these environments. When there is a strong process of détente in Continental Europe, or even a transcendence of détente into integration or unification, the element of "Norden as low-tension area" will tend to disappear. In fact, the increasing maritime tensions in the Northern Waters in the 1980s have been reduced less by the recent changes than have the tensions in Central Europe.

It might therefore even be possible for these areas to change places in mental geography.

When democracy becomes a household word in wider and wider parts of Europe, the democracy element in the negative Nordic identity weakens. If there has been anything specifically "Nordic" about democracy, it might be a stronger egalitarian connotation than elsewhere in conceptions of it; if so, that contrast, too, is weakening today.

The Nordic identity may also be threatened by a number of *competing identities*. We have already referred to the four circles intersecting in Norden: the Arctic, the North Atlantic, the Baltic/Hanseatic and the European. Different Nordic countries have always given different relative weight to these, whether because of economic factors or national security considerations in the traditional narrow sense. This is why the "grand schemes" have always failed. In some cases, these circles not only intersect but even divide Norden, at least if we look at it in purely institutional terms, such as NATO (Denmark, Iceland, Norway versus Finland and Sweden) or the EC (Denmark minus the Faroe Islands and Greenland versus all the rest).

At least some of these circles will get increasing saliency in the future. After 1992, different aspects of the European Union will be an example. In this case, one may make two different scenarios of each kind. The division of memberships in Norden may remain the same, in which case one scenario consists in Denmark "drifting away" from Norden, and another one in the survival of Nordic patterns of cooperation, for example as a consequence of successful agreements between the EC and EFTA.

In the other main case, all or most of the Nordic countries may become members of the EC in the 1990s. This may make for better possibilities to extend "the Nordic caucus" from the UN context to the EC. On the other hand, it may also make Norden a periphery in Europe – and in addition a fragmented periphery.

POSSIBLE IDENTITY CONFLICTS

Analytically speaking, there are *three different types of identity conflicts.* Identities may be at least partly incompatible, so that there has to be something of a choice between them. The main Nordic example has – so far – been Denmark in its position between Norden and Europe, and the Danish approach to this has been three-pronged.

One reaction has been *to deny that any conflict exists,* and another one has been to work hard to avoid that it becomes visible. This is usually done by trying to nudge EC and Nordic positions closer to each other when they seem to be on their way to disagreeing in the UN or elsewhere (Denmark seeing itself as a "bridge builder"). The third tactic has been to try to prevent the necessity for choice from ever arising. It is exemplified in the recent Danish hard-selling of EC membership to the other Nordic countries. Another example may be found in Norway sometimes lying closer to the North Atlantic mainstream than do the other Nordic NATO members – and occasionally being seen as being more "hawkish" than befits a member of the Nordic club.

Another type of identity conflict might be described as *"flooding."* This is where the Nordic identity appears as a sub-identity of a wider one, e.g., "European." There may be no direct conflict today; the fear is rather that the wider identity will increase so much in saliency that the "middle level" Nordic identity will become insignificant and disappear. In other parts of Europe, this can be found as a positive identity strategy, for example when the Catalans largely insist on being "directly European," minimizing the Spanish elements of identity in favour of the lower, Catalan, and the higher, European, level.

In all Nordic countries, however, there is a widespread (but unevenly distributed) fear that becoming too European would threaten the national identities. This fear is sometimes also extended to the Nordic level of identity. The North Atlantic and Arctic circles seem to contain less of such a risk of "flooding." It might be there for the Baltic/Hanseatic circle; on the other hand, Norwegian and Icelandic identities would be more likely to be partly incompatible with this possible identity than to become nested in it.

A third case may be termed *"overextension."* In the core EC countries, there is much concern that too much and too rapid extension of the EC would lead to a weakening and dissolution of (its version of) European identity, for which reason the phases of "widening" of EC have alternated with phases of "deepening" of it.

For example, Moslem Turkey will probably remain indigestible, notwithstanding its NATO membership. In the Nordic case, it turned out to be possible to include Finland without suffering from indigestion. The inclusion of the Baltic republics in a "wider Nordic house" might pose a problem here. If it were only a matter of Estonia, which is in several respects closest to Norden, it might get in on the tail of Finland, just as Finland once got in on the tail of Sweden. Latvia might pose more of a problem; and going all the way to Catholic Lithuania would probably be too much.

THREATS TO NORDIC IDENTITY: THE HARD SIDE

So, both the positive and the negative identity elements are threatened, and various kinds of identity conflicts are likely to emerge. But there is more to be said when we now switch the focus to the hard aspects of Nordic identity.

The pattern of dense interaction may be broken up by competition with other interaction. The obvious primary menaces in this respect are the EC and, on the national level, Germany. During the past two decades, the developments of Nordic trade patterns have not contained any great changes. In fact, it is Norway that has drastically increased its EC trade relative to Nordic trade, whereas Denmark has changed very little and differs very little from Sweden.

There are some fears, however, that the transformation of the EC in 1992 might present a radically new situation in this respect: the present heavy flow of Swedish takeovers of Danish enterprises is but one indication of this. In the present context, the main scenario consists in Denmark being "pried off"

Norden – but even in this context, it is possible to write scenarios where the other Nordic countries drift apart from each other with respect to trade or other interaction.

If the present context represents the Scylla, the Charybdis is defined by all the Nordic countries becoming EC members. The most optimistic analysis, presently energetically propagated by the Danish government, concludes that this would improve the possibilities of Nordic unity. The worst case analysis is that it would make all the Nordic countries peripheral, with the normal tendencies of peripheries to drift apart from each other. In addition, the obligations deriving from EC membership would make it more difficult to counteract these tendencies on a Nordic basis, e.g., by banning various forms of preferential treatment.

THREATS TO THE COMMON INTERESTS

Let us finally look at the threats to the "common interests" element of Nordic unity. We have already pointed out that it has normally been too limited to permit any grand Nordic schemes, while, on the other hand, the present web of Nordic cooperation has survived a number of divisions (NATO, the EC, etc.) that would have been more fatal to other groupings of small countries. There are two main types of factors that might threaten continued survival: some versions of European transformation and the maritime/nuclear strategies of the superpowers and other big nations.

In the European case, one scenario consists of a return to a Cold War pattern. This, in itself, would not mean much change: it is precisely in the context of such a pattern that the Nordic countries have long training in formal and informal cooperation.

Another scenario is a fragmented Europe, with three or more power blocs, probably including a division of NATO. This would pose a definite threat to Nordic unity, since Denmark would not have much alternative to following the German choices, whatever they would be. The other Nordic countries would have greater latitude, and probably would not let "Nordic solidarity" make them follow Denmark into such a close dependence on Germany.

The third main scenario, (Western) Europe as a global pole, would also pose some threats to the cohesion of Norden, but this time because it would be more problematic to the non-members of the EC than to Denmark remaining in it.

The second main threat to the "common interests" would have to do with military strategic concerns. If a continued Central European détente or integration is accompanied by an unabated – or even strengthened – maritime and nuclear superpower rivalry in the North, the traditional "Nordic balance" pattern might break down, and each state would have to fend for itself. Norwegian fears of ending up behind the Soviet defence line would then lead to Norway getting even closer than now to NATO – whether like present one, expanded or reduced – around the USA and the UK. Denmark would primarily look to Germany, whether inside or outside NATO. Finland would stick to the primacy of having good neighbour relations with the USSR, or – if or when it dissolves – with Russia.

Sweden, finally, would be internally split, but would in all likelihood coordinate its behaviour more with Norway than with any other Nordic country. This would not mean Sweden going as far as NATO membership or anything resembling it; but the new Swedish behaviour would be likely to arouse Soviet/Russian fears on that account, which would spell the end of (at least the traditional pattern of) informal all-Nordic cooperation in military security matters.

SUMMING UP: WHAT SCENARIOS TELL US WHAT?

We may thus find a number of potential developments that might weaken various factors behind the present Nordic cohesion. If all of them occurred at the same time, then the dissolution of Norden as partially self-contained region would be a fact. But would they?

To some extent this is an empirical question, which would need further investigation – and even then might not be possible to answer. To some extent, however, it is a matter of how the scenarios are constructed. Do several of the undermining factors occur in any single scenario? Where do we find most of them?

The "return to the Cold War" scenario does contain a risk of divergent military strategic interests; but on the other hand, it would also be likely to regenerate the "Nordic balance pattern," and it would make it less likely that Nordic countries entered the EC or that "Norden" was extended to include one or more of the Baltic republics.

All of Norden getting into the EC, and hence the risk of "flooding" has the highest probability in the "transcendence" scenario. That scenario, on the other hand, makes a further extension of Norden unlikely, and would probably reduce the superpower or big power rivalry in the North. It is also likely to generate a Nordic caucus in the EC, economic common interests having been strengthened.

A deepened economic division (between Denmark and the others) appears to be most of a risk in the "fragmented Europe" scenario – but in this scenario there are fewer risks of flooding or overextension. In a situation where English and German would be the first foreign languages in different countries and in different generations, the tradition of Scandinavian languages would probably be strengthened.

It therefore appears likely that Norden will be subjected to at least some undermining factors, with different combinations of them in different scenarios. This is, abstractly speaking, nothing new to Norden, where the "grand schemes" have always lost out in competition with extra-regional factors, even if some combinations might be new.

At the same time, it is unlikely that Norden will experience any maximal combination of undermining factors, since different factors belong to different scenarios. The dissolution of Norden, thus, cannot be excluded, but neither does it appear very probable within the foreseeable future.

13

Experimental Politics After the Cold War
A Peace Zone in Cooperation With the United Nations

Johan Galtung & Jan Øberg

A BIRD'S EYE VIEW OF THE NORDICS IN THE WORLD

Culturally, economically, anthropologically, linguistically, historically, politically and socially, the peoples of the Nordic region ("Norden") have some affinities with one another and a distinctness from the rest of Europe. The collectivity of Danes, Swedes and Norwegians (from ancient times called Skandia, today often called Scandinavia, sometimes including the Finns) together with the Icelanders, Greenlanders, Faraoese, the Sami nation, the Ålanders and so on make up central Norden with about 0.5% of the world's population.

We Nordics must for centuries, perhaps for millennia, have seemed to others somewhat like Spitsbergen today, or Greenland: an *Ultima Thule*, far beyond the last outpost. And yet we were there, and still are. All in all, we shall count nine Nordic nations, eight of which are members of the Nordic Council. The ninth, the Sami – to our great shame – is still not. They come in *four layers or circles:*

– there is a *core pair* of two countries; Denmark and Sweden. They were never dominated by any other Nordic country, and after centuries of warfare, finally settled on the present border with The Sound (Øresund) as the dividing line. Then there are the *six dominated parts*, which we can conveniently divide into two groups:

– *three countries*, Norway, Finland and Iceland which regained autonomy only in this century – from Danish and Swedish, Swedish and Russian, and from Danish control respectively;

– *three island countries*, Åland, the Faeroe Islands and Greenland which are still under Finnish, Danish and Danish control, respectively (and Svalbard under Norwegian control); and, finally:

– there is *a nation*, the Samuit nation, consisting of the Sami and Inuit (Eskimo) nations in Greenland, Norway, Sweden and Finland in the Arctic part of the Nordic countries.

The composition of the Nordic group is complicated, but not very complicated. Today there is no or very little distinction between the first and the second circle; that all (or mostly) belongs to history. Not being autonomous to the point of being a UN member is important, however, and this is the case for the third circle, the island countries. And not having any of the instruments of statehood, as is the case for the Arctic peoples, is very important. There is conflict material here, and there are still struggles to be fought – let us hope with no violence from any side.

On the whole the shape of the Nordic system seems clear. For the foreseeable future it is very hard to imagine any part of the system trying to control any other part or parts. Direct dominance is on the way out in the Nordic world. What is possible is some form of *fusion*, with all or some of them coming more closely together; or some kind of *fission*, in the sense of more decentralization inside countries, with some parts less dependent on the capitals in these relatively solidly-built nation-states. Preserving a basic pattern of equality, there would still be room for some fusion and some fission processes after all nine have attained full membership in the Nordic Council and the Samuit nation has acquired more of those instruments (a flag, a centre, a university, internal autonomy with legislative, executive and judicial powers of their own, less ruled by a "host country" national parliament where they are left without representation or badly represented).

Leaving that aside, our focus is on the possible fusion and fission processes, in the light of the historical and global contexts. But first some more words about intra-Nordic history.

There is the Golden Age, in a certain sense – the Viking Era, with the West Vikings expanding westwards, to Normandy and the British Isles and, of course, to Iceland and Greenland, even into *Vinland*, presumably America of today, and the East Vikings expanding eastwards, into Russia, Novgorod and onwards. Then they went further south, both of them, and met at Constantinople. They were traders and pirates mainly, with the exception of the Athens of the North, Iceland, which had not only intellectual, artistic and literary traditions, but also a democracy still very highly visible in that remarkable, enduring demonstration of the truth in the *Small Is Beautiful* thesis.

Norway was not able to keep up with this expansionist tradition, possibly because of the weakness of the country's nobility fighting each other, being cut down by kings jealous of their potential power, and being heavily hit by the Black Death. Denmark and Sweden continued the tradition, expanding northwards, westwards, southwards, and eastwards, all over – including into the Nordic system itself. This they divided between the two of them, with Norway passing from one to the other in 1814, ultimately only having the Sami to boss. The others did not engage in such ventures. And, except for the period 1939–45, the whole region has escaped foreign occupation. And *that* requires some explanation.

THE WORLD AS SEEN FROM NORDEN – FOUR CIRCLES

For that purpose, let us now place the nine Nordic countries in the centre of the world, and look at them – in a very Nordic-centric manner – as surrounded by three circles. In other words, the world as seen from the (real) North.

The *first circle* surrounding the Nordic countries comprises North-Western Europe and North America. These are the famous "countries with which it is natural to compare ourselves," the reference group so to speak. Protestant, rich, democratic – the way we see ourselves.

The *second circle* would take in Eastern and Southern Europe. For historical reasons and – probably – also for futurological reasons, it makes sense to include the North African and West Asian countries surrounding the Mediterranean. After all, they have very little in common with the countries south of Sahara and the countries east of Mesopotamia, respectively. Historically it was the deserts and the mountain ranges that were divisive, not the Mediterranean. Catholic and Orthodox, Islamic and Jewish; medium rich and medium democratic – but visible, to us.

The *third circle* would take the rest of the world: South America, the Caribbean, Africa south of the Sahara, Asia east of Mesopotamia, and the Pacific Islands. All these parts are remote. We do not think many people in the Nordic countries feel themselves influenced by the consequences of actions of the third circle. And they would feel threatened if they did, as during the oil crisis of 1973–1974. They prefer to see themselves as causes, for instance through missionary activities and development assistance.

They may feel themselves *moved by* second circle history, and as *part* of first circle history; but neither *part of*, nor moved by, the third circle. Also, the periphery of the second circle is remote, such as North Africa, West Asia and the non-Russian Soviet Union, except for the Baltic states. This is all quite well reflected in standard textbooks in history and geography which would also have a "rest of the world" category. Nordic expansionism, even colonialism, would tend to be soft-pedalled, however – as would the predatory exploits by the Vikings. Only Latin America is Christian, generally the third circle is seen as pagan, poor, undemocratic.

On the one hand, then, there is the *Nordic system* with its internal differentiation and history, important to its inhabitants even if less so to the surrounding world. On the other hand, there is a *world system*, also with its internal differentiation and history, in which the Nordic system is embedded.

Partly because of the modest size of the Nordic system, partly because of its peripheral location – less important as a fact in our age with rapid transportation/communication – the world system has had considerably more impact on the Nordic system than vice versa, with the possible exception of the Viking period.

This statement is not so trivial as it may sound. The underlying assumption is a certain openness to the outside so as to be influenced and shaped, yet not so much that total absorption takes place. The Nordic system still retains a certain specificity – perhaps best observed at one of the peaks in "Nordicity," that little speck in the Atlantic known as the Faeroe Islands. Go there, and return happier, wiser. *Very* small can be *very* beautiful.

To summarize, then:

(1) The general policy of the Nordic countries has been to be accepted by the first circle, North-Western Europe and North America, sharing most of their (changing) views of the second and third circles.
(2) The relation to the first circle has been characterized by:
- *politically–militarily:* seek friendship with the stronger countries, also for protection against second and third circles;
- *economically:* make use of the openings to the second and the third circles provided by the stronger countries in the first circle;
- *culturally:* be up-to-date and "imprintable" with all new ideas.
(3) The relation to the second circle has been characterized by:
politically–militarily: preparedness and defensiveness;
economically: relatively low levels of interaction;
culturally: arrogance.
(4) The relation to the third circle has been characterized by participation in exploitative trade patterns and missionarism, the two currently coming together in "development assistance."
(5) The rise of the second circle against the First after World Wars I and II was seen as a threat and defined as a fight between democracy and totalitarian/ authoritarian fascist or communist dictatorship, not in terms of their struggle for political, economic, or cultural autonomy.

(6) The rise of the third circle against the first after World War II was seen as a threat and increasingly evaluated in (individual) human rights terms, less in terms of struggle for political, economic and cultural autonomy.

(7) The two processes together cannot, in the longer run, fail to reduce the relative position of the first circle in the world system, politically, militarily, economically and culturally. In the military field, the most dramatic example is the Soviet nuclear challenge, still there after INF in 1987 and Europe in 1989 but perhaps turning into a Russian, or Ukrainian challenge? In the economic field, the most dramatic example is the challenge from the outer third circle, the fourth world in the south-eastern corner of the world, Japan and her neighbours. And in the cultural field, the most dramatic challenge is the one from alternative social cosmologies, *Weltanschauungen*, in the Third World, expressing itself, for instance, in 'New Age' ideas. But the first circle still remains stronger.

(8) The long-term consequences of these processes are, of course, difficult to predict, depending on alignment patterns between the three circles and the three types of power. But *die Welt von gestern* is no longer there.

WHAT SHOULD THE NORDIC COUNTRIES DO?

Shall the Nordic countries continue riding *piggy-back*, to use that excellent Americanism, on the imperialist pig? Four piglets, to limit ourselves to the Big Four in the Nordic countries, sitting on the back of the first circle; on top of that big, big one? Riding piggy-back is fine as long as the pig is strong and healthy. But what happens when the pig gets feeble, old and/or unhealthy; and/or there are many other pigs, not to mention other animals?

Off-hand there are three clear possible courses for the piglets to take:

A) Continue riding piggy-back, on the same pig, come what may.

B) Changing to some other new, more promising, pig but continuing riding piggy-back.
C) Jumping off the pig, fending for themselves.

There is no reason why these three courses of action should exclude each other in the real world, if perhaps not in the realm of pigs. Just to the contrary, they can be seen as complementary, only that the argument would then be a less one-sided concentration on (A) to the exclusion of the other two.

Thus, wise Nordic policy would probably be to keep most of the first circle ties, developing more ties to the second and third circles while *at the same time* developing more self-reliance. Self-reliance,[1] not self-sufficiency – the latter means autarchy – and should only be seen as a capacity to be developed, to meet world crises in a rational way. Concretely, this would mean much better economic and cultural ties to the Soviet Union or what it transforms itself into eventually – learning from the Finns – to Eastern Europe and to Southern Europe, the latter probably coming along not too badly. And it means much, much better economic and cultural ties to the whole third circle, both its poor parts in the Third World and its rich parts in the South-east and East Asian Fourth World.

Why all this talk about visions when things actually are functioning not too badly after all? Nobody in his or her right mind can talk about a real crisis in the Nordic countries *anno* 1991 or 1992. Answer: because non-crisis may turn into crisis given the long-term trends of the total world system, not for the world as a whole, but for those who have benefited most from the system now being challenged, the First World, and more particularly the first circle of North-Western Europe and North American countries. And the Nordic nations, all nine of them, lie within that circle. Moreover, visions should be discussed precisely when we are in relatively tranquil waters. When the going gets rough, as during the Gulf Crisis and War, there is no time to discuss visions; and as a consequence relations will be more ritualistic, almost instinctive. Social change is the legitimate child of a crisis into which is injected a vision – but gestation takes time, not to mention the courtship period. Now is the time to start, not when the crisis is there.

To elaborate a vision, we need assumptions beyond the obvious that we want qualitatively better societies, with a higher quality of life and of nature, in general, for the whole Nordic area. The sticky problem is that this should be at the expense of no other part of the world. Often that turns out to be the difference between right-wing and left-wing policies, the latter having more solidarity with countries, people, and nature elsewhere.

Of course we want this. But we also want some kind of security, some guarantee that our state of affairs can last. We want some basis that is relatively invulnerable, like a family building their house strong enough to withstand the shocks, insults from nature – perhaps not the shock that comes once a century but at least those that come once a decade. And this is precisely where self-reliance enters: make your society so that you are able to survive on your own resources in times of crisis, and act in times of non-crisis so that the crises are less like to hit you.

By producing as much as possible locally and nationally, you will become more careful ecologically. And you will become less dependent and less aggressive abroad, since you depend less on foreign raw materials and markets. On the next page is one vision of the Nordic countries as a self-reliant peace zone.

Five important dimensions or qualities are here combined with four social spaces: the whole world; the Nordic countries as a region; nine nations, and the local level – the latter not necessarily always the same as the municipalities of today. Some may have to undergo fission in order to be "local" enough; others may undergo fusion. In some cases borders will have to be redrawn. But these are processes going on all the time, anyhow: nothing particularly new.

There is nothing particularly dramatic contained in this vision, nor is anything very dramatic needed in our view. These are only some proposals about how to relate these four social spaces to each other within the social structure provided *so that the social structure itself can withstand some of the shocks that may be on the cards, also for us.*

RELATIONS

	ECONOMIC	POLITICAL	MILITARY	CULTURAL	ECOLOGICAL
WORLD system	Equitable exchange with all	More positive less negative sanctions	Non-provocative defensive defence	Open to the whole world	Cooperate with UNEP
NORDIC system	Regional self-reliance	A Nordic confederation with parliament, executive, judiciary	A Nordic defence Union, non-aligned	Nordic cultural institutions	Cooperate with EFTA, EC, etc.
NATIONAL system	National self-reliance	More federal structure, direct and indirect democracy	Conventional para-military and non-military defence	Much more surplus to culture	Strong national norms and rules
LOCAL system	Local self-reliance	More local autonomy and direct relations	Strong local basis	Strong local basis	Strong local norms and rules

And there we necessarily touch on the three major forms of power: exchange power in the realm of economics, coercive power in the realm of politics and military affairs, and idea power in the realm of culture.

The questions to be approached in the remainder of this chapter are the following: can we find a concept or at least some rather open-ended framework that carries relevant messages for and to all the twenty boxes in the Table promoting Nordicity without imposing it on others? Can we translate it into practical proposals of immediate relevance for the 1990s in which we live – perhaps the most challenging decade since 1945 because the Cold War between the East and West, within the Occident, has faded away and tremendous new energies *can* be converted for solving problems that will otherwise just grow worse and already threaten the very survival of the biosphere and ourselves?

Or, on a more pessimistic note: can we imagine a concept that will also create a new security should changes in Europe lead to series of new directly as well as structurally violent problems? A concept that is both an opportunity and, if things go wrong, a protective shield – but very different from that of the Cold War era?

TOWARDS A NORDIC PEACE ZONE BY THE YEAR 2010

We start out by arguing that there are very promising features of Nordic politics which must be preserved because they hold potentials not yet utilized. Simultaneously, we are also aware that things cannot continue as previously; the simple fact is that the world around us is rapidly undergoing deep and increasingly unpredictable change. Thus, the challenge is to devise a strategy and some goals which are compatible with change but preserve the best of what there is and which will represent both fission and fusion, both Nordicity and globalism – a strategy that can be pursued with boldness and caution.

After all we have been through, who knows what is "realistic"? Anyone who back in, say 1985, had predicted the changes that we have witnessed in the international system since then would have been met with the argument that that was certainly not "realistic" to expect. We have learnt that international politics is a lot less predictable than many a theoretician and "Realpolitik" practitioner seemed to believe. *Experimental politics* one may call it, i.e., taking initiatives and setting in motion processes the result of which cannot be foreseen in any detail, will be needed. What motivates this type of politics? A recognition that things must change, that new methods are needed to solve new and complex problems and that we all have a duty to take bold – but well-conceived and well-publicized – initiatives to save the Earth and help bring about a humane global order.

Ventures such as this demand *less* intellectual and political courage today than before since the major lesson the historic last five years of East–West relations transmit to us is this: change is necessary, it is possible and, if carried out with vision and determination and without violence, it is itself a confidence-building measure and not a destabilizing factor. Crisis-resolution, i.e., the determined effort to redress local, national or regional wrongs in a number of respects, *can* lead to new opportunities not only for the actor alone but for a much larger community.[2]

WHY A PEACE ZONE?

Because the Cold War is gone, we must turn to the other challenges, and we don't want it to reappear. Humanity is in need of arrangements in which human beings can regain a democratic right to self-determination – a free political space in which the need for developing a more democratic and humane world order, honouring legal as well as ethical norms such as those built into the united Nations Charter, can be explored.

The larger Nordic region is an ideal place because of the rather unique image others hold of it as comparatively democratic, egalitarian, welfare-oriented, with an above-average commitment to assist developing countries, already nuclear weapons free (except for – presumably – short periods), not militarized in a conspicuous sense, not "colonialist" – only ignorant about itself as an overdeveloped society. All this is not meant as self-righteousness, but as an evaluation in relative terms, in the sense that a committed peace policy here would be more credible than if coming out of most other regions.

In security political terms it has been an active region. At the same time we must admit that a number of important issues have not moved very far the last ten or twenty years. Since 1963 a Nordic nuclear weapons free zone has been discussed on an on-and-off basis. But there is still no such zone. A number of parties, some movements and research institutes advocate new defensive defence structures. In quite a few respects the Nordic countries are already fairly defensive. However, a real shift in defence thinking has not taken place. Neither have non-violence and civil resistance, desirable as they undoubtedly are, gained their way to the minds of the general publics of the Nordic countries.

Taking stock of the transformation all around the Nordic region during the last five years, the lack of change in security, development and foreign policy – and thinking – is, indeed, enigmatic.

By way of intuition and some vision, a peace zone in the larger Nordic area – and in the minds of each of us – could serve as a meeting place, a confluence of trends and aspirations of at least some of these rather fundamental and existential issues. It could help us not only to address important security and peace issues within a long-term perspective; it could also help us reshape the ways in which we think about and struggle for a better world.

Therefore, a peace zone should not be seen as just another political item or "point on the peace agenda" but as a framework around all the Nordic countries for the next twenty years or so. It should serve us in opening a new scope and depth and thereby welcoming many new groups into this – indeed historical – process of overall change of our societies.

THE CONCEPT OF A PEACE ZONE

If for a moment we stick to the political discourse a peace zone implies, among other things:

• A geographically defined area in which there exists a community of nations which maintain peace themselves and have no expectations of violent conflict-resolution among themselves.

• They operate within a framework of political, cultural, economic and cultural cooperation.

• They exercise mutual military restraint, including possibly defensive military and civilian defence.

• Agreements with outside powers are important for the viability of the zone, so that it is respected by non-zone participants and, possibly, by world opinion and international organizations, including the UN. The latter is often expected to be instrumental in setting in motion a zone-building process or maintaining or monitoring activities in the zone.

• Further, states within a zone could cooperate on developing a code of conduct and confidence-building measures and on appealing to other states to take similar initiatives. Some of the main elements in such activities could be renunciation of all threats or use of force, reductions of military troops, disengagement zones, non-aggression pacts, no first use of mass-destructive weapons, halting further escalation of arsenals, eliminating parts of or all foreign military presence in the zone, regulating activities of foreign nations within the zone, etc.

• In concrete cases peace zone countries can engage in Third Party activity, as a go-between in conflicts elsewhere, their motives being less questionable.

• A zone implies the land/sea territory, the airspace above, and the ocean floor within a limit. It can be established by one process and agreement procedure or by stepwise initiatives expanding from a nucleus to every larger part of a region.

• As part of peace zone processes and operations one can imagine various types of consultative procedures, a system of regional conferences, monitoring and verification arrangements, appeal procedures in case of violations of the zone provisions, peace-keeping forces and international bodies of observers, etc.

• Zones of peace aim to increase security within the zone but also that of others in the world community. They must, of course, comply with the UN Charter, with international law and with the laws and regulations of the nations participating in it. But within these provisions, it is clearly an aim of peace zone arrangements to introduce innovations and stimulate others to recognize new peace-promoting principles for the international system. The zone is anything but static.

A "zone of peace" is a framework concept. It contains both the "best" of what is already found today and it opens up vistas. Its establishment sets a good example for others to respect or imitate. It can be discussed whether or to what degree it is compatible with present norms and policies. The establishment of such a zone in Norden is a flexible project that can start out with small steps rather than a grand design but which, if pursued with honesty and commitment, ultimately cannot but lead to a rather fundamental change in the policies and status of the Nordic region.

It is a comprehensive design for leaving deterrence and militarization behind, stimulating and helping others do likewise. It is an opting out, but much more so *an entering into a new "human/transnational/ecological security + self-reliant development = peace policy."*

The zone countries acquire their credibility through taking bold steps first themselves instead of appealing to others. They don't do so only for local or national reasons but strike a compromise in the sense of balancing their own interests with global concerns in a manner which is fundamentally new compared with today's – outdated – "national security" paradigm. In several senses this is consistent with the safe strategy of GRIT – Graduated Reciprocation in Tension-Reduction that Charles Osgood has developed in 1962 (see reference 2).

A peace zone is an expression of *integrative common security and peace policy options.* It is ultimately a "grand design," but its advantage is that it can be developed stepwise. It comes from within, not as a consequence of somebody else taking initiatives. And it can never be so constructed that it threatens others. At the same time it resists defensively to be the object or part of the threat systems of others.

The "Common Security" Report of the Palme Commission states about zones of peace that: "Political difficulties that might seem to militate against its realization in the immediate future should not, in our views, inhibit groups of countries from continuing their work towards the establishment of such zones as a long-term objective" (p. 171). Initiatives like the ones we discuss here would take common security a step further – into new fields of application, into an integrated strategy and into the higher international, global level.

Quite important, too, is the fact that it is a concept that *opens up for UN participation and peace-keeping arrangements which could embody truly global thinking.* Robert C. Johansen, University of Notre Dame, Indiana has come forward with the following six proposals to strengthen the United Nations:[3]

1) Establish a permanent UN peace-keeping force, a transnational force individually recruited among volunteers throughout the world who could be sent by the Secretary-General to any tension area at any time without advance Security Council consent.

2) Create an international monitoring and research agency which by means of on-site inspection and advanced surveillance technology could warn and possibly deter surprise attacks. It should also prevent nuclear smuggling, investigate suspicious military events, check on the abuse of intelligence reports and conduct a variety of research programmes.

3) Create the status of UN-protected countries, i.e., smaller countries could be more effectively protected by UN peacekeeping forces than by costly national military means. They could turn their own forces into purely defensive structures and adhere to international limitation. They could lessen their military burdens considerably and devote scarce resources to development, i.e., alleviate the conditions that often lead to domestic or international violence without feeling weakened. It would certainly be much more difficult to invade countries or regions so protected, and UN peace-keeping forces would not contribute to the arms race.

4) Empower the UN Secretary-General to pursue peaceful settlement more actively, not least by means of a corps of unarmed, experienced observer-diplomats working in addition to the armed peace-keeping forces. The UN capacity for mediation at an early stage would be significant.

5) Demilitarize the common heritage and establish a modest degree of global governance over ecologically vital areas such as outer space, Antarctica and the high seas; establish zones of military activity roughly the size of the exclusive economic zones at sea.

6) Convene a conference to strengthen world security institutions to nurture such arrangements, set a global agenda and lay plans for supplementing and eventually replacing national forces with more effective UN peace-keeping arrangements.

A very important step towards realizing a zone of peace will be to call upon the assistance of the United Nations and its member states to monitor the Nordic countries throughout the process. We find it essential that changes in the Nordic area *contributes to a more vigorous United Nations* according to the principles outlined by Johansen and the TFF (see reference 3). For instance, an element of UN protection of the zone would not only help the zone but also contribute to the development of *global security-democratic management*. It would give the world community a stake in the success of the Nordic zone.

Such local and regional arrangements that include a vitalization of UN functions have become more important than ever because of the tragic misuse of the UN Charter, its letter as well as its principles, during the Gulf Crisis and War of 1990-91.

The regions in which such zones have been established or discussed, so far, are among others the Indian Ocean (1971), South East Asia (1971), Central America (1982) and the Pacific. Several of them have come about as instruments of big power politics.

Be that as it may, it is most unfortunate that zones of peace have so far been ignored or declared irrelevant for *developed* countries and regions. In the wake of the Cold War, however, it is exactly here they should now proliferate as instruments for safeguarding people and societies through turbulent change. It must not be overlooked that these changes have not led to the scrapping of nuclear weapons, of NATO, of offensive doctrines everywhere but, rather, seem to lead to the proliferation of nationalist-oriented states and more – not fewer – nuclear powers and national armies.

Having come so far, we want to emphasize as clearly as we possibly can that a peace zone goes far beyond the field of traditional security concerns. Its integrative perspective on security issues and economy, ecology, culture and other aspects of interaction (= human and social development) is its real strength. Peace cannot be achieved by arrangements pertaining only to defence or purely military issues. It is a matter of overall social structures, developments and trends.

The zone, therefore, should include all kinds of activities related to cooperation and confidence-building measures in the civilian sphere – cooperation about solving ecological problems which threaten, in the long run, all zone countries and states adjacent to the zone. It should intensify cooperative projects in economic, technological, raw materials, energy, transport and communications areas, as well as, naturally, give way to intra- and extra-zone exchanges of peoples, ideas, scientific results, etc. – *all of it being so shaped that it has a peace-dimension built into it.*

If, in numerous ways, important transnational issues were dealt with within such a framework we could develop our abilities, through concrete practices instead of rhetoric, to live peacefully and with mutual benefits together. By increasing the number, size and scope of cooperative bonds, serious conflicts and misunderstandings could be prevented from developing or getting out of hand.

We have known it, but not really found ways to practise what we know: that true peace is built through a web of interdependencies, cooperations and trust, not by means of military defence no matter how impressive it looks. It would embody the philosophy that "if you want peace, prepare for peace" and, thereby, be a viable, cohesive strategy towards the abolition not only of various forms of direct violence but also structural violence.

The whole idea would be to a) use civil society's interdependencies, common interests and problem-solving situations pertaining to all as a lever for integrated common security, unity in diversity, peaceful co-existence and global development, and b) to make the steps to violent conflict resolution so high and so numerous that its probability would tend towards zero.[4]

There is no end to it. A peace zone is not the goal, it is the way. Precisely that quality should prevent it from becoming just another point on the agenda of any single movement or government. And that is important because the zone idea is so much richer, more flexible and open-ended. It is a concept through which our sensibilities and empathy with the future can unfold.

THE FIRST STEPS HAVE ALREADY BEEN TAKEN

The work for Zones of Peace will not start by signing treaties or stipulating a fixed "plan of action." It has to slowly gain broad citizen support and mature organically at many levels. It must reach those not already convinced, the elites, yes, but also the majority for whom the issue of peace otherwise comes far down the list of daily priorities.

It is important to keep in mind that a lot is already being done in the Nordic and other regional communities. In order not to waste social energy, it is important to take stock of what is already on the agenda and continue from there.

The Nordic region is so much more than five nation-states and it can be seen from so many perspectives other than those of governments and security elites. Here we offer some:

1. *The concept of Norden could be expanded.* There is, of course, Denmark, Norway, Finland, Iceland and Sweden. But then there is also, as mentioned, Åland, Greenland and the Faroe Islands and Scotland. There is the vast Arctic territories reaching Canada and there is Spitsbergen (Svalbard) and the most southern Bear Island; there are not negligible parts of the Soviet Union, including for instance Murmansk in the North, the St Petersburg region, and the three new states of Lithuania, Estonia and Latvia; and, of course, there is Poland, the northern parts of reunited Germany, the Netherlands and Belgium. And there is Jan Mayen, the Shetland and Orkney Islands, the Hebrides – and several smaller territories.

Within this area we find tremendous variation in economic structure, culture, life styles, development achievements, natural resource base, transport systems, ethnic groups, traditions and history, languages, etc. And we find a considerable variation in terms of threat perception, defence and security – from complete demilitarization at Åland, dog sleighs in Greenland and the absence of national military forces in Iceland to nuclear weapons in the adjacent waters and in Murmansk, from various types of membership of

NATO and (earlier) the Warsaw Pact to neutrality positions. And we find very different links to the European Community.

We are in no way advocating a formal recognition of this expanded Norden as a substitute for the present; the point is to help us keep in mind that there are relevant "circles" of security and development far larger than those brought into the mainstream debates since 1945. The reason? Simply that we all become more interdependent and, as they say, the world is shrinking. As another chapter evidences, the whole Arctic area is of considerable importance for peoples geographically far away from it.

Thus, in a number of respects the larger Nordic region is already a collection or patchwork of more or less independently chosen and practised alternatives. We shall now take a quick glance at the scattered evidence of those features – all of which are compatible with the idea of a zone of peace in the region.

2. *The region itself is already an exception in several respects*. First it is much less militarized than many other regions of the globe. *Iceland* has no national defence but is a member of NATO. Norwegian *Svalbard* is demilitarized by the 1920 Treaty which is signed by many countries. *Greenland* is defended mainly by patrol flights and dog sleighs – while also a host to American conventional and nuclear-linked installations. This gigantic island is particularly relevant for strategic warning, anti-submarine warfare capacity, some nuclear warfare planning and for military research. The *Faeroe Islands*, granted home rule in 1948, hosts NATO facilities but has recently declared themselves a nuclear weapons free zone in peace, crisis and war time. Several other islands and groups have a considerable potential strategic relevance hosting, e.g., air bases, but none are heavily militarized. *Åland* situated between Finland and Sweden was demilitarized in 1850. Its neutrality will be supported and defended by Finland in case of war.

3. *Denmark and Norway share some self-imposed limitations*. They are members of NATO but they do not allow the stationing of foreign military troops in peace time. Neither do they permit nuclear weapons – although transiting and harbour visits by nuclear-equipped vessels permit the United States to pursue its arrogant "neither confirm nor deny" policy. Just as Denmark has obliged herself to keep a low military profile at the Bornholm

---

Island in the Baltic, Finnmark in the very north-east of Norway has limited personnel; no military exercises and no NATO planes should go east of the 24th degree of longitude. No foreign naval vessels are permitted there either.

4. Finland and "Finlandization" is not so bad after all, actually it can serve as inspiration. Finland's neutrality policy is based on the quite sensible premise that "a small country cannot primarily build its security on the power of weapons" as the 1976 defence committee report stated it. Politics in command, in other words. Finland has consistently, from the formation of the "Paasikivi-Kekkonen Line" in 1946, striven to maintain her integrity and stay out of the great power conflict. It recognized the security interests of its big neighbour in the East, having established a trustful relationship in several ways with the purpose pointed to by former president Kekkonen, thus: "The better we can gain the trust of the Soviet Union in Finland as a peaceful neighbour, the better our opportunities for close co-operation with Western countries."

That this policy is now – by 1991 – in crisis because of the disintegration of that Eastern neighbour is not a proof that the principles on which it was based were fundamentally wrong. They will have to be applied to the new circumstances and supplemented with new principles and policies. It is a general mistake made by many commentators, that neutrality is dead because "there are no longer two blocs to be neutral between." The main aim of politics must still be to work for conflict-resolution, war-prevention and stability in peace time and keep out of war should it anyhow occur and involve one's neighbours.

The FCMA Treaty with the Soviet Union is not a military alliance since, according to Article 1 of the treaty, a) Finland's defence operates only on Finnish territory; b) it does not start operating until consultations have been held, i.e. there is no automatic switch to military cooperation; c) it only takes action the moment a threat against Finland and/or the Soviet Union has been recognized (this is, however, a stipulation the interpretation of which is being debated), and d) Finland is first and foremost to carry through its self-defence and call upon Soviet assistance only when her own strength is no longer sufficient.

Finland, furthermore, is obliged to care for her own defence within the neutrality obligation, the FCMA Treaty and the Paris Peace Treaty of 1947 which limits her to having only defensive military means and a certain amount of them. The neutrality policy profile has traditionally been an active one. It is considered desirable and fairly credible with all parties at the same time as the peace policies of the country are respected worldwide. The consistent plea for a Nordic nuclear weapons free zone, the hosting of the CSCE conference leading to the Helsinki Agreement of 1975 – all are examples of this active concern, a voice of common sense and a plea for détente. Finland has found her own security in helping others feeling safe.

Obviously, these are outdated political operationalizations by now. But, again, some of the unorthodox ideas and principles underlying it do hold value today. A flexible re-interpretation of them coupled with a series of new elements and initiatives will be needed. The tendency to throw out the baby with the bath water in turbulent times, as is also the case with "Nordicity" now the Cold War is gone, may not turn out to be the safest strategy. Rather, there is a point in realizing potentials that, for a variety of reasons, could not be realized during that period but which have now become more relevant – and possible.

Interestingly enough and in consequence of such traditions, the Finnish people – according to public opinion surveys – seems to hold rather non-polarized enemy images.[5] In summary, Finland's security philosophy is about defensiveness, limitation, about not developing enemy images, not hosting particularly attractive installations, upholding integrity, self-defence, de-coupling from big power conflicts, recognizing the defence interests of her neighbours, nuclear freedom, "politics-before-arms," neutrality through trust-building with the East and cooperation with the West, balanced trade, no military-industrial complex, domestic support for official policies by citizens whose images of friends and foes are far from polarized, and an active disarmament and foreign policy. And, so far, still comparatively low military expenditures and exports. How all this will fare after the Cold War has disappeared remains to be seen.

The world would be safer if many other countries did somewhat the same as Finland used to do. Each would be more secure and the collectivity would not feel threatened. More countries would seek security through trust-building and cooperation, through acknowledging the legitimate interests of others and through being useful to them. We are well aware that there are specific historic reasons and many others cannot embark on policies similar to Finland's – or they would create instability if they did. But would it be far-fetched to suggest that the combination of pure self-defence with FCMA treaty-like obligations could serve as an inspiration for European NATO allies in their search for more up-to-date relations among themselves and with the United States in the era after the Cold War – provided NATO is to exist in the future, that is?

FURTHER STEPS TOWARD A WORLD ORDER VISION

How could Norden get the process started and sustain it? How to develop a programme without ending up in rigidity? How can we avoid step no. 1 standing alone because step no. 2 is never taken? And who would be the social carriers of a process towards such a zone of peace in the region?

Several of the ideas presented elsewhere in this volume would fit excellently into the framework of a peace zone in this region. For instance, that regions must network more, that emphasis be placed on eco-security cooperation and that self-reliant cultural exchange be intensified.

We offer the following, deliberately short, guiding ideas as an implicit *plädoyer* for innovation of world order initiatives:

1. All interested parties set in motion *a process of elaborate consultations* between all kinds of forces for change, including leading decision-makers, social movements, bureaucrats and experts in security, economy, ecology, culture, etc. It is critically important to refine the general idea and give it more substance than we have managed here.

2. Start up *a process of "interviewing" the world around Norden –* governments, NGOs and experts – about their views on the importance and desirability of Norden (and other regions) taking such an important step in the direction of combining regional and global responsibility. This in itself

would be a confidence-building measure, a criss-crossing dialogue throughout the expanded Norden and with its neighbours.

3. When it has become abundantly clear that there is a serious and widespread positive attitude to such an idea, *a regional conference* with all important parties should be arranged in order to find out under which forms to launch such an initiative from different regions, including the Nordic.

4. This process may end up in *a global statement by "we, the peoples"* to the effect that this is what we wish our governments do and the world around us to respect. This in itself would be an important contribution to regaining a sort of local-global normativity. It could be seen as one among several steps towards an international democracy; a "critical mass" would form through all thinkable initiatives within the larger zone framework.

5. Within the larger Norden, governments would be urged to *declare in front of the UN General Assembly*, in the Nordic Council, the EC and wherever else in the region, their joint or unilateral initiative to take, say, a five-year "break away from history" and experiment *under full international control* – by the UN or otherwise – with changes in the direction of developing, in concrete terms, such a zone. Thus, a new type of *political space* would be provided. The declaration should, of course, offer a vision, but also emphasize that present treaty obligations and binding agreements which the countries and regions are part of remain unchanged.

Such a declaration could be seen as one advocating a "parallel politics" since a peace zone cannot be the only project of Norden. But then, again, neither is it a safe strategy for each when all rush like lemmings to the European Union. A peace zone project, rather, emphasizes the "con" in the word confederation.

6. *Procedures, political and administrative bodies* should be set up to secure control and *complete openness to the world community*. This experimental zone, which is what it would be to begin with, should invite observers, through the United Nations, from the East and West, North and South to monitor constantly and be informed about all initiatives within the region well in advance, so that no-one anywhere could misunderstand what the Nordic countries or their wider region were up to.

This would be peace-*keeping*, but it would also be peace-*building* – something the United Nations has had no chance to engage in before. It would be an important expression of global dialectics, a local-global thinking and action which elevates security to the level it should truly aim at: humanity's. National efforts, in this way, stimulate changes in UN peace-keeping which is not only badly needed, but is also possible now the two big obstacles for UN reforms, decolonization and the Cold War, belong to history. The restructuring of the world organization would support changes in regions and viceversa.

The whole point would be to establish a free space and a free time – a zone and a time – to set the process in motion, closely monitored and supported by world opinion and the United Nations. No-one outside the zone would take advantage of such a situation. No-one would find it meaningful to destroy such a process by military means, occupation or nuclear terror.

Such a multi-layer approach would be facilitated and brought down to earth if two steps were taken at an early stage:

7. Parliaments in this expanded Norden should establish multidisciplinary global policy committees with experts, politicians, public servants and representatives of movements, minorities, refugees, children and youth, charged with raising issues, presenting proposals, holding hearings, etc. related to all the nation's policies and programmes before the UN and its agencies, examining and criticizing performance when necessary. These committees would have a general perspective but would specialize in influencing day-to-day policies, making them compatible with the long-range goals of a peace zone. They should be given the right and the means to conduct *"global impact assessment"* of national decision-making, preferably in cooperation with UN agencies and regional bodies.

There is, for example, no doubt that consumerism in the North must be kept in check in order to enable the global system to go in the direction of sustainable development. If such parliamentary bodies could make their influence felt in policy-making we would have come a long way in *introducing a transnational, UN-related dimension into national decision-making which embodies in itself the norms of a peace zone.*

8. It could also be coupled or combined with *setting up UN "embassies" in member states with transnationally recruited teams* who could monitor security and development policies and actions and report back to regional organizations, UN agencies and central UN bodies on these matters: they could place their views, advice and analyses at the disposal of governmental, non-governmental groups and associations, as well as explain UN decisions to the media. In other words, a sort of "go-between" in each country, with consultative and observer status and no more. To make the presence of the UN and its norm system felt locally – balancing the government's representatives at the UN – is an obvious solution to the problem of the much too low UN profile worldwide.

Impossible? Unrealistic? Utopian? Perhaps, but is it more so than, let's say, present-day policies for national security, planning for limited and unlimited wars to "win" a victory, interventions and fighting in Third World countries, or the view that the present philosophies and policies of economy, ecology and development will carry us safely through the next 45 years in much the same way as they did the last 45 years?

There may be numerous other ways of going about it. We consider it more important to take the first step than knowing where it will end. Since we are all imperfect and experimenting, there should be a margin for mistakes. To reduce the probability of committing serious mistakes in such a process it is important that the regional Experimental Zones for Peace mature through dialogue, networking, cooperation and good will. Means are "ends-in-the-making" as Gandhi stated; a peace zone would be a pioneering instrument in the never-ending process of building peace and inviting others to follow suit in their own manner.

The need for bold initiatives and the chance that we succeed with them is larger than ever since World War II. If not meeting them now, when? If not we in the privileged North, who?

NOTES AND REFERENCES

1. See Galtung, O'Brien, Preiswerk, *Self-Reliance*, London, Bougle-d'Ouverture, 1980, for a discussion of the politics of self-reliance and Galtung, Johan, *There Are Alternatives*, Spokesman, Nottingham 1984, chapter 5 on defensive defence and self-reliance.

2. Charles Osgood's 15 principles for unilateral disarmament initiatives which are strikingly similar to Mikhail Gorbachev's overall strategy in this field, is an illustration, see Osgood, *An Alternative to War and Surrender*, Urbana, University of Illinois Press, 1962 or a summary by Juergen Dedring in his *Recent Advances in Peace and Conflict Research: A Critical Survey*, Sage Publications, London 1976.

3. See *TFF Newsletter*, "Creating a Durable Peace-Keeping System" 1988. For a more comprehensive view, see TFF Statement No. 5, *A United Nations of the Future. What We the Peoples and Governments Can Do to Help the UN Help Ourselves*, TFF 1991.

4. See e.g. Dietrich Fischer, Wilhelm Nolte and Jan Øberg, *"Winning Peace: Strategies and Ethics for a Nuclear-Free World,"* Crane Russak, New York 1989, in which these principles are elaborated.

5. According to opinion surveys by Tampere Peace Research Institute (TAPRI). They identify the threat in the combined games of superpowers, risks of accidental war, developments of new technology and the nuclearization of regional politics. Polls show that the Finns rank their friends in this manner: Sweden, the Soviet Union, Norway, Denmark and the United States. It also has a more balanced trade than the other Nordic countries. The five most important importers of Finnish goods are the Soviet Union, Sweden, England, the FRG and Norway.

14

Redefining Norden

Sverre Lodgaard

NORDEN IN A PERIOD OF TRANSITION

Transitions from wartime to peacetime are the classical periods of opportunity for new policies. In the second half of the 1980s, the *Cold* War ended: then, on its heels came a *hot* war in the Persian Gulf involving – in one way or another – states in most parts of the world. Moving from one world order to another, the scope for international reconstruction, and for new and better approaches to critical problems, is substantial.

So is the scope for things to go wrong. To the extent that the new political map of Europe will be shaped by crises – by the impact of the Gulf War, a more or less turbulent breakdown of the Soviet Union, and desperate pressures for immigration from Eastern Europe or across the Mediterranean – the organizational solutions may turn out to be suboptimal. To the extent that it will be shaped by growing interdependence, unfolding in a more "logical" manner now that the East–West confrontation is gone, reconstruction may be better founded and longer lasting.

In the post-World War II order, the Nordic countries fared relatively well. Assuming a positive relationship between means and ends – as most people tend to do – it therefore will take much to set the Nordic countries on a different course. Successful policies should be continued: until the need for new departures is well demonstrated, it is prudent to opt for more of the same.

Moreover, what the Nordic countries have done, with some success, in the past has been to *fend off adverse trends* relevant to their own area. They have no similar experience in *advancing positive ones*. Therefore, the Nordic countries can be expected to move cautiously, responding to rather than spearheading new developments.

The Nordic countries are not unaffected by the ongoing reorganization of international affairs. In economic matters, the magnetism of the European Community is strongly felt in all of them. There is the risk, however, that the Nordic countries will accommodate with a rush to Community rules and policies and become full members without paying sufficient attention to the *political* dimensions of the reconstruction of Europe. It is a peculiar form of reductionism in all Nordic countries that this reconstruction is being discussed as a matter of economic adaptation to the EC, and little more.

In reality, the questions are much broader. To appreciate fully the range of new options and to exploit the attractive ones, we will need radical departures from the philosophies, concepts and practices of the post-World War II era.

In the following, we shall present the case for *redefining* Norden. First, by arguing that Norden must retrieve and articulate its own identity: if not, Nordic cooperation may vanish and the Nordic countries may find themselves drifting into the new world order. Then, by considering the implications of changes in our surroundings, chiefly as seen and generated by Bonn and Brussels, but also by Moscow and Washington. Finally, the structure of a revised and extended Norden will be examined together with some of its functions.

NORDIC IDENTITY

Identity Lost

In the old system of East–West confrontation, Norden developed a political identity by being different from the rest of the system. Norden defined itself in contrast to the rest of Europe: it represented a modification of the confrontation, essentially by limiting Soviet involvement in Finland and US involvement in Norway. The Nordic countries exercised a balance of unused options, and managed to convince the superpowers that this was in their own interest.[1] The level of confrontation was lower in Northern than in Central Europe, and Norden tried to shield itself from precarious conflict manifestations on the Central Front.

Now, by the 1990s, Norden can no longer define itself in such terms. This is clearly spelled out by almost all the authors in this volume and shall not be elaborated on here.

In Central Europe, major force withdrawals and reductions are taking place, while in the high North military postures have not changed much. In the North, force levels have in fact become relatively *un*favourable. There, the USA and the USSR still confront each other. In a sense, Norden has become divided into Southern Norden – comprising the South of Norway, most of Sweden and Finland, and Denmark, which is increasingly influenced by the new cooperative setting in Central Europe – and Northern Norden which remains of great military significance to the main adversaries of the Cold War.[2]

A New Identity?

If Norden can no longer define itself in terms of *what it is not*, then what *is* the basis of Nordic identity? Politically, Norden will have to find its identity as part of Europe, as an element of the new processes unfolding in this region. More precisely, Norden must find a new identity within the CSCE area, the USA and Canada being important actors in Northern Europe and the high

North for the foreseeable future. However, while North-Western Europe and North America constituted the prime Nordic "reference group" in the old order (see Galtung & Øberg in this volume), in the new system the EC is likely to be allotted that role.

In the old order, Norden was divided between East and West, although less sharply so than in Central Europe. In the new system, there will still be penchants and preferences towards the East and towards the West – Eastern Norden and Western Norden – but these cleavages are likely to be weaker, revolving around a new pole: the EC.

In the post-war period, Nordic identity was based on a number of achievements: among them were prosperity – in terms of overall level and distribution of wealth *(folkhemmet)*, well-functioning democratic systems, a remarkable degree of political stability and porous borders that facilitated exchange and cooperation among the five Nordic countries without central, supranational institutions.

However, in most of these respects, Norden is no longer so outstanding. The so-called Nordic model that won fame in the 1960s is not much of a distinctive feature in the 1990s. For sure, Norden is still doing well: but when trends get mixed, the model value gets blurred and the sources of identity ambiguous.

Unless we can establish our Nordic identity in more fundamental terms than military, political and economic achievements – which tend to come and go – Norden may not remain a viable formation in international affairs for much longer.

Since 1945, the division of Europe and the cosmopolitanism of the North-Western world developed at the expense of Nordic consciousness, putting Nordic identities aside, into irrelevance. Now that the Cold War is gone, it is time to rediscover our roots. In a sense, the peoples and governments of Norden ought to forget what they have learnt and, instead, try to remember what they have forgotten.[3] Nordic intellectuals have been good at discovering the world. Now they should be equally good at rediscovering themselves. If they cannot retrieve a stronger identity, the Nordic countries will become drifting objects rather than goal-oriented subjects in the ongoing transformation of the world.

What Do We Find in Our Annals?

First, we have Edda and Kalevala, pagan myths, evangelical Christianity, a common language, literary traditions transcending Nordic boundaries, common histories of art and drama: either we have this heritage in common or we are familiar with each other's traditions and upbringing. Second, Nordic culture is stained by the geography and climate of the region, and inspired by summer nights, birch trees and Northern Lights.[4] It is characterized by a down-to-earth realism required by long winters and a harsh environment. Third, the gaps between the cultural elites and ordinary people are less pronounced than in countries further south. For instance, the Nordic countries have not had philosophical, religious or intellectual elites who lacked contact with the producing classes, no equivalent to the monks and philosophical enclaves in Central and Southern Europe.[5] Fourth, more than elsewhere, peasants in the Nordic countries have owned their land, and agriculture is not only a matter of food: it is also a matter of population distribution and cultural landscapes (in countries like Australia, Argentina, Canada and the United States it has become industry). Fifth, political unions have come and gone. Wars, too, have come and gone in large numbers – but in this century they have been taken off the agenda and replaced by a Nordic security community. The Nordic countries no longer threaten each other.

What Does It Mean Today?

First, common history, common language, common culture and no threats: no doubt, this amounts to a Nordic identity. Moreover, it translates into a Nordic sociometry: porous borders and a great deal of interaction. A degree of cohesion which means that national and regional identities are not in contradiction to Scandinavian or Nordic ones. The peoples of the Nordic area constitute a community which is enriched and strengthened by the variations as much as by the commonalities: the way people tend to see them, the differences amidst the commonalities become a resource.

Translated to the political level, we may therefore conceive of the Nordic system as a specific setting or arena of political discourse (see Joenniemi in this volume), not only as a formation manifesting common interests. *Getting* rid of international straitjackets, *we are entitled to ask for something more: a discourse aimed at re-establishing the contents and demographic scope of Nordic identity and at crystallizing new directions for the development of modern societies.* But we are, admittedly, increasingly lacking vision – and we also lack strong common action to pave the way for Nordic ideals.

Second, we share humanitarian, egalitarian and democratic values. In Norden, these values have been developed, refined and treasured over long periods of time. In these respects, we have stronger traditions to uphold and convey to the outside world than most others. However, we cannot claim particularly convincing strategies for promoting them. *Generally, political strategy and political architecture – dynamic thinking for the long term – is more of a tradition in Central Europe than in the Nordic area.* Compared with Germany in particular, political thinking in our ultra-stable societies tends to be more static in nature.

Third, the norm of peaceful change is strong in the Nordic area. Not only is Norden a security community: war is no longer an option in the foreign affairs of these countries, except under the UN flag. On the other hand, the same may be said for many other European countries. And like so many others, the Nordic countries are sometimes dragged into big-power military ventures, their non-violent principles notwithstanding. In the Gulf War, the UN stamp on the coalition forces facilitated and legitimized support for a military operation that was, in essence, designed and run by the United States.

Fourth, all this amounts to a call for further research into the question of Nordic identity. We need a better understanding of our cultural codes and a greater awareness of the meaning of being Nordic. We need a broader discussion of the political implications of our Nordic heritage. These are matters that have suffered from neglect for decades. They cannot be retrieved and crystallized overnight. However, in view of the ongoing international reconstruction – of all the things that may happen for good or bad – they have become matters of urgency.

THE EUROPEAN SURROUNDINGS

The EC – Extension and Integration

Some observers of international affairs – those of the Realist school – hold that the end of the Cold War means a return to old-fashioned power politics, with dominant powers competing for influence and pursuing their own national interests. This conception of relations between nations is historically well founded. To some extent, it is still being adhered to.

However, it is inconsistent with the requirements of an increasingly interdependent world. Interestingly enough, few people have been so unable to relate to the radical changes of the past five years as those who fancy themselves realists. Their paradigm and way of thinking fail to explain important processes in world affairs.

Europe will have to come to grips with the question of how to balance or accommodate the interests of a united Germany. This is primarily a task for the EC. One way of achieving it is through adoption of new members. The EC has 12 members and can have 20, and extensions may be orchestrated in some kind of balancing game. However, coalitions are frequently shifting – as indeed Brussels wants them to be. So adopting new members to "balance" Germany may well fall victim to short-lived alignments of the moment.

Another approach would be to push integration towards an economic and political union, amalgamating Germany of 78 million people into a Community of 330 million. This is the French approach, and this is very much the direction things are moving now with Maastricht, December 1991 being one historical station. It is German policy, too: Germany itself wants economic union to be accompanied by a political union comprising foreign affairs in general and security policy in particular. While recognizing the balance-of-power elements in current developments, interdependence and integration weigh more heavily.

Another reason for pursuing the objective of economic and political union is that some sort of union is needed to compete effectively with the United States and Japan. Sluggish economic growth may trigger stiff competition between these powers. At worst, it may lead to protectionism, trade wars, economic chauvinism and political irredentism. We may see more aggressive exploitation of natural resources to gain competitive edges, and less concern for the environment.

It follows that the EC will be keenly interested in gaining access to natural resources in other parts of the world. For unless history changes dramatically to the better, this economic giant will exploit resources and populations in adjoining areas in the East and South and energy resources in the North which will enrich the centres while depriving the peripheries of the possibility of self-reliant development.

It should be noted, however, that *within* the Community, substantial sums are transferred to the poor from among the rich – chiefly to countries in the South. Internally, it is a moot question whether or to what extent the EC is heading for centre growth and periphery degradation. Externally, there is little to suggest that history will not be repeated. However, in the European economic space, the borderlines between internal and external economic behaviour may not be so sharp.

In Community history, the adoption of new members and the deepening of integration have taken place more or less in parallel. At important junctures, package deals have been struck.[6] The two processes are likely to proceed in conjunction in the future. Possibly, institutionalization of relations with third countries may enter such package deals as well. For instance, Germany is interested in institutionalizing relations with the USSR/Russia and with the Central European states, while France and Italy are keen on integration in depth to tie Germany up in joint decision-making. One solution may be a package containing both elements.

There is little doubt that *integration* will proceed both in domain and in depth. The EC will become *the pole* in European affairs: to a large extent, it already is centre-stage. This is the likely prospect. Carried to its theoretical conclusion, the integration processes will eventually make the EC a subject in international law, thereby producing a formidable revision of the state boundaries in Europe. At the other extreme, *fragmentation* may substitute for integration and produce a return to balance-of-power politics, with small-power accommodation to and cooperation with big neighbouring states.

High Politics: The Organization of European Security
In periods of consensus about security policy, functional cooperation in the EC has seen progress, while in periods of discord, it has stagnated.[7] Today, the disagreements on security issues which do exist have not prevented functional integration from proceeding at considerable speed. However, the ongoing transformation of European affairs leaves a great deal of uncertainty about the future organization of European security.

What is to become of NATO, the EC/WEU and the CSCE in the field of security policy? The answers to such questions will shape the future of the new European security order. It certainly seems that the role of NATO is diminishing while the EC/WEU is assuming a greater role. However, the EC/WEU will rely more on economic and political means of security policy and less on military means than the United States does. One reason is that this is the integration sequence, beginning at the economic end and finishing at the military. Another is that today there is no threat to Germany. For this reason and because of economic commitments in the East, Bonn is unlikely to invest very much in military forces. And a third is that growing interdependence makes military means less suitable. As a German politician recently remarked to French officials: "What is the use of "force de frappe" when we have the Bundesbank?"

For the time being, it seems that issues of security policy will be channelled through the WEU. For instance, in April 1991 the EC summit asked the WEU to find the best route for aid to Kurdish refugees. For some time, this may constitute an important example of so-called *variable geometry*: as the Community has become a Community of 12 and may grow larger, simultaneous deepening of integration is taking place in smaller circles, the Bonn–Paris axis being at the core. At some later stage, the idea is to absorb WEU cooperation into the Community organs proper. If not before, the EC will get its military dimension then.

Should the CSCE assume a stronger role in the security field, this may constrain the military dimension of the EC. The functions of the CSCE are bound to change. Its role in economic cooperation is going to disappear as the systemic differences wither. Issues concerning human rights and freedoms will remain on the agenda, but they will be handled increasingly by the

Council of Europe as East European countries are becoming members of this organization. What remains, then, are issues of environmental security and politico-military security. As far as those issues are concerned, the CSCE is likely to become more important.

The Paris summit took the first steps towards institutionalizing the CSCE. But they were modest steps. Among the big powers, the United States was not prepared to give the CSCE any major boost. The USA is concerned about the incorporation of military issues into the EC/WEU, because this will reduce the role of NATO and US influence in Europe. Still, the United States seems to be betting on NATO: this organization has proven an effective instrument of US foreign policy over several decades.

Even if the threat from the East is gone, there are some residues of the Cold War to deal with. The future is uncertain, very much because the future of the Soviet Union is an open question, and so NATO may function as an insurance premium. Its infrastructure can be useful in organizing US participation in extra-European contingencies. Anyway, big organizations can always be counted upon to invent new functions to justify their existence. However, the main value of NATO for the United States may after all be as an instrument of US influence in Europe. In maintaining this instrument, the United States can count on a solid amount of organizational inertia.

Will the United States succeed in keeping a viable NATO? There are two simple reasons for doubting this. First, the NATO of 1991 is clearly overdone, and largely irrelevant. Most of its original rationale is gone. Second, Europe is increasingly going to assert its independence. The EC is the main vehicle for that; the integration process has gained strong momentum; and NATO is standing in its way. Not that European leaders will put it that sharply. For some time to come, NATO will remain a fact, and the USA will use it to stem military cooperation within the EC/WEU. Therefore, putting their house in order, the leading actors of the EC will repeat that NATO enhances stability, while trimming it shorter and shorter.

During the recent transformation of Europe, the United States has accommodated as much as necessary and as little as possible. If EC integration progresses to incorporate issues of military security, this recipe may no longer be sufficient. At some stage, then, the EC/WEU might push

NATO to the sidelines and leave the United States in a weak diplomatic position – not to say outmanoeuvred.

This prospect leads into an argument for the US investing more in the CSCE. The USA is a *bona fide* member of the CSCE, and if the CSCE were to become the main framework of European security, the USA might cooperate with the USSR to constrain the EC. Its economy in a shambles and the union in jeopardy, the Soviet Union is unlikely to re-emerge as a serious rival in the foreseeable future. The EC, on the other hand, is already well on its way to becoming that. Therefore, there is some weight behind the argument that a strong CSCE is needed to prevent the EC from becoming a fully-fledged combination of economic, political and military power.

The United States is the only power to command such a combination. To make the significance of the CSCE more compatible with the weight that the USA would claim for itself in European affairs, a European Security Council comprising the main actors of the region might be established under its auspices.

NORDEN REDEFINED

1. Integration and Decentralization

Europe has seen a breakthrough for the concept of *common security*. Common solutions are increasingly found to common problems. Originally launched to solicit new departures in the field of military security, the concept is equally valid where environmental security is concerned. Common fates in the nuclear age and growing interdependence across the board of functional matters have changed our conceptions of self-interest. This translates into political accommodation, tighter functional cooperation and integration.

In the EC, integration and decentralization are simultaneous developments. *Unification spells differentiation. More opportunities are created for the Europe of the subregions.* There will be more possibilities for overlapping patterns of cooperation, and more possibilities for overlapping identities. More of what is found, for instance, in Catalonia: there, people are first of all Catalonians; then they perceive of themselves as Europeans; and finally they are Spaniards, too. Or in Slovakia: the Slovaks may identify themselves as belonging to Slovakia, Czechoslovakia, Central Europe or Europe. Historically, this is not unique. The Habsburg Empire allowed for much of the same.

A critical factor in this connection has been the transformation of the European security system. Until recently, cooperation in Europe was conditioned by the division of the continent into East and West. Today, European security is increasingly a matter of Europe's relations with the rest of the world. For sure, there has been a revival of ethnic conflicts, nationality clashes and territorial disputes in Eastern Europe and in the Soviet Union. Also, new conflict formations may emerge between prosperous centres and exploited peripheries in the East.

Thus, in the traditional inter-state sense, security cleavages within Europe have been much reduced. This opens up to a Europe of subregions: to new frameworks of cooperation and cultural identity.

In part, these new frameworks of cooperation are state-centred. The so-called "Pentagonale group" is a case in point. Here the governments of Italy, (parts of former) Yugoslavia, Austria, Hungary and Czechoslovakia are working together across old dividing lines. In part, the cooperating units are districts or *Länder*. In Germany, the *Länder* are developing networks of cooperation beyond the German/EC borders. This may be a practical proposition: different *Länder* extend their activities each into their own neighbourhood.

That makes sense in terms of "high politics" as well. Had the networking been left to the Federal authorities, traditional fears of German domination could have been strengthened, leading to countervailing action in countries such as the Soviet Union/Russia and France. The smoothest way "from Bismarck to D-mark" may therefore go via the *Länder*. Other important actors are German banks; *Länder* like Schleswig-Holstein and Baden-Wurttemberg are competing for financial support of subregional development projects.

2. *The Nordic Cultural Community*

In the North, conditions now exist for an extension of the Nordic cultural community. The Estonians can be re-integrated. They may identify themselves as Estonians, as Balts or as a Nordic people. The Latvians might do much the same. Lithuania, however, is less Nordic. The Samuit nation should be more attended to. Also, Karelia still harbours Nordic sentiments, although ethnic Karelians have now become a small minority there (10%).

Other peoples in the north-western parts of the Soviet Union should be invited to revive and express their cultural origins and identities: some of them have had Nordic affiliations, and may want to revive them. The strength of Norden as a cultural community lies not only in its unity, but in its unity in diversity. Therefore, as the imposition of high politics on the area is lifted, a strong case emerges for a comprehensive operational definition of the Nordic cultural community.

3. *Environmental Cooperation in the Baltic Area*

In the field of environmental security, the Baltic area constitutes an eco-geographical region, defined as the Baltic Sea and its drainage area. The environmental problems call on all states around the Baltic Sea for joint action. All seven of the Baltic littoral states have entered into two major treaties: the Convention of 1973 on Fishing and the Conservation of the Living Resources in the Baltic Sea and the Straits; and the Convention of 1974 on the Protection of the Maritime Environment of the Baltic Sea Area. Each of them is implemented more or less adequately by a Commission, the Baltic Sea Fishery Commission situated in Gdansk and the Baltic Marine Environment Protection Commission situated in Helsinki.[8] These arrangements probably provide an adequate formal basis for regional environmental protection. Major investments in environmental protection have now begun to flow eastwards, where the main sources of pollution are located.

★ ★ ★ ★ ★ ★ ★ ★ ★ ★ ★ ★ ★ ★ ★

---

4. Economic Cooperation – Revival of Northern Europe?
Economically, there is no special future for the three non-EC Nordic countries Finland, Sweden and Norway. The main question for them is how to connect with the EC, not how to connect with each other.

More realistically, Norden of the five may launch a concerted effort for economic development in the larger Northern European area. This may involve new and interesting actor constellations: governments, German *Länder* (Schleswig-Holstein, Mecklenburg-Vorpommern), the newly independent Estonia, Latvia, Lithuania, the Russian Republic (the Leningrad area), an autonomous Soviet republic (Karelia), banks (such as the Nordic Investment Bank and Deutsche Bank), firms – and the EC. For cooperation to gather momentum, it would have to be *both* a state and a non-state process.

Also, cooperation would have to be of non-German as well as German origin. Networking solely out of Germany would be neither feasible nor desirable. Today, German economic commitments are simply too big for the D-mark to flow easily northwards, and governments and other actors further north would wish to be in on new cooperative ventures from the beginning. Looking to the North European Club as a forerunner, a North European Council might be established which comprises different categories of actors.[9]

The ideological rationale for such a formation has been aired for some time already. It is called "Hansa-Europe" and is discussed elsewhere in this book. Hansa-Europe may help legitimize new practical arrangements in the larger North European area.[10]

The historical Hansa-Europe was a cooperative network between towns or cities. It does not appeal so much to the *capitals* of Northern Europe since they are closely identified with their states and with the state system. In addition to the cities on the southern shores of the Baltic, it has greater appeal to Bergen, Gothenburg, Malmö, Karlskrona, and Turku. Hansa–Europe had strong Slavic elements as well: Novgorod was part of the Hansa. In similar fashion, a modern version of the Hansa may set out to link Europe and the Russian *hinterland*.

The Hansa notion can provide an *image* of how Norden may be redefined to regain relevance and significance. It invites new variations on an old theme that had been forgotten: it directs the visions and actions of businessmen, political activists, students, culturally and historically interested elites and laypersons in new directions.

5. *The Military Face of Norden: North Versus South*

While the centrifugal forces of the old East–West system have become weaker, the division of Norden into a northern and a southern military arena has become more distinct.[11]

Northern Scandinavia, northern Finland, maritime Iceland and Greenland all bear the imprint of bipolar US–Soviet strategic rivalry. The Southern parts, on the other hand, rather belong to the Central European setting. While the latter is undergoing fundamental reconstruction, the former still retains its essential features such as flight routes for air-breathing forces, patrol areas for strategic missile submarines, early warning facilities for intercontinental ballistic missiles and a complex pattern of strategies and counter-strategies for strategic warfare. Thus, Norden is affected by security arrangements that are increasingly different, and that follow different kinds of logic: in the North the logic of *deterrence by retaliation*, in the South the logic of *common security and deterrence by denial* (non-offensive defence).

In the 1980s, the United States adopted a forward maritime strategy which emphasized massive, offensive SSN and carrier group operations in the North. At the beginning of the 1990s, Soviet as well as US maritime ambitions in northern waters remain high. The Soviet aircraft carrier programme has been extended, and air forces from the former Central Front are being transferred to the Kola peninsula. Nuclear-tipped SLCM deployments continue, and much the same goes for strategic bomber forces and ALCMs.

This underlines the strategic significance of the Scandinavian peninsula, because pre-planned flight routes go through Nordic air space, and because the threat that US bombers pose to Soviet mobile ICBMs may shift Soviet priorities towards SSBNs in northern waters. For both powers, limited access to Continental Europe tends to preserve their military interests in the High North. It remains to be seen how these factors will be influenced by the outcome of the ongoing disintegration of the Soviet Union and the emergence of one or more nuclear powers such as Russia and the Ukraine.

---

6. Political Orientations – East Versus West

Politically, Norden is also divided into an East and a West. *Eastern* Norden - Finland, Sweden and continental Denmark – has a distinct European orientation, towards the EC and, possibly, towards enhanced Baltic cooperation. *Western* Norden – Iceland, Greenland and Norway – turns more in the Atlantic direction. For these actors and communities, cooperation with the United States on security matters has tended to determine their international orientation in general. To Icelanders, Greenlanders and people in Northern Norway, US-related military infrastructure may seem more attractive – economically and in terms of overseas communication – than old colonial relations to Denmark and to the rest of Europe.

The real dividing line between Eastern and Western Norden goes somewhere through the middle of Norway. *Atlanticism* and *Europeanism* are no longer the same thing, no longer compatible in all essential respects: feeling the magnetism of the EC, Norway is facing a tough choice between the two. Either it links up more firmly with the evolving European security system, or it chooses to stay at a distance, exposing itself to bilateral US–Soviet (Russian) relations and relying heavily on the United States for its politico-military security for the future. There is strong popular support in Norway for the security framework now on the decline (NATO), and much scepticism towards the ascendant framework (EC/WEU).

Sweden's intelligence cooperation with the United States, and its military-industrial ties to the same nation, have been very close throughout the post-war period – closer, it seems, than US–German ties. Membership in the EC would make these ties weaker. In a sense, therefore, Swedish neutrality would not be jeopardized as much as some observers have assumed. Neutrality would be affected, but in a different way, depending on relations between Germany/EC and the Soviet Union/Russia, and on whether or not the EC/WEU is to assume important military functions.

Should the CSCE become an increasingly significant framework of European security, the military dimension of the EC/WEU may be limited; this would mean that Sweden's neutrality concerns – to the extent that they exist today – would be much alleviated if not eliminated. The same holds true for Finland. Also in Norway, the EC membership issue would become somewhat less intractable. In Central and Southern Europe, the term *union* has positive connotations of cooperation and common gain. But to many Norwegians, it still has a tinge of subordination, inferiority and undue constraint.

CONCLUSIONS

The farewell to the Cold War spells new frameworks of cooperation and identity: where the Cold War cut Norden short, the net may again be cast wide. Integration spells decentralization and regionalism: Nordic cooperation is getting a new chance that is more in line with cultural propensities and environmental and economic requirements.

In many parts of Europe, people are reviving their identities. The Nordic peoples must retrieve their identity, too. This leads beyond Norden of the five. If Nordic cooperation is extended to encompass not only cultural commonalities, but unity in diversity as well, it may stand to gain much. Identity formation is a fundamental value in itself. New participants can, moreover, make Nordic institutions richer and more vivid.

The Baltic area is an eco-geographical region. The requirements of environmental security therefore extend all around the Baltic Sea. Economically, we may be in for a similar development. Inspired by the economic history of the Hanseatic period, the entire Baltic area as well as the trade routes into Russia could become part of the Nordic meeting ground. "Hansa-Europe" may capture no particularly strong economic rationale under contemporary circumstances. However, cultural, economic and environmental needs *in combination with* historical inspirations combine into a vision for the reconstruction of Northern Europe that may become a powerful incentive for political action.

But we must also ask: *How fragile is such a comprehensive concept of Norden? Which are its limitations?*

Militarily, it is the imprint of US–Soviet strategic rivalry in the High North. The military dynamics there testify to the maintenance of a system of nuclear deterrence. However, this system is no longer a dominant element in big power relations and at the time of writing we don't know what the outcome will be of all the turbulence in the Soviet Union. Be that as it may, it should not be allowed to have the same strong imprint on Northern Norden in the future that it has had.

In a sense, this imprint is as strong or as weak as we *perceive* it to be: tuning themselves to the new political realities, the Nordic countries would be well advised to adopt an attitude of *benign neglect*. This would move the bipolar logic into the background – a much needed policy.

It would reduce the centrifugal forces in the area, alleviate the division between Eastern and Western Norden and facilitate the development of relations to the rest of Europe. Further, it would reduce dependence on the United States and help integrate the Nordic area into the evolving European security system. Confidence and Security Building Measures (CSBMs) and arms control agreements may have similar effects, linking the Nordic countries more closely to the emerging, future European security order.

Politically, one of the main limitations is the course that Western Norden – notably Norway – may choose. In the old political order, the Nordic countries were too differently positioned for foreign affairs to be discussed in the Nordic Council. Nordic cooperation was devoted to intra-Nordic matters among the five member states – security policy being left out.

But in the new Europe, networking and responsibilities of an external nature – towards adjoining areas – may become the main task. In a sense, Nordic cooperation may be turned inside out. Thus, if Sweden, Finland and Norway become members of the EC, the Nordic Council and other Nordic institutions would lose most of their present functions, while Norden of the five would be expected to assume special responsibilities for developments in neighbouring areas to the east and south. *Will political coherence in Norden be strong enough to manage that?*

Norway may choose not to join the EC. Then, Western Norden is likely to remain Atlanticist. Most of Norden would become entirely European, and somewhat more Eastern, whereas the Western rim of Scandinavia would be in the realm of the Atlantic politics, closer to US interests. A strong CSCE supported by the USA could alleviate the Norwegian dilemma and help reduce the cleavage along the Norwegian–Swedish border. However, this would not eliminate the new political demarcation line – and it may, moreover, prove to be wishful thinking.

NOTES AND REFERENCES

1. Ole Wæver, "Region, Sub-region and Proto-Region: Security Dynamics in Northern Europe in the 1980s and 1990s," paper for the annual conference of the British International Studies Association, Newcastle, December 1990.

2. Before World War II, the Nordic countries perceived themselves as distinctly different from the Soviet Union and Germany. Today there is no basis for such a self-perception in relation to Germany, and the Soviet Union represents no stable unit of comparison or contra-distinction.

3. Edvard Hoem, "Nordisk eigenart" in *Nordisk kulturell identitet*, report from a seminar held in Oslo, October 19–21, 1988.

4. Hoem, op. cit.

5. Søren Sørensen, "Norden i historiskt perspektiv," in Nordisk kulturell identitet.

6. In 1987, new members simultaneously with project 1992: establishment of the integrated Inner Market. In 1972, new members simultaneously with a broadening of the integration process to include new issue areas.

7. Martin Sæter, "Funksjonalisme og maktpolitikk i Nord-Europa" in Pertti Joenniemi and Unto Vesa (eds.), *Säkerhetsutveckling i Östersjöområdet*, Tampere Peace Research Institute, Research report No. 35, 1988.

8. Arthur Westing (ed.), *Comprehensive Security for the Baltic: An Environmental Approach*, Sage Publications, London 1989.

9. The North European Club, under the leadership of Minister President Björn Engholm of Schleswig-Holstein and dr. Pehr Gyllenhammar, has discussed economic, educational, communicational and other issues pertaining to the Northern European area.

10. See for instance Pertti Joenniemi, "Regionalization in the Baltic Area. Actors and Policies" in Pertti Joenniemi (ed.), *Cooperation in the Baltic Sea Region. Needs and Prospects*, Tampere Peace Research Institute, Research Report No. 42, 1991.

11. Ola Tunander, "The Two Nordens: The North and the South, or the East and the West," in *Bulletin of Peace Proposals*, No. 1, March 1991.

15

Redefining the Problem
A Sceptical Contribution

Jan Øberg

PEACE DIVIDEND AND THE END OF THE COLD WAR: EXCUSE ME, BUT – ?

There was much talk about a 'peace dividend' after the Cold War came to an end, but this period has witnessed no grand aid schemes to help those in need, whether in the Eastern bloc, the Third World, or in the poorer regions of the Western hemisphere.

The Soviet Union carried through unilateral transarmament, withdrew from Afghanistan, and dissolved its empire and the Warsaw Pact. Major reforms were carried through in the political, economic, social and cultural life of the country from 1985 to 1991. The majority of NATO nations have reduced their military budgets too and most arms export markets are shrinking. This is all true and good.

But we still live with militarism, nuclearism, deterrence strategies, the Star Wars project, tens of thousands of nuclear weapons and interventionism. Every day some ten wars rage worldwide, now also in the heart of Europe, in former Yugoslavia.

There has been no peace dividend and little genuinely 'new thinking' outside the Eastern bloc. What Mikhail Gorbachev got in return for his setting in motion what could well be the largest historical experiment this century was a reunited Germany, a revived West European Union, a new intervention force under NATO, ever-increasing demands from the West as preconditions for economic aid - that never really materialized, the last chance probably being the G-7 meeting in London just a few weeks before the disastrous coup attempt in Moscow.

Instead, the West has celebrated its so-called 'victory' in the Cold War and the demise of socialism. The West chose to interpret socialism or Marxism as 100% bad or false and, as a consequence, capitalism, the market and liberalism as 100% good, following a primitive specious logic: if they failed, we must be a success; if their system was wrong, ours must be right!

Little has changed at a deeper level. Soul-searching is not in a characteristic of winners. Take, for example, the perception of national interests. Some see them best served by independence, others by integration into federal or union formations. Local, national or regional considerations take precedence over urgent global needs and problem-solving. There is a new search for 'identities' – local, national or European. Humankind, however, is not a reference point of those identities, although we all share in the fate of the Earth.

The economic and military concerns of societies and the international community take precedence over ethical, ecological, cultural and non-violent concerns. Concepts of power, economic growth and underlying Westernness have changed only marginally, if at all. We still belong to the First World.

Thus, if we define the problem in terms of culture, mentality and worldview, the Cold War is not over. The West is preserving the code and will be able, within months, to find a substitute for communism and the Warsaw Pact. Cold wars do not derive their energies from having one permanent enemy image only; enemies may come and go. The day before it was Japan or the Chinese 'yellow peril,' yesterday it was the Soviet Union and its allies. Tomorrow?

Among the candidates, old and new, I could imagine Libya (again), Iraq (continued), Cuba (as usual); there could be a civilizational conflict between

Christian capitalist 'enlightenment' on the one hand and Islamic feudal 'fundamentalism' on the other. The contemporary foundation was laid during the oil crisis in the early 1970s, but the historical roots are centuries old and very firm. Furthermore, the focus could be some new state or union of states in the former Soviet Union – for instance a nuclear-based, authoritarian nationalist-fascist/socialist formation in some of the ethnic trouble spots along the borders between the former union and its Muslim neighbours. Yet another could be North Korea or, in the economic field taking a long-term perspective, Japan and the growing economies of the Pacific.

Finally, the Cold War that ended was the one between the East and the West in the European–Atlantic sphere. The Cold War on the Eastern, Oriental wing did not end - the structures created by the Second World War have far from disappeared, although rapid progress is seen in the relations between the two Koreas.

NEW PROJECTS OR OLD PROJECTS?

'Europe' is a strange term. As schoolchildren we learned that Europe stretched from the Arctic to the coasts of Northern Africa. In some sense, Swedes have always belonged to Europe, we would say, but they themselves talk now enthusiastically about becoming 'members of Europe.'

Becoming part – or a member - of 'Europe' has a ring of *the inevitable*. This 'Europe' is the European Community, EC, striving to become a European Union and, consequently, a 'United States of Europe.' The founding fathers had that dream; the fathers of the 'New Europe' today have that vision and the designation was used in, e.g., Chancellor Kohl's CDU Dresden Manifest of December 1991.

In a simple sense it is an old project. For decades the EC suffered from 'Euro-sclerosis,' from a top-heavy bureaucracy occupied mainly with agricultural sector problems and fighting 'mountains' of meat, butter and cereals. Suddenly, it gained attention from all sides, and even proud and independent-minded countries like Sweden switched attitudes overnight and said: It is either Brussels or the Stone Age. What had happened?

Nothing happened within the EC itself. True, a step-by-step process had taken place involving, among other things, direct elections to the European Parliament, the Single European Act and the Maastricht results. But the trigger was, again, Mikhail Gorbachev with his vision of a reformed, Europe-oriented Soviet Union, the 'Sinatra doctrine' for the former allies, his insistence on introducing the market economy and cooperating with all his neighbours from China to Norway – all summed up in the catchy concept of a 'new European home' related to a reformed United Nations. Gorbachev gave Europe, the EC, a new sense of purpose and addressed the regions, too – the Nordic countries in the Murmansk and Helsinki speeches.

In another, deeper, sense it is also an old project.

Neither the empire, nor the union which integrates and harmonizes millions, not to mention the superpower, are fundamentally new ideas. They drive on 'grandeur,' sheer bigness and verticality, on being isomorphic with supranational economic trends of modern capitalism and transmitting a sense of 'modernity' and civilizing zeal.

Their basic philosophy is this: many actors face a lot of somewhat similar problems that they cannot solve individually. They have been created by themselves and by the accumulated consequences of their collective actions over a long period. To solve them we do *not* need a horizontal structure for consultation, coordination and cooperation that aims to preserve diversity and develop unity. What we need is a transnational, vertical, centralized top-down leadership which, in order to function effectively, must imply increasing unity at the cost of diversity. And, of course, it is all possible only if there is an out-group – a 'they' or 'the others' – who can be exploited or marginalized.

Inevitability is evident in this reasoning. *Goal rationality*, to use Max Weber's term, is far more important than value rationality. The important thing is to get all the actors to act in unison – 'speak with one voice' – and to have goals and purposes (among them the building of *the Organization* itself) that guide the activity. Whether there was and remains a correspondence between the goals and the means – let us say, between the problems Europe must solve and the setting up of the European Union – increasingly becomes an irrelevant issue. Rationality becomes, simply, everything that furthers the goal of building a Eurocentric organization and sentiments that embody the optimum satisfaction of as many members as possible.

No doubt, most people today see the EC as the answer. 'If we do not join it fully and unconditionally we will be left behind and only through this type of organization can our large common problems find their solution,' it is argued. A sceptic – and sceptics there must be in this Europe whose identity is historically infused with scepticism, doubt and self-criticism – would probably ask: if the EC is the answer, what was the question? If it is the solution, what are the problems it is likely to solve?

Value rationality would not give priority to organization and form but to content and values. It would ask first: what norms and values are more important to further? What is productive thinking and action with respect to the realization of these values? If Europe had started out there, is it so self-evident that it would have formed the EC as 'the answer'? One does not have to be 'anti-EC' to raise that question, just a curious sociologist, or anthropologist or ethicist.

The EC is an old project. It builds on old European virtues such as modernity (whatever that actually is), materialism, science and technology, a vertical, contract-based dream of imperial peace among 'us' versus 'them,' it builds on faith, knowledge, enlightenment – and on historically unique brutality against and arrogance *vis-à-vis* other cultures. And it builds on dialogue among its own members.

Thus, everybody is inevitably knocking on the door but not to sell something, rather to get something. With exclusivity, power becomes the ability to hand out membership cards to those who meet the criteria set up by the club management.

All this is now questioned by a larger non-European world ascending to power. It is is only partly infused with European values and has a historical memory (some would call it a traumatic memory) of what Europe did – e.g. in India, China, America, the Middle East and Africa during the last 500 to

800 years. In the year 2010, 'Europe' – the present EC – will make up 3% of the world's population and we are already less than 5% of Earth's land.

If there is one European value that will not be self-evident in tomorrow's world, it is that of universalizing European values. The fascination the Japanese seem to have with Mozart, French cuisine, Italian design or German social engineering should not be confused with the universalization of European values. True, many parts of the world – particularly the centres of the peripheries – have adapted, assimilated, been curious about Europe.

But having European values imposed, being bullied because they don't think like Westerners and Christians, because they don't have multi-party systems or respect for human rights the way European-based law and ethics expect them to is no proof of the inevitability of universalization of European values.

The EC is – at least, *also* – a protective shield in an increasingly non-European world, a world in which European virtues such as hard work, economic growth, cultural diversity, principled ethics, devotion to religious and other life-values are increasingly found *outside* Europe. We find them in much richer variation because they have been shaped there through dialogue with Europe, imprinted with European values, but they have retained at least something of their own identity. Europe itself, on the other hand, has not received – or been receptive to – any major non-European cultural dynamics.

Eastern Europe and the Soviet Union also struggle to revive old projects. While we in the West struggle to revive the old *supranational* federation with imperial sentiments, in the East they dissolve the old federations, as in Yugoslavia and the Soviet Union, and assert their *national* identities. And while it is believed in EC Europe – also by many in this book - that the counter stream to EC will be the re-linking of *regions*, the counter stream in the Eastern bloc seems to be re-linking the *nations* to new (con-) federative structures or a new union replacing the Soviet Union while in Eastern Europe people look to the EC with their newly-acquired national identities.

The founding fathers of the new union, or commonwealth, in Minsk proclaim that their project is the *sine qua non* of solving their problems. In this they resemble their fellow union-builders in Brussels and Maastricht. We are supposed to believe that the content is new, because the form is. Whether things have really changed remains to be seen. It is not self-evident that these gigantic organizational transformations are the most appropriate means to achieve viable solutions to the real problems of either Europe, now or in the future. Neither can we take for granted that they will not create new problems.

POLITICS OR THE MARKET: THE RISK OF OVER-EXTENSION

Admittedly, most of the world is in a mess by the early 1990s. The responsibility for managing enormously complex and gigantic social systems is increasingly placed in the hands of the few - be it Yeltsin, Kravtchuk, Delors, Kohl or Bush. The systems are now so big that definitions of democracy will have to be stretched and twisted. First, accountability to citizens of power elites and decision procedures become increasingly difficult.

Second, the knowledge each citizen commands about the central issues and their implications diminishes in proportion to the wealth of information. According to opinion polls from December 1991, 63% of the Swedes find it very difficult to take a stand on EC issues although they find the information they get from the media reliable and sufficient.

Under circumstances such as these the market becomes *politically* attractive. When we let the market take care of society's functions, way beyond the economic sphere, we diffuse our responsibilities – not to speak of the civilizationally regressive effects of turning deeply human, social and cultural values over to the market.

The market and democratic societies are supposed to go hand in hand. Could it be that the market undermines democratic politics, particularly when introduced *ad absurdum*, not as an instrument but as an ideological goal? With the demise of socialism, market forces gain strength as a social myth and as a technocratic tool. The myth says that Adam Smith's 'invisible hand' will optimize the satisfaction of all people and their 'utility functions.' In and of itself it plays the role of God – the invisible regulator making everything good if only we have faith in it.

However, the free market does not exist, except perhaps at the local market squares where we buy our vegetables, cheese and flowers. But that is no problem because the *political* function of 'the free market' is not to be a market but to serve as a hidden ideological glue in an era marked by junk academia that seriously discusses whether ideology and history is dead or not.

So, there *is* a problem. If there is no 'other' ideology, what is our own ideology and identity? If everybody wants to become part of what they believe to be a free market in the West, in the world economy, if we are all to become identical economic players on one single world system – what is the use of dialogue? What is the point of conducting an ethics-based or value-oriented debate when the market proliferates horizontally to virtually all countries, when old economies disappear and no new ones appear and when the market penetrates vertically down in every fibre of our society and every corner of our living? A monologising Europe, Europe the Inevitable, Europe the Market, the Union, the Europe that speaks with One Voice is all we need.

If this trend continues much longer European citizens will be faced with the choice between democracy/politics and markets/economism. This is, indeed, a paradox, and in *Europe* of all places, the cradle of democracy. Letting the market take over, as a matter of inevitability, is to give up politics and the value-based human community.

Another type of over-extension or overloading is now becoming evident. Directly and indirectly, the West Europeans have caused ever-rising expectations with the peoples of Eastern Europe, the Soviet Union and the poorer EC regions. The only economic system possible was their free market and high-productivity industries pouring out plenty of consumer goods and providing social services, all supported by effective financial institutions and social policies.

A finance minister of the FRG in the 1990s was of the opinion that a fraction of Germany's economic growth surplus would be more than enough to finance the increase to FRG levels of the GDR sisters and brothers.

The dreams were not fulfilled and they will not be in the foreseeable future. Even Germany's strong economy is heavily burdened with the re-unification process and living conditions have turned to the worse all over the Eastern bloc where people just one year ago happily embraced Chancellor Kohl. There has been much rhetoric but no substantial 'Marshall-like' aid programmes or transfer of needed resources, technology, etc. The West tell its fellow-Europeans that, at least in the short run, everything will have to get even worse before they can get better. But in the long run?

It is highly doubtful that the EC ever will be able to meet the rising expectations, expectations that were developed in the shadow of the victor's self-congratulatory manners. What they are told in the Soviet Union and Eastern Europe, now that things are worse than they ever were under the old system, is that they will have to endure much more hardship before they can achieve higher living standards. But for how long, with what frustrations – and could it ever result in anything but second-class citizenry in the New Europe?

NEW CONFLICT FORMATIONS

The new Europe embodies a dream of peace. By 1991, however, one may argue that it is heading for a variety of new conflicts. There is the trend, already visible, towards a First Europe (Maastricht, Brussels, Strasbourg), a Second Europe (around the Mediterranean), a Third Europe (Eastern Europe and the Balkans) and a Fourth Europe (Minsk, Moscow, St Petersburg).

Second, there is social upheaval and human rights violations in former communist countries, predominantly against former communists (Czechoslovakia, Eastern Germany, Baltic states); there are nationalist and

---

ethnocratic policies (in some of the mentioned plus, e.g., Croatia and Serbia), and there are problems of minorities in almost all EC countries. Nuclear weapons and arsenals of former federations are escaping control; nazism, anti-Semitism, xenophobic sentiments rear their ugly heads again, both in the East and the West.

Third, there are about 20 million unemployed within the EC alone. With the majority of peoples in this four-layer Europe, democratic procedures are not that well-established. Free elections and multi-party systems have brought many to power who, yesteryear, were not exactly known for their liberalism or internationalism. They thrive on nationalism, chauvinism and on age-old psycho-political animosity directed against other nationalities.

Changing *forms* may, indeed, be a necessity when *contents* undergo change and problems must be solved. In processes we witnessed in Eastern Europe and the former Soviet Union during 1991, few had concrete workable programmes or plans with which to fill the new structures. Old unions can be dissolved and new ones proclaimed in their place, but it was not self-evident why the new structures were totally superior when it comes to finding solutions to the problems.

As our need for effective conflict-resolution increases, the need for weapons will decrease. But neither the remaining superpower nor the newly born nation-states are likely to be the first candidates to practise non-violence or mediation, provide negotiation forums or conflict mitigation.

EC policies *vis-à-vis* the Gulf War and the war in Croatia indicate how far statesmen still are from understanding conflicts or helping bring about solutions without getting involved. The EC has no procedures, no statutes or UN-like charter, no experience and no troops for peace-keeping. The consistently inconsistent policies of member states probably undermined the efforts of the EC-appointed mediator, Lord Carrington.

The fact that the first major EC conflict-mediation attempts were a failure has been used as an argument for further integration of the community; it is said to prove that there is a need for speaking more determinedly with one voice. Indeed, it has also served as an argument for recognizing Croatia and Slovenia as independent states. Again, the organization is seen as the problem – not the lack of understanding of conflict structures and history in former Yugoslavia or what conflict-resolution (mediation) is actually about.

Neither can one seriously argue that the EC has been particularly responsive to the changes in the Soviet Union during the last 5–6 years. 'We could not have foreseen it,' everybody says about perestroika and glasnost. The same may also be said about the dissolution of the union and what follows from that. However, reacting only will not suffice in the troublesome future of this new Europe. Turning inward, like in Maastricht – where it looked as though England's industrial and labour relations were the most important issue of all – while neighbouring countries go through potentially very dangerous processes appears puzzling even now and I believe it will be even more so to historians in the future.

The new Europe is overloaded with security organizations of the past such as NATO, the West European Union (WEU) and the CSCE (a process fit to soften and stabilize the consequences of the old bloc-Europe, but one that deserves a boost now), and outdated strategies of deterrence and national defence. Little is in the making for future tasks - early warning, conflict-control, war-prevention, conflict-resolution, non-violence, alternative defensive defence, ecological security, emergency relief aid - not to mention inter-cultural dialogue.

Imagine that 'Minsk Europe' and 'Maastricht Europe' develop into empires. What will their internal conflict structures and cooperation structures be like? And will they have exclusively friendly relations with each other or will we see some kind of new (old) bloc structure emerge? Just as there are certain layers in the West, layers can also be discerned in the new union/commonwealth arrangements in Minsk.

Thus, Russia, the Ukraine, Belorussia, the founding members make the centre. Within that, the western part of Russia is the centre and Siberia the periphery full of natural resources. These three command 73% of the people in the former Soviet Union, 80% of the Gross Domestic Product, 74% of the agricultural output, 89% of the foreign exports and more than 90% of the oil.

Depending on indicators, one can imagine various rank orders. If we choose economic and industrial potential it would probably look like this: Russia, Ukraine, Georgia as 'First Class,' Belorussia, Kazakhstan, Moldavia,

---

Armenia and Azerbaijan as 'Second Class,' and Uzbekistan, Turkmenistan, Kirghizia and Tadzhikistan as 'Third Class.' With other indicators, e.g., the possession of nuclear weapons, the rank order will change. And then there are other structures such as nationality and religion, more or less overlapping.

At the time of the creation of this commonwealth, in December 1991, we did not know what the peace-keeping modes of operation or organization would be in such an empire. The control of nuclear forces and warheads was far from the only problem.

It is difficult to see what is actually new in 'new Europe' in these respects. It is not very reassuring that we seem to be unable to find any genuinely new approach anywhere to security, defence, war-prevention or conflict-resolution in what could well be a quagmire of conflicts, new and old, throughout the continent.

CONTRADICTIONS EVERYWHERE

1. *Unity in Diversity or Uniformity*

Europeans believe that one-party political systems invariably lead to dictatorship, no matter the time, space or culture. As we know this thesis has wide empirical support. We prefer the pluralism of more parties, or at least two as in the United States. We want free choice.

But not so when it comes to choosing one's own path or when it comes to the economy. Freedom of choice is incompatible with the inevitability of our times. Where there is only one way and one system, there is not real choice. The public debate in Sweden 1989–91 is an excellent illustration of this dilemma.

In economics, too, uniformity is preached; each and everybody should preferably confess their faith in the free market, in liberalization, privatization, growth, freedom of movement for people, services, goods and capital, the division of labour, global sourcing and interdependence. National economics is the queen of university disciplines although national economies hardly exist any more.

The EC opts for one Central Bank and one currency from 1999. No 'unity in diversity' survives – an otherwise deeply European philosophical principle. Uniformity and standardization in a one-economy world system is rewarded. Integrate, marketize – or perish! Obviously, all this contradicts common sense derived from what we know about social and ecological systems. Simply, if one central element in this one system malfunctions, everybody will be drawn in and down. Economic mono-cultures are fragile, but look strong because of their universal appearance. And some subsystem somewhere will always fail, sometime.

This could well be a profound reason why capitalism has not been very eager to get involved in the Soviet Union. Getting stuck there, sucked into a project too large – and fundamentally different from exploiting already structurally underdeveloped Third World peoples – could be suicidal for problem-ridden world capitalism. Japanese capitalism is much stronger, but they have their reasons for not engaging themselves (yet?) in the Soviet Union – perhaps waiting for the West to build the infrastructure after which they will enter the market for consumer goods.

In summary, combine unity in *uniformity* with this *Zeitgeist* of *inevitability* – 'there is only one organization, one goal, one way and we have to be there', add to it *ever bigger units* and centralizing *materialism* in an increasingly non-European world – and we have something to which a professional peace researcher and politician would – inevitably! – react with deep concern.

2. Universal but Only for the Few

'What millions cannot have, we should not have,' Gandhi once said. What he meant was that societies ought not strive for such *levels* of material welfare or use such *means* to achieve it that others were prevented from attaining their welfare goals.

A quick glance in the serious global reports about the developmental and environmental 'state of the Earth' offers all necessary and sufficient evidence that the global system would break down should 5.3 billion people try to achieve living standards comparable with those now found to be 'natural' in Europe and other OECD countries. Six to eight more globes would be needed. EC Europe is only possible as long as others do not act like Europeans. To illustrate, there are now 400 million cars on Earth, owned by only 8% of the people. What would happen if the remaining 92% insisted on having and using cars like we do?

The deeply moral dilemma we are driving at here is this: can we tell our brothers and sisters in Eastern Europe and the former Soviet Union *not* to aspire for living standards such as ours? Are we morally equipped to argue that it leads to environmental decay, is built on the exploitation of peoples in the peripheries and creates new diseases and human alienation – and continue living like we do here? Can we tell them that they *can* become part of our system and reach our levels within some decades – knowing full well that the carrying capacity of the Earth will probably be impaired if they did?

Some may see the EC as the answer, but it is not the answer to dilemmas such as these. The EC as an idea appeals to nations, states and regions, to capital, goods and services, but certainly not to the *world* or global community, not to humankind. In this sense it is exclusivist ('a rich men's club'), parochial.

The historic EC as well as this new Europe, has an *anti-Eastern foundation*. It is rather *ignorant* of this Eastern bloc now (history, I think will judge Maastricht as an almost autistic exercize, EC domestic policies with no relevance whatsoever to the larger world). It is an effort to *assert itself vis-à-vis* the United States, it is strongly *anti-Japanese* and *ignorant* about the Third World beyond its own economic interests. In civilizational terms it could be seen as an attempt to make possible in the short run what will be impossible in the long run, namely limitless material growth and self-assertive Westernness.

Only if we in Western Europe are also willing to go through paradigmatic and systematic transformation of *our* system and cooperate with the emerging new formations elsewhere, can we hope to solve the dilemma above.

In this paradoxical sense we Western Europeans need the reformed Eastern Europe and new actors in the East. Not their old system, but neither should they simply take over ours as it is. Together, at this turning point in history, we could create something new together, something compatible with a global common future in a deep sense. But one precondition is that the West deliberately chooses to become less self-assured and more self-critical.

The breakdown in the East is an opportunity for the West. Not for exploitation, but for self-criticism and cooperation. The EC does not point in the direction of true sustainability or optimal, differentiated growth, i.e., *growth* where needed and *stabilization* where possible and *reduction* of luxury production and consumption where extraction, production, consumption and disposal processes cause irreversible damage to people, the environment and other cultures.

NEW AND OLD IDENTITIES IN THE NEW OLD EUROPE

The 'new Europe' emerging is not so new. It represents a new organizational form, a new marketing of the old system(s) and its civilizational code. One may actually say that the EC is modelled on Germany with a Central Bank like the Bundesbank, a federal political structure, with a parliament gaining strength, and an EC police force like the Bundeskriminalamt. The Europeanized Germany was an important goal; the main way of reaching it seems to be to Germanize the organization of Europe.

New projects are actually often old. Croatia and Slovenia want to become nation-states, states created on the basis of one leading majority nationality, 'hard' borders, national defence, currency and centralization. Political energy is tapped in age-old national history, and most peoples in former Yugoslavia base their wish for independent states on history rather than on a vision or a programme pertaining to the future.

The European identity is not in focus to remind us that we are Europeans. We knew and know that that is the case. Rather, it is a concept that helps us cope with the fact that our Europe is a shrinking part of the world, that we have to think in a *common European* way in order to survive in the larger world. Self assertion in what is perceived as an increasingly hostile environment is an important driving force in both cases, but on a different level.

Where earlier international relations professionals talked about the 'billiard ball model', we now see – in this volume too – that the computer with its images and games might be a better metaphor. In the whole debate about the new Europe there is a question about how Europe can be 'seen' or 'perceived' or 'interpreted.' We tend to see new links, regions, connections, networks and people 'linking-up' in new ways.

Perceptions and interpretations are needed. But we must also ask questions about substance: what *is* it? Who are the actors? What are their motives? About cosmology: what does it *mean?* About implications: how will it change the future – our own, that of others and that of the globe? In comparison with these questions, perceptional analyses appear non-committal. Metaphors *are* not reality.

What would be new, instead?

If approached analytically from the point of view of the evolution of human society, *it would be something new if the new Europe was built on a vision going fundamentally beyond itself.* Just as a local community has to identify with the nation-state of which it is a part, nation-states have to identify with the international system of which they are a part. Part of their identity reaches beyond themselves.

The new Europe seems to identify with some kind of smallest common denominator of 'European-ness' – a unity of identification based on harmonization, uniformity and modernity.

For Europeans it is important in and of itself to be modern, to search for what is new, to be progressive. Sweden since 1945 can be taken as an extreme case with its emphasis on social engineering, tearing up old city centres and building modern environments, making use of the computer, treating social outsiders according to modern educational theory, being very advanced in technology for civilian and military uses and practising old concepts in new ways.

To Sweden, Europe is the new thing. Sweden's 'future' is Europe, not Sweden or the Nordic countries. The trend now is to Europeanize Sweden and – inevitably – to try to Swedify the EC where possible. But Europe is 'in.' The way to keep Sweden dynamic is to integrate it as much and as quickly as possible with the new Europe. The train is rolling to Brussels – inevitably.

The change in self-perception is surprising to anyone who cares to see it. During recent decades the Swedes knew they were different, did things better and had their own ideas – cars, neutrality, international solidarity, a welfare model and a mixed economy – following a 'Third Path,' not socialist, not capitalist, but in between in Swedish fashion. To be a real Swede today implies to be more European than other Europeans.

Regionalization is often perceived (for instance, by some of the authors in this volume) as a healthy or necessary counterstream, as an exciting dialectic, or as something good surfacing now precisely because supra-nationalization is on the European agenda.

The identification point of regionalization is, however, still 'Europe.' Business, towns and cities, citizens and associations of various kinds link up and form regional networks, but they do so within this Europe. Proudly, we hope, they will display plurality – show us different 'ways of being European.'

In other words, they have no identification points beyond the new Europe itself, only within it. In the best cases the regions will succeed in their small identity–formation projects and preserve various aspects of plural Europe, but only in 'low politics' areas; their only frame of reference will be the 'Europe' where 'high politics' take place. In the worst cases they will be parochial units regressing into folklore, becoming some kind of future cultural zoos where we can observe 'how we once lived.'

One does not have to be 'anti-European' or 'anti-EC' to raise such an issue in 1991-92, although I deliberately do it somewhat provocatively here. What I fear is that world events and the breakdown of neighbouring systems could well lead Europe to be more inward-looking and European than ever, much less visionary and experimental than before. In a civilizational sense the world is closing in on the 3% Europeans. And the EC, in response, is closing itself.

The new Europe, its regions, supranational institutions will only be new if:

• it manages to go beyond itself in terms of identification and sees itself as an open region of the world community;
• its 'mind,' its collective consciousness, is infused with non-European values, and it is receptive in an entirely new manner (in all areas and not only when it comes to different cuisines);
• its organizational form becomes increasingly transnational instead of supranational, i.e., if it embodies fewer references to the nation-states and more to the regions *and*, at the same time, to the global community.

It is often said that we identify ourselves by being different from others. There is a necessary, logical truth in this. But the other side of the coin is that we have no identity outside the human community, outside values that we share, beyond our shared lives. We are someone because we *identify*, i.e., we stress contrasts and our individual uniqueness. But we are also someone because we *empathize*, i.e., we try to understand the position of others and their perceptions of us and we stress our similarities with others, with the larger community.

When we identify we ask: who am I? When we empathize we ask: Who are they? When we combine these dimensions we get images of both, we get to know them through empathy, through seriously trying to put ourselves in their position and to see how we differ and how we are alike. We learn to see them as they see themselves, we learn to see ourselves as they see us, and we learn more about ourselves – precisely through balancing identification and empathy.

The present 'Euro-phoria' is Euro-centric and grapples only with identity. What we need in today's world is empathy, from which flows care, reconciliation, compassion, cooperation, peace, and a willingness to share in conflict-resolution, not win or lose. This goes for the human, political community. At the even higher level, nature – Gaia – could serve as a point of identification–empathy. As a matter of fact we cannot do without relating to it with empathy.

NORDEN: BEING NORDIC IN OLD AND NEW WAYS

Norden is Europe. Our identity is Northern European. Some of the authors in this book insist that we are different as societies and as security policy actors, that we have survived so well during the Cold War era because we are different to some extent. And some draw the conclusion that the Cold War was the framework within which all this worked out fine, but that now something new will be needed.

What distinguishes Norden within this framework? I would like to believe that it is *the Nordic capacity for empathy*, for identification beyond ourselves, even beyond our European-ness, reaching the larger world. Many fundamental world order values have been and are practised by the Nordic region – peaceful conflict-resolution, equality of trade, open borders, low militarization, decent welfare for all, etc.

Within the limits of the post-1945 world, the Nordic region practised some alternatives (see Chapter 13). In small ways – but fairly big ways considering our political size – we acted a little bit as if the Cold War did not exist. We had lively discussion about nuclear freedom in a world shaped by nuclearism. We practised democracy and citizens' participation in a welfare order which neither the United States nor certainly the Soviet Union ever achieved.

Norden is now – inevitably – being drawn into the new Europe. Sweden, Finland and Norway, soon the Baltic states and – why not? – Iceland will be swept into the EC by the same winds. Our comparative advantage in that process will not be our basic Europeanness, our identity. It will be our empathy, our historical ability to identify with those who are different, our compassion, our environmental consciousness, our humanitarian solidarity with the poor peoples of the Earth. Finally, we are still small and have quite an experience in how to do things a little bit outside the mainstream.

If *these* qualities are swept away and said to 'belong only to the Cold War era', the prospects for Norden in Europe are bleak - for us, for Europe and for those we used to empathize with. Concepts such as the Baltic region or Hansa cooperation point fruitfully in the direction of a 'new way' of being European, and may serve as a good substitute for obsolete Nordic ways of coping with the Cold War framework.

But if it develops into a parochial Baltic-centrism, taking its inspiration predominantly from the past ('Hansa') and not from the needs and challenges of the future, if it is not infused with new concepts of politics such as defensiveness, non-violence, new economics, self-reliance, the genuine search for the progression of democracy and the balancing of material and other civilizational dimensions, etc. – then, why should we have it? Is it simply 'the best we can get out of the present situation,' a compensation for coping with the inevitability of being sucked into 'Europe'?

The challenge to Norden, whatever its members' relation to new Europe is this: how do we preserve and offensively develop thinking and policies that give expression to the age-old capacity of Norden to empathize with issues and problems beyond ourselves and even beyond Europe?

Our identity will survive in this Europe because it is part and parcel of it. But will our empathy?

Index

Index